Economics Directorate
Information Directorate
(eds)

 NATO

Regional Development in the USSR.
TRENDS AND PROSPECTS

Colloquium
25-27 April 1979
Brussels

 OTAN

Le Developpement Regional en URSS.
Tendances et Perspectives

Colloque
25-27 Avril 1979
Bruxelles

Oriental Research Partners
Newtonville, Mass.
1979

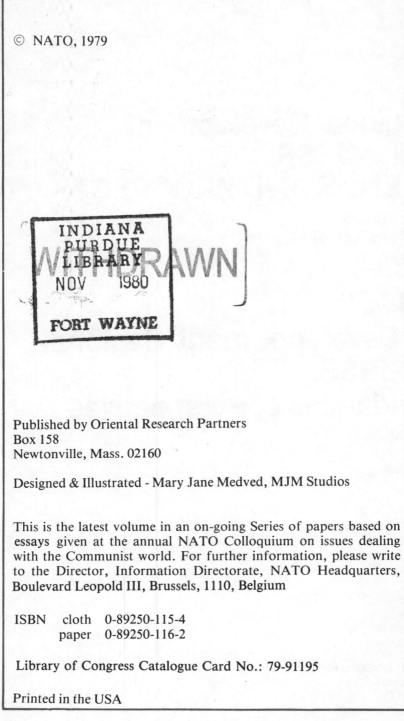

Published by Oriental Research Partners
Box 158
Newtonville, Mass. 02160

Designed & Illustrated - Mary Jane Medved, MJM Studios

This is the latest volume in an on-going Series of papers based on essays given at the annual NATO Colloquium on issues dealing with the Communist world. For further information, please write to the Director, Information Directorate, NATO Headquarters, Boulevard Leopold III, Brussels, 1110, Belgium

ISBN   cloth   0-89250-115-4
        paper   0-89250-116-2

Library of Congress Catalogue Card No.: 79-91195

Printed in the USA

Table of Contents

Trade Aspects of Regionalization

Summary

Comment
A Review of the NATO Colloquium

 James Ellis

The Soviet Union is notable for its uneven distribution of resources. Ninety percent of the land is unsuited for cultivation, and most of its vast mineral wealth lies outside areas of concentrated population. Consequently, its overall economic growth will depend very much on its success in carrying out plans for regional economic development.

With this situation in mind, the NATO Economics Directorate, which organizes a colloquium each year designed to foster discussion of topics of current interest relating to the Soviet and East European economies, chose as the theme of its eighth colloquium, Regional Development in the USSR. It was held between 25-27 April at NATO's Brussels Headquarters, under the Chairmanship of Monsieur J-N. Gibault, director of the Economics Directorate, and presented in cooperation with NATO's Information Directorate.

Participating at the colloquium (from left to right); Mr. Petrignani, Deputy Secretary General of NATO; Mr. Gibault, Director of NATO's Economics Directorate; Mr. Joseph, Assistant Director of the Economics Directorate; Dr. Vogel, Director of the Bundesinstitut Fur Ostwissenschaftliche und internationale Studien at Cologne.

In brief, the colloquium concluded that the problem of regional economic development in the Soviet Union is basically one of a maldistribution and growing shortage of labor in certain areas, which cannot be overcome by increased investment alone. But in seeking inducements to provide for an adequate regional labor supply, Soviet planners are frequently at odds with their policy of eliminating inequities in living standards. These problems are exacerbated by transport difficulties and an inefficient distribution network, as well as planners' hesitancy in integrating regional economies for the maximum benefit of the nation as a whole.

Regional Living Standards

Soviet efforts to raise regional standards of living are complicated by the fact that, in contrast to the heavily farmed regions, the greater part of the rural areas contain altogether some 140,000 small settlements each with an average population of only 125. As a result, much of the population has to make long journeys to remote cities to find required goods and services. The search for jobs closer to supply centers probably accounts for a substantial proportion of the USSR's annual labor turnover rate of some 14-15 million people.

Although living conditions in general appear to be improving and divergences to be lessening, it will take fifteen to twenty years to reach basic equality in living standards. In the meantime, the Soviet Government is trying to develop social amenities in the more populated rural districts. In doing so, however, it causes additional difficulties for those living in the thinly settled areas where services are being reduced.

Wage levels among the Soviet republics vary by as much as one-fifth above or below the national average, and sometimes even higher in remote Far East areas, despite uniform wage policies and continuing wage reforms. Within each republic, moreover, wages tend to vary much more widely, especially in the agricultural sector, although here they may be augmented by earnings derived from private plots.

Costs of living also tend to diverge considerably throughout the country, partly because of marked differences in climate, and also because of variations in family size. Even allowing for regional adjustments by the Soviet Government to compensate for living costs, wages probably do not vary enough to make up for these differences, especially in the more populated areas of Central Asia and the Caucasus.

Retail trade in the Soviet Union is generally increasing and improving although it is still far behind Western standards in quality and quantity of goods; its development in some regions is hindered by the rural population's continuing invasion of the cities to buy up goods. Partly as a result of inadequate sales outlets, savings in the rural areas tend to increase more quickly than the turnover of retail trade.

Increasing levels of savings throughout the Soviet Union may reflect a rising standard of living, or may point to wide-spread intentions eventually to purchase durable consumer goods, such as cars and television sets, in which case severe supply difficulties could arise for such items in the future. To a certain extent, people probably save because they cannot immediately find the goods they want to buy.

In sum, although living standards appear to have increased substantially throughout the Soviet Union in the past two decades, there has been little reduction in the divergence of real income from region to region, largely because of differing regional living costs and patterns of population growth. Furthermore, insufficient supplies of goods and services in certain areas lead to retail trade distortions and high savings rates. Social inequalities resulting from these conditions must ultimately affect labor standards.

Regional Investment

In the Soviet Union's investment policy, emphasis has been placed on developing basic resources and industrial capacity throughout the country, rather than on giving specialized attention to particular regions according to their comparative economic advantages. Soviet investment decisions thus tend to work against regional economic specialization and division of labor which could form the basis for an integrated, more productive economy.

Soviet agriculture, in particular, varies among regions as to its level of development and output. Besides the effect of climate, regional divergences in agricultural output appear to be due to differences in fertilizer use, in labor mobility, and in birth rates and consequent size of the labor supply. A primary barrier to regional specialization in agriculture, which would help compensate for differences in output, is the absence of adequate transportation, storage, and processing facilities. To upgrade these, however, requires additional extensive investment, to the detriment of other national economic priorities.

Furthermore, because of a uniform pricing system throughout the country, there is not incentive to move state-produced agricultural commodities and other items to regions where they are scarce and would otherwise fetch a higher price. The absence of pricing based on supply and demand therefore forms an additional barrier to the expansion of markets and to regional specialization.

In these circumstances, regional specialization for nationwide markets can only be effected by planning decisions. But in the view of Soviet planners, regional specialization should not be stressed without first establishing production of basic commodities in each region. Even now, Soviet investment priorities can be divided into three groups which do not emphasize regional specialization: exploitation of vital raw materials resources, development of priority industries, and growth of other industries.

In any case, it is evident that Soviet approaches to regional investment and resource development are failing to promote rapid economic growth. Soviet growth rates are definitely slowing and, according to United States Government estimates, will decline to around 2 percent a year by 1985, or half of the present rate of around 4 percent by Soviet reckoning. Indeed, economic results for the first six months of the year show that plan targets have not generally been met and the overall economic performance has been very disappointing to Soviet planners.

Because high growth rates tend to depend on energy-intensive industries, Soviet planners may deliberately set lower targets in order to allow the country to switch from such industries; or they might concentrate, as they have to a certain extent in the past, on selective investment in regional industries with promising rates of growth. Such tactics, however, would not solve the problem of creating sustained long-term growth, which might be achieved through regional specialization and nation-wide managerial reform.

Labor Versus Natural Resources

Soviet economic development is hindered by the fact that the regions where natural resources are concentrated are usually those of low population density. Eighty percent of the USSR's energy resources, for instance, are east of the Ural Mountains, but 80 percent of the country's energy consumption takes place west of the Urals.

During the last thirty years, the Soviet approach to resource development has followed two main patterns: shifting the population to areas where the resources are being exploited; and moving extracted resources west to the historic population centers. The first approach was applied in Stalin's time, when it was facilitated by a large pool of forced labor and stringent controls on population movements. After Stalin, with most controls on internal migration relaxed, planners have followed the second approach. Now, they favor maintaining only a minimum labor force at the site of resource extraction, moving the resources by rail or an ever-growing pipeline network to established industrial centers for further processing.

Regardless of the approach used, the overall annual increase in the USSR's labor supply, according to some estimates, will probably be less than 0.5 percent in the 1980's, rising to about 1 percent a year by the end of the century. The agricultural sector, the traditional supplier of additional manpower, will probably not be able to provide an adequate number of workers for regions intended for resource development even though the percentage of the civilian labor force in agriculture will probably continue to decline from its current 25 percent to around 20 percent by 1990.

Additional manpower for regional economic development, therefore, will have to come from regions with a relatively high labor supply—the Uzbek, Tadzhik, and Kirgiz Republics of Central Asia, Moldavia, and certain autonomous republics of the Russian Soviet Federal Socialist Republic. By 1984, other areas of the Soviet Union will begin experiencing labor supply shortages, which will have to be mostly overcome by transfers from these regions, although the need for some of these transfers might be allayed by large infusions of capital.

Planners trying to encourage labor migration to areas of resource development are hindered by the fact that workers are often reluctant to go where they are needed, partly because of difficulties in obtaining permission for a change of residence, but more because of harsh climate and a lack of amenities in these areas of the country.

Nonetheless, labor mobility appears to be growing. At least 12 million Soviet citizens now migrate annually, largely from the North to the South—from the areas of low labor supply to those already crowded by large populations. On the other hand, there is negligible worker movement from the West to the East—to the primary areas of resource development. These migration patterns suggest that the regional labor supply situation in the 1980's could worsen unless the Soviet Government finds effective measures to counter them.

Resource Development in Siberia

One of the principal regions for the development of resources in the 1980's, both for domestic use and for export, will be Siberia. First a center of the Soviet iron and steel industry in the 1930's, then the country's principal area of investment for the oil and gas industry in the 1970's, Siberia is the source of an impressive portion of the USSR's energy and mineral wealth. In 1975 alone, it provided 40 percent of the country's hydro-electric power, 34 percent of its coal, 34 percent of its roundwood, and over half of such metals as aluminum, cobalt, nickel and tin.

Aware of the importance of the region, Soviet planners have earmarked around one-third of gross investment for Siberia during the 1976-1980 period, and will probably invest even more there in the next five-year period. Discussions continue with United States and Japanese firms, for instance, for the exploitation of the immense Yakutia gas reserves, a project which will cost the USSR $4-5 billion.

Principal constraints on Siberian development are the region's environment, labor supply, and transport system. Because of difficulties in dealing with the climate, projects originally planned for installation in the permafrost are now being relocated to more hospitable areas. Moreover, workers can usually be attracted to Siberia for only short periods of time, in order to gain extra earnings. Finally, the traditional means of transport in Siberia, waterways, is limited in its effectiveness because of the seasons. seasons.

However, there have been recent major transportation developments in Siberia, such as a railway spur from the Trans-Siberian Railway to Urengoy, the region's first north-south railroad; and the Baikal-Amur Mainline (BAM), providing access to the Pacific and enhancing Soviet export capabilities. The BAM will help Siberia grow as an exporting region, because the present Trans-Siberian Railway and terminal at Vladivostok is geographically remote from centers of Siberian resource extraction. A final important development affecting transport in Siberia is the use of powerful new ice-breakers, which give rise to the prospect of virtually year-round operation on the Arctic Sea route from the mineral-rich region of Noril'sk.

Transport and the Role of the Military

Railways continue to be the principal means of transportation in the USSR, and so will play a key role in regional economic development and eventual national economic integration. By contrast, few new highways are constructed each year, because Soviet planners put little emphasis on road building. As a consequence, Soviet Central Asia will probably be relatively neglected in transport development over the next twenty years, and the Soviet railways will continue to be heavily charged with both the long-distance transport of agricultural commodities and the movement of industrial freight.

The development of the Soviet railway system has been troubled by a number of difficulties, however, not the least of which is that planners tend to demand too much of it. For instance, on a cost basis, more Kuzbass coal should be burned beyond the Urals, according to the calculations of Soviet planners; but it is not, partially because of east-west rail bottlenecks. The problem is alleviated to some extent by new slurry pipelines, which carry finely ground coal in water.

Another difficulty has been that the railways built under Khrushchev's virgin-lands agricultural development scheme were narrow-gauge and therefore cheaper, but economically inefficient, consequently, they have had to be replaced by regular-gauge railroads. In addition, the Soviet railway system is lacking in capable management and specialization: only 15 percent of Soviet rolling stock is designed for specialized freight, although for effective service the figure should be nearer 25 percent. Such short-comings have caused the Soviet railway system to be thus far more of an obstacle than an aid to regional economic development.

Since progress on the BAM and other railways has been slowed and in some cases interrupted by other investment priorities, it has been suggested that such projects might be completed even ahead of schedule through the employment of military resources and equipment. Indeed, military man-power might be called on to help solve other Soviet regional development problems, such as assisting with manpower redistribution. It is questionable, however, whether the Soviet military leaders would allow it to be employed in these ways, since they like to keep a certain amount of man-power in reserve to respond to sudden emergencies.

Regionalization and Foreign Trade

Although the composition of Soviet foreign trade is only weakly linked to the economic development of the regions, the potential total volume of foreign trade is also very much dependent on the adequacy of the Soviet transport system. The average distance of travel within the USSR of export-ed goods, for instance, is as much as twice that of the same goods destined for domestic use. Certain large regional development projects, such as the Yakutia Gas Project, would not be economically feasible in the absence of anticipated export earnings, in turn dependent on specially-designed trans-port facilities.

Partially because of Soviet slowness in developing adequate transport, however, Soviet foreign trade still represents a relatively small percentage of the USSR's industrial output. It accounts for only around 4 percent of estimated Soviet Gross National Product, as compared to 12 percent for the United States, and much higher percentages for European countries.

The relatively low level of Soviet foreign trade is also partly at-tributable to planners' aversion to the uncertainties of foreign markets, and to their desire to avoid problems in product design, packaging, and marketing for foreign tastes. Thus, potential regional export industries have not been developed to the extent they might have been, even though more investment in such industries could have led to greater regional economic development.

In the future, the Soviet Union will probably continue to import Western technology and goods to help make up for lacks in its industrial capacity and labor supply, and to help improve regional standards of living. As living standards continue to rise, moreover, imports will probably have to be increased still further to satisfy insistent consumer demand. Export production, however, probably cannot expand rapidly enough to keep pace. Hence, a chronic balance of trade deficit might act as a continuing restraint on Soviet regional economic development, perhaps to the end of the century.

USSR:
Urban Rural Population
by Republic, 1940-1977
(in Percent)

	1940		1970		1977	
	Urban	Rural	Urban	Rural	Urban	Rural
USSR (total)	33	67	56	44	62	38
RSFSR	34	66	62	38	69	31
Ukraine	34	66	55	45	61	39
Belorussia	21	79	43	57	53	47
Uzbekistan	25	75	37	63	39	61
Kazakhastan	30	70	50	50	54	46
Georgia	31	69	48	52	51	49
Azerbaidjan	37	63	50	50	52	48
Lithuania	23	77	50	50	58	42
Moldavia	13	87	32	68	38	62
Latvia	35	65	62	38	67	38
Kirgizstan	22	78	37	63	39	61
Tadjikistan	19	81	37	63	36	64
Armenia	28	72	59	41	64	36
Turkmenistan	35	65	48	52	48	52
Estonia	34	66	65	35	69	31

Source: Official Soviet statistics

To help make up for its trade deficit the USSR will increasingly insist on product buy-back arrangements with Western firms. The value of such transactions is expected to grow from its present level of around $1 billion annually to $4 billion by 1985. In present world economic conditions, however, where many Western plants are operating below capacity, the growth of such compensation arrangements is bound to have repercussions on Western markets.

In short, the success of Soviet regional economic development plans will depend on a number of factors, such as labor supply, Soviet investment policy, regional living standards, and the rate of evolution of natural resource extraction, transport, and foreign trade. Because of the complexities involved in each of these matters, it is difficult to predict how they will affect the growth of the Soviet economy as a whole. In the meantime, in order to hold down ever-increasing costs, Soviet planners will doubtless continue to insist on making the maximum use of existing resources and minimizing transport costs.

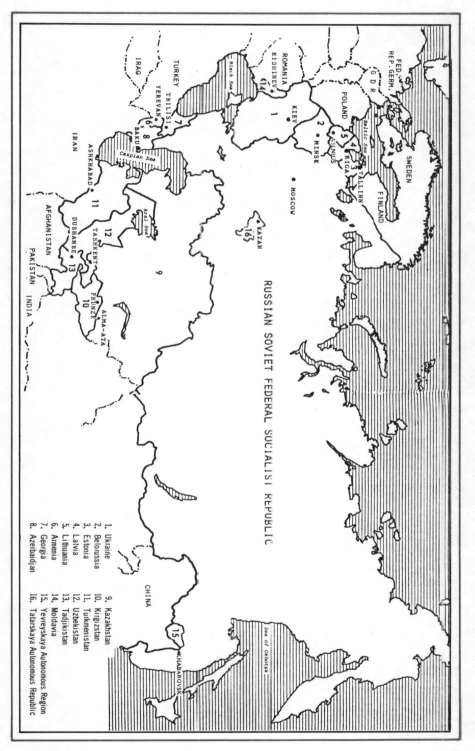

RUSSIAN SOVIET FEDERAL SOCIALIST REPUBLIC

1. Ukraine
2. Belorussia
3. Estonia
4. Latvia
5. Lithuania
6. Armenia
7. Georgia
8. Azerbaidjan
9. Kazakhstan
10. Kirgizstan
11. Turkmenistan
12. Uzbekistan
13. Tadjikistan
14. Moldavia
15. Yevreyskaya Autonomous Region
16. Tatarskaya Autonomous Republic

Introduction
Soviet Regional Development Policy in the Tenth Five-Year Plan and Beyond

Dr. Theodore Shabad

Regional development usually displays marked differences within large countries, but in the Soviet Union the regional policy issue has played a particularly important role because of the extraordinary diversity of lands, climate and other environmental conditions and the uneven distribution of resources, population, agriculture, industry and transportation. The basic fact of life in the Soviet Union is that nearly 90 percent of the territory is unsuited for cultivation, being either too cold or too dry, too wet or too mountainous. The bulk of agricultural activity is concentrated in the so-called fertile triangle, which has its base on the western borders and comes to a point in the southern zone of Western Siberia. This farming wedge is also the historical area of settlement and, in turn, has become the focus of most economic activity. On the other hand, much of the natural resource potential, including fuels and energy, timber and water, is found in the sparsely populated or entirely uninhabited eastern regions. The aims of regional policy through the Soviet period have been to devise methods for reconciling the spatial discrepancy between the distribution of population and economic activity, on the one hand, and the distribution of resources, on the other hand. Although the methods used to achieve this aim have varied in detail, two basic approaches may be distinguished. Under Stalin, regional policy was guided by the doctrine of uniform development, which called essentially for equalizing levels of economic activity by shifting population to sources of fuels and raw materials in the eastern regions and building up new centers of human activity on that basis. This approach was facilitated to some extent by strict controls over population movements, including the availability of a large pool of forced labor that could be used as a maneuverable, even though highly inefficient, work force in economic development projects. After Stalin, when most controls over migration were relaxed, Soviet planners found it more difficult to attract population to outlying regions, especially in the absence of adequate housing and other services. The planners, to use a highly simplified model, came to the realization that it was more difficult to move resources to the historical centers of economic activity. As a result, the focus of economic development shifted back to the populated regions and lower priority was given to the previous doctrine of integrating the resource-rich pioneering areas into the mainstream of economic life.

Given the sequence of these two basic approaches to regional development, Soviet policy can be examined through several prisms, some of which will be discussed in greater detail in the present Colloquium:

(1) the issue of regional living standards and income differentials;

(2) regional investment patterns and the issue of regional self-sufficiency as opposed to specialization and a geographical division of labor;

(3) the basic spatial discrepancy between labor resources and natural resources and raw materials;

(4) the significance of transport infrastructure in regional development, with particular focus on the role of the Baikal-Amur Mainline;

(5) the interplay between foreign trade and regional policy.

Since each of these themes will be the subject of special presentations, comments by co-rapporteurs and general discussion, the following introductory comments will be limited to some general propositions on regional development policy as they appear to evolve during the current, 10th Five Year Plan (1976-1980) and into the 1980's.

Although the equalization of living levels among regions and between urban and rural areas continues to be an avowed objective, the problem is far from resolved. Serious differentials persist both in real incomes and in the availability of services between republics, with the Baltic republics and some of the Central Asian republics at opposite poles, and within republics, specifically between the developed western regions and the under-developed eastern regions of the RSFSR. Moreover, inequalities remain between urban and rural areas. Rural services are particularly inadequate in regions distinguished by a large number of very small settlements, for example, the Non-Chernozem (Non-Black Soil) Zone of north-central European Russia, and in regions with wide dispersion of rural settlement, as in parts of Siberia. Part of the current program to upgrade the rural economy of the Non-Chernozem Zone, one of the major regional development projects of the 10th five-year plan, is to improve rural services in a region that has 142,500 rural inhabited places, with a mean population of 125 each. Most of these places obviously lack the capacity to provide even a minimum standard of services. "As a result," Soviet rural planners have commented, "the great majority of places makes use of service establishments in other places. The rural population is thus forced to make service trips not only to nearby rural service centers or to the central settlements of collective and state farms, but also to present or former administrative seats of rayons (minor civil divisions), to small and middle-size urban places, to oblast capitals and to Moscow."[1] The long-term objective of planners is to eliminate the many small settlements, and to reduce the system of rural places to a total of 23,800, with a mean population of 400. The long-term aim of planners is to achieve a situation in which Moscow will no longer be the single, ultimate shopping center for the nation.

Other Soviet writers have complained that the official normative guidelines used in the Soviet Union for the design, planning and construction of development projects, including service networks, are not sufficiently differentiated for the great diversity of physical and socio-economic conditions. Design and construction norms for rural service establishments are being applied equally to densely populated areas in the western regions, where the settlement system is closely meshed, and to widely dispersed rural settlement in Siberia. As a result, mean distance between settlements was largely ignored, and services were far less accessible in the eastern than in the western regions.[2]

While much of the current focus is on ways of improving living standards in rural and outlying areas, there is also a school of thought that favors limitations on the population movement to remote regions on the ground that it is too costly to provide the amenities that would be needed to attract a labor force. No more lip service is being given to the old doctrine of promoting equal development and population distribution. The present view, at least among Moscow planners if not among local boosters, is that the work force in resource areas should be limited to the bare minimum required to extract and transport the resources and that any processing and manufacturing activities be located in regions where population is already settled, and housing, schools, medical facilities and other services can be provided at lower cost. To demonstrate this point, a Soviet geographer analyzed the locational pattern of the nation's resource potential and other economic factors, and found virtually no correlation between resources and industry, but very high correlation between population and industry.[3]

With respect to the issue of autarky, or economic self-sufficiency, significant changes of policy have occurred. The autarky of regions was an integral aspect of the former doctrine of equal regional development and it may be said, only with slight exaggeration, that there was a time when Soviet economic planners envisaged a situation in which each major region would provide for its own needs in virtually all sectors, with its own little coal basin, its own little steel plant, and so forth. But, just as the Soviet Union has moved in recent years toward greater integration with the world economy, there has been greater emphasis on regional specialization within the Soviet Union. In terms of broad East-West terms, the eastern regions, particularly Siberia, are now looked on as primarily purveyors of fuels, energy and raw materials, while the western regions are viewed mainly in terms of their manufacturing potential, especially as regards skill-intensive types of industries. This basic division of functions does not imply a total abandonment of the principle of regional integration, which is akin to autarky. Aside from giving priority to specialization industries, regions are still being encouraged to provide for their needs to the maximum extent possible. The 10th Five-Year Plan, for example, called for a special effort to develop whatever fuels and energy reserves may be identified in the European USSR to reduce the dependence on long hauls from Siberia. This aim continues to be projected into the

1980's under the guidelines for the long-term economic program running to 1990.[4] However, the realities seem to be that the western resource potential is approaching depletion, and the western regions will become increasingly dependent on long hauls of fuels from the east and, if the technology can be worked out, on long-distance transmission of electricity from the east.

Conversely, the long-term economic program calls for a greater effort to meet the need of the eastern regions through the local production of such commodities as refined oil products, building materials, processed foods, livestock products, potatoes and vegetables to reduce the long-distance hauls of these goods from the western regions. Regional integration is also being stressed in the sense that an effort is to be made to coordinate regional machinery output with regional needs. For example, the projected development of large lignite strip mines in the Kansk-Achinsk Basin of southern Siberia will require large-capacity excavating machinery and haulers, and plans are being made for the construction of such a heavy-equipment plant at Krasnoyarsk. In view of the oil and gas development in West Siberia and the projected construction of large petrochemical complexes at Tobol'sk and Tomsk, more equipment for these industries is to be produced within Siberia.

In terms of regional investment policy, the present stress on intensification of production (reduction of labor input per unit of output) and on modernization of plant and equipment is expected to favor the further development of the older industrial regions of the USSR, where most of the nation's productive capacity is concentrated.[5] One of the issues that has been holding up completion of the long-term development program scheduled for the 1980's is the need for channeling more investment into the improvement of the plant and equipment of the European regions. The Gosplan directive on further study of development prospects called for "more thorough work on the question of developing industries in the European part of the USSR through retooling and reconstruction of existing establishments."[6]

The renewed western focus of investment in most manufacturing has even called into question any major new investment in iron and steel and in some chemicals in the eastern regions. New iron and steel developments in the east are being questioned on the ground that, contrary to most raw-material resources, the eastern regions appear to be poor in high-grade, accessible iron-ore resources. In contrast to most energy and raw material flows, which run from east to west, iron-ore movements are running from west to east as the major ore producing districts in the European USSR must ship increasing amounts of iron ore to existing steelmaking plants in the Urals and Siberia. The only prospective eastern steel development would be a projected Far Eastern complex oriented mainly for export; the Soviet Union has sought to interest Japan in such a complex, which would be based on coking coal from the Neryungri strip mine of southern Yakutia and newly discovered Yakutian ore resources and would export iron and steel projects to

Japan on a compensation basis.[7] Japan, with surplus steel capacity at the present time, has been cool to the proposal.

In the case of chemicals, the eastward movement of new capacity in synthetic resins, plastics and fibers was originally envisaged because of the large water requirements of such activities and the problem of pollution in the western regions, where water resources are more limited. However, the new emphasis on modernization of existing plant rather than the construction of new plant and advances being made in recycling technology appear to have raised questions about the eastward movement of the chemical industry, with the exception of major petrochemical complexes based directly on the use of feedstocks from the West Siberian oil and gas fields.[8] The long-term development program running through the 1980's points up the controversy over the future location of steel and chemicals by calling for "more careful study of the prospects of steel and chemicals in the eastern regions, especially as regards the iron-ore supply and the time required for the construction of new establishments in these industries."[9]

New investment is also likely to consider to a greater degree than in the past the distribution of labor resources. In contrast to the old view that population can always be drawn by one means or another to future development projects, Soviet writers now imply that the distribution of population should be given greater weight as a focus of new investment. "If redistribution [of population] is out of the question," one labor specialist writes, "then appropriate changes must be made in the planned volumes and proportions of economic production in light of the actual labor resource situation."[10] Other Soviet writers call on planners to pay more attention to people's residential preferences in view of the evident problems of controlling migration processes. "A great deal has been written about the fact that existing patterns of southward migration run directly contrary to the task of opening up the natural resources of the eastern regions," A. S. Akhiyezer, a sociologist, and P. M. Il'yin, a geographer, write. "We are evidently dealing here with a conflict between the desire of people to live and work in particular sets of places, i.e. a system of territorial evaluations perceived by large numbers of people, and the evaluations that have been incorporated into the state economic plan."[11]

Gosplan USSR, evidently aware of the problem of drawing permanent settlers to the eastern regions, has asked for "fuller analysis of the problem of supplying the projected eastern developments with labor resources and more precise information on the measures that would be required to induce people to settle there permanently--housing, social-cultural institutions, municipal and retailing facilities, additional benefits for permanent settlers, etc."[12]

A crucial problem in this context is that of the rapidly growing labor potential of Central Asia and the inadequate opportunities for

19

employment in the region. The Soviet Government continues to appear undecided on whether to try to encourage out-migration of the admittedly immobile Central Asian population or to provide more regional investment in productive capacity. A recent issue of the main planning journal clearly illustrates the continuing dilemma.[13] An editorial article contrasts the need for retooling of existing industrial establishments in the European regions with the need for new industrial construction in Central Asia to absorb the local labor resources. However L. Kostin, a First Deputy Chairman of the State Committee for Labor and Social Problems, writing in the same issue says that accelerated industrial construction in Central Asia "would not be advisable on a large scale since industrial location is known to depend on a whole range of factors" other than population distribution. Kostin calls instead for greater efforts to train young Central Asians in industrial skills and have them spend their training period in other parts of the Soviet Union, where employment opportunities would presumably be greater. However, the outlook for even such temporary out-migration of Central Asians appears dim since they have shown reluctance even to move to urban centers within Central Asia; in the end, greater investment in agricultural and light-industry activities in small Central Asian settlements may be the optimal approach to solving the Central Asian problem.[14]

Transportation has, of course, always been a crucial element in regional development policy. During the days of the doctrine of uniform development, grandiose plans were formulated for the construction of railroads in outlying regions in an effort to provide all parts of the Soviet Union with transport access. These projects, made possible in part by the availability of forced labor, did not always have an economic rationale. The early plans for the construction of the Baikal-Amur Mainline, for example, were formulated as part of the old program of uniform transport development. The western and eastern extremities of the original BAM project were in fact completed before the mass use of forced labor was abolished in the middle 1950's, but the completion of the railroad under the new conditions lacked an economic rationale at the time, and work was interrupted for 20 years. Another old railroad project of that type was the Salekhard-Igarka line in the northern part of West Siberia. That railroad had reached the future gas fields of West Siberia by the time its progress was halted. When the gas resources were discovered 10 years later, there was talk about rehabilitating the abandoned project to aid in the development of the gas fields. But in the end, it was decided to build a new approach railroad from the south.

When the BAM project was revived in the early 1970's, the rationale was totally different. It was no longer viewed simply as an element in a vast Siberian railroad net that would insure the uniform development of the eastern regions; its revival, motivated to a large extent by detente and the prospect of expanded East-West trade, particularly the use of the railways in Siberia as a 'land bridge' for containers from Europe to Asia, was also designed to open up new resource areas in the southeast quadrant of Siberia for export to the Pacific Basin, particularly Japan. Yet, the relevance of the BAM to the Soviet domestic economy under present conditions is greatly reduced by the sheer friction of distance since it serves a region thousands of miles from the nation's economic centers in the USSR. Nor is the BAM being viewed as a development axis for a string of new population centers. On the contrary, Soviet planners are quite explicit that the new railroad, though running only about 100 to 200 miles to the north of the Trans-Siberian mainline, passes through territory that is not attractive for human settlement. The work force along the railroad is to be limited to a minimum necessary to extract raw materials and service the rail facilities. Any activities requiring greater labor inputs, such as processing of materials, would be located in more hospitable environments to the south.

The decision to proceed with the construction of the BAM can thus be assessed as an important clue to current Soviet regional policy in the Far East. In discussing the rationale for the BAM, Soviet planners make no mention of the western regions of the USSR. N. N. Nekrasov, chairman of the Council for the Study of Productive Forces, which is the preplanning research agency of Gosplan USSR, described the function of the BAM as follows: "The construction of this railroad is of great economic significance for the development of new regions in Siberia and the Far East. It will help open up huge natural resources--the South Yakutian coal basin, the Aldan iron-ore basin, the Udokan copper deposit and many others. The BAM will link the principal industrial regions of Siberia that produce energy-intensive goods with the ports of the Pacific coast, thus strengthening the international economic linkages of Siberia and the Far East."[15]

This discussion of the BAM brings us to the trade aspects of Soviet regional policy. Two aspects may be distinguished here (1) a general westward trend fostered by increasing interplay between the Soviet Union and its East European allies, and (2) an apparently new emphasis on seaboard development as the Soviet Union looks increasingly to interaction with the rest of the world.

The westward shift related to economic integration within the Council for Mutual Economic Assistance (CMEA) reinforces the general westward trend of economic activity toward the European USSR and the new policy of introducing more investment in heavily populated areas. However, in contrast to the older industrial regions of central Russia, where the emphasis is on modernization of existing plant and equipment, the industrialization of the western borderlands often requires new construction in historically underindustrialized, but well populated regions. Belorussia and the western Ukraine probably offer the best examples of the buildup of industry in proximity to the East European allies. The industrialization of the western borderlands takes several forms, including technological linkages across the international border (as in the chemical arrangement between Kalush in the western Ukraine and Leninvaros in Hungary), the construction of machinery industries serving the CMEA market, and the program of developing nuclear power stations to feed electricity into the unified CMEA power system.[16]

The shift toward seacoasts, presenting a departure from the traditional interior continental location of economic activity in the Soviet Union, is evident both in academic interest in maritime development[17] and in greater attention given to the seacoasts under the 10th Five-Year Plan, affecting linkages both with the East European allies and with Western countries.[18] These seaboard-oriented developments comprise new port construction, including the expansion of facilities in the Baltic port of Ventspils (crude-oil exports, chemical exports and imports), the construction of the new chemical port of Yuzhnyy near Odessa on the Black Sea, and the inauguration of rail-ferry service between Ilyichevsk (near Odessa) and Varna (Bulgaria). But there is also evidence of a shift of industrial activity toward seacoasts as the Soviet Union interacts more with the rest of the world, especially in exports and imports of raw materials, for which seaboard locations are logical breaking points. A good example is the alumina plant under construction at the Black Sea port of Nikolayev in the Ukraine. It will convert Guinean bauxite into alumina, an intermediate product, for shipment to the aluminum reduction plant under construction at Sayanogorsk in southern Siberia. Other examples are the chemical plants associated with the two new chemical ship terminals at Ventspils and Yuzhnyy. This seaward trend, already evident on the western coasts, is also expected to be fostered on the Pacific coast by the construction of the BAM. This apparent new focus of economic activity coincides with a migratory trend toward seacoasts. This tendency is most evident in the coastal regions of the Black Sea, which have been distinguished by net in-migraiton motivated in part by a search for warmer climate. The in-migration trend is also evident in the Baltic region, although there it is opposed by the indigenous republics on the ground that a large Russian influx will lead to the dilution of the indigenous populations. Finally, in the case of the Pacific coast, the Soviet Far East has consistently recorded net in-migration, being generally less harsh in environment than the rest of Siberia.

In summary, the principal factors in Soviet regional policy that appear to be emerging at the present time are the resource-oriented development of Siberia and other eastern regions, the increasing importance of population distribution in the allocation of manufacturing investment, and the growing importance of international trade in regional development, as evidenced both by the industrialization of the western borderlands adjoining Eastern Europe and by the unusual interest displayed in seacoast development.

Footnotes

1. A.M. Lola and T.M. Savina, "Regulation and prospects of transformation of rural settlement in the Non-Chernozem Zone of the RSFSR", *Soviet Geography*,

(March 1979), 170-183; quotation from p. 176.

2. K.P. Kosmachev and V.P. Mosunov, "Evaluation of spatial differences in the setting of normative guidelines for planning and construction", *Soviet Geography*, (September, 1978), 463-470.

3. T.G. Runova, "Location of the natural resource potential of the USSR in relation to the geography of productive forces", *Soviet Geography*. (February 1976), 73-85.

4 *Planove Khoziaistovo* (library of Congress system) is not the same transliteration system as the rest of the paper. I used the *Board of Geographic Names* system, which is in official U.S. Government use.

5. A.A. Mints, "A predictive hypotheses of economic development in the European part of the USSR", *Soviet Geography*, (January 1976) 1-28.

6. *Planovoe Khoziastvo*, 6(1977), 154-5.

7. *The New York Times*, Feb. 17, 1979.

8. N.V. Alisov, "Spatial aspects of the new Soviet strategy of intensification of industrial production", *Soviet Geography*, (January 1979), 1-6.

9. *Planovoye Khoziastvo*, 6(1977), 154-5.

10. N.A. Salikova, "Methodological problems in the geography of labor resources", *Soviet Geography*, (June 1977), 401.

11. A.S. Akhiyezer and P.M. Il'yin, "Social evaluation of territory under the conditions of the scientific and technical revolution", *Soviet Geography*, (December 1975), 656.

12. *Planovoe Khoziastvo*, 6 (1977), 154-5.

13. *Planovoe Khoziastvo*, 12 (1978), 5, 19.

14. Theodore Shabad, "Some aspects of Central Asian manpower and urbanization", *Soviet Geography*, (February 1979), 113-124.

15. N.N. Nekrasov, *Regional'naia ekoromika*, (Moscow, 1978), p. 322.

16. Theodore Shabad, "Regional policy and CMEA integration", *Soviet Geography*, (April 1979).

17. V.V. Pokshishevskiy, "Theoretical aspects of attracting population to seacoasts and the measurement of that attraction", *Soviet Geography*, (March 1976), 145-153; O.N. Krivoruchko, "Maritime economic systems of the USSR", *Soviet Geography*. (March 1976, 153-159.

18. Theodore Shabad, "Some geographical aspects of the new Soviet five-year plan", *Soviet Geography*, (March 1978), 202-204.

Dr. Gertrude Schroeder

Current Position:
Professor of Economics, University of Virginia, Charlottesville, Va., 22901

Main field of work:
Soviet economic development, regional Territorial Production Complexes, regional standards of living in the USSR.

Regional Living Standards
Regional Differences in Income in the USSR in the 1970's
Professor Gertrude Schroeder

I. Introduction

Regional differences in incomes in the Soviet Union are of interest for several reasons. First, one wishes to assess the success of oft-stated Soviet policies to narrow such differences. Second, regional differences, along with rural-urban differences, are an important factor in any assessment of the USSR's likely ability to effect rural-urban and inter-regional employment transfers in the period of severe labor stringency that it faces in the 1980's. Finally, one wishes to learn how the USSR stands in comparison with other countries in respect to these kinds of income differences. Unfortunately, the available data are skimpy and unsatisfactory. Although average monthly wages by branch of the economy in the state sector are now published for all republics for recent years, similar data for lower-level units (oblasts, krays, ASSR's) are sparse. Also scarce are statistics on incomes of collective farmers, who constitute about one-fifth of the civilian labor force. Not all republics release data even on earnings in the public sector of collective farms, and almost no official statistics have been published on incomes from private activities, which still contribute substantially to rural incomes. Hence, in trying to measure farm incomes by regions, one must rely on a few studies published by Soviet researchers, whose data are ill-explained and sometimes conflict. Since the USSR does not systematically provide regional price information, these studies also must be relied on to appraise regional differences in real incomes. Finally, with existing information there is no way to estimate urban and rural income differences by region; one merely can try to provide some notions about the relative size of agricultural and non-agricultural incomes. The results are tenuous, at best.

This paper will build on and extend previous work in this area done by the author and others.[1] The following sections consider (1) differences in wages of the state labor force (workers and employees) in republics and some sub-regions (2) indicators of regional differences in agricultural and non-agricultural incomes and (3) the impact of regional differences in the cost of living on relative money incomes. Attention will also be paid to the effects of transfer payments and similar benefits on regional income disparities.

II. Wages of the State Labor Force

Soviet wage policy establishes uniform basic wage rates, bonus arrangements and job classification systems for each branch in the state sector. Regional differences in average earnings and also in earnings in particular sectors, therefore, arise largely from differences in the structure of economic activity as reflected in employment and skill mixes, from variations in the administration of the wage and bonus systems in practice, and from explicit regional wage coefficients and supplements that apply to certain geographic areas. In the early 1970's, these coefficients, which then were supposed to apply only to earnings up to 300 rubles per month, ranged from 10 to 20 percent in the Urals, southern regions of West Siberia, Kazakhstan and Central Asia to 100 percent in the islands of the Arctic Ocean.[2] In addition, income supplements related to length of service applied in certain Far Northern areas. When first introduced, the coefficients affected only wages in heavy industry; later, lower coefficients were introduced for light industry. In the 1970's, the USSR began a program to gradually extend the regional coefficients to all workers in the applicable area, to introduce them along with length of service supplements in certain regions where they did not exist before, and to raise the coefficients in some cases. This program has not yet been completed, and information on the differentials that will finally apply in various regions has not been published. Evidently, the coefficients are not uniform among sectors in a given region. The revision and extension of regional coefficients and supplements is being carried out simultaneously with a program to increase the minimum wage, adjust middle-level differentials and raise wages in most of the non-productive branches (e.g., education, health). These developments mean that regional differentials in average earnings are currently in a state of flux.

Data on average annual earnings by republic during 1960-1975 have been presented and discussed in previous papers.[3] The findings were that differences among the republics were narrow, well within the range found in other countries at similar levels of development, and that not much change in relative levels had occurred in this period. Table 1 shows average monthly earnings by republic for 1970-78. As a consequence of the extension of regional wage coefficients and supplements, earnings differentials have widened during the 1970's. The coefficient of variation rose from 0.082 in 1970 to 0.102 in 1978. These findings are greatly influenced by the fact that one "region"--the RSFSR--accounts for over three-fifths of the total wage bill, as well as by the fact that a reform of the wage system was in process. A more definitive measure of relative levels and trends can be made, when data for 1980 are published and when more data for geographic sub-units of the republics can be compiled. In the interim, the data given in Tables 2 and 3 extend our knowledge about regional wage variations in important ways. Available statistics now permit us to learn how wages vary among the 15 republics by branch of the economy (Table 2). Only Kazakhstan does not

Table 1
Average Monthly Wages in the USSR and Republics
1970, 1975 and 1978

| | Rubles | | | Percentages | | |
	1970	1975	1978	1970	1975	1978
USSR	122	146	160	100	100	100
RSFSR	126	153	168	103	105	105
Ukraine	115	134	146	94	92	91
Belorussia	106	126	141	87	86	88
Uzbekistan	115	137	148	94	94	92
Kazakhstan	124	148	160	101	102	100
Georgia	106	118	134	87	81	84
Azerbaidjan	110	125	138	90	86	86
Lithuania	120	142	158	98	97	99
Moldavia	103	117	129	84	80	81
Latvia	126	146	161	103	100	101
Kirgizia	113	134	144	92	93	90
Tadjikistan	118	136	141	96	93	88
Armenia	123	139	153	100	96	96
Turkmenia	130	158	171	170	111	107
Estonia	135	160	178	111	110	111

Source: Compiled from annual statistical handbooks and plan fulfillment reports published by the USSR and republics.

release such information.   As might be expected from the uniformity characteristic of Soviet wage-setting, high-wage republics tend to have high wages in nearly all branches, and low-wage republics tend to pay relatively low wages in most branches. Thus, the highest wages are paid in Estonia, on the average and also in 8 of the 13 branches. Conversely, Moldavia with the lowest average wage, also had the lowest wages in 5 branches. For the most part, industry transportation and construction rank highest in all republics, and trade, housing-communal economy and health rank lowest.

Table 3 presents fragmentary data on average wages in 3 cities, 18 oblasts and 4 other administrative units, mainly for 1975. These data are taken from published statistical handbooks of the units that happened to be available to the author; a number of others are known to have been published, but were not available. Despite their small number and random selection, they provide an important addition to our knowledge about wages in entities below the republic level. A casual inspection indicates, as Soviet economists assert,[4] that regional wage differences are much wider than revealed by data for republics alone. In 1975, wages for 19 administrative units ranged from 19 percent below the USSR average to 139 percent above it. This contrasts with a range among the republics from 20 percent below the national average in Moldavia to 11 percent above in Turkmenia. The impact of regional wage coefficients and supplement is clearly evident in the relatively very high wages paid in Magadan, Murmansk and Skhalin Oblasts. Wage data by branch of the economy, available for most of these administrative units, generally conform to the pattern characteristic of the republics.

Table 2
Average Monthly Wages by Republic and Branch, 1975

	Total	Industry	Agriculture	Transport-ation	Commun-ication	Construct-tion	Trade and Related Activities
USSR	145.8	162.2	126.8	173.5	123.6	176.8	108.7
RSFSR	153.2	167.9	134.6	185.2	130.8	183.1	113.6
Ukraine	133.5	153.0	115.2	147.4	111.1	155.9	99.3
Belorussia	126.0	138.7	95.8	146.8	107.0	153.7	102.0
Uzbekistan	136.6	151.9	121.0	171.7	122.3	178.9	106.2
Kazakhstan	148.5						
Georgia	118.5	138.4	79.3	146.0	92.9	173.5	96.0
Azerbaidjan	125.1	140.0	99.5	142.0	97.9	174.8	92.2
Lithuania	142.3	155.4	116.6	165.2	107.1	179.7	108.5
Moldavia	117.0	129.0	99.1	141.8	103.7	139.4	98.0
Latvia	146.4	154.5	129.4	173.3	114.7	185.3	111.4
Kirgizia	134.2	153.7	112.1	165.9	127.0	164.2	103.6
Tadjikistan	136.2	147.8	110.7	169.5	119.9	172.7	109.0
Armenia	138.6	156.4	101.2	153.5	110.1	205.9	98.9
Turkmenia	158.4	169.6	174.6	180.5	143.0	203.5	116.2
Estonia	159.8	185.9	179.4	198.5	141.1	203.6	118.4

	Housing-Health Communal Economy		Education& Culture	Science	Credit and Insurance	Adminis-Tration
USSR	109.0	102.3	122.9	157.5	133.8	131.8
RSFSR	113.4	107.4	125.2	162.1	142.8	138.5
Urkaine	101.0	91.6	117.3	142.4	121.9	116.8
Belorussia	100.8	95.1	118.2	127.8	118.5	118.2
Uzbekistan	100.5	98.7	123.4	146.2	113.9	122.2
Kazakhstan						
Georgia	92.8	89.6	118.1	134.8	105.8	113.8
Azerbaidjan	83.4	92.4	132.1	143.8	126.5	130.0
Lithuania	112.1	108.1	129.4			132.3
Moldavia	96.7	94.7	114.8	126.3	127.9	119.0
Latvia	117.6	107.3	127.3	141.4	131.5	132.1
Kirgizia	102.3	97.1	124.7	145.9	116.4	122.4
Tadjikstan	98.6	106.4	133.6	148.2	118.3	122.5
Armenia	92.3	109.9	124.5	140.2	117.3	123.2
Turkmenia	118.9	110.9	142.2	165.7	114.1	132.3
Estonia	131.5	114.1	131.6	154.6	136.9	146.5

Sources: Annual statistical handbooks of the republics. Data for Turkmenia pertain to 1974. The average wage there was 161.5 in 1975.

Table 3
Average Monthly Wages of State Employees
in Various Geographical Areas, 1973 and 1975

Area	Year	Average Monthly Wage (rubles)	Percent Urban
USSR	1975	145.8	61
Moscow (city)	1975	160.0	100
Leningrad (city)	1975	150.1	100
Orenburg Oblast	1975	145.6	60
Kaliningrad O.	1975	139.4	77
Magadan O.	1975	348.3	78
Murmansk O.	1975	274.0	89
Novosibirsk O.	1975	160.5	71
Leningrad O.	1975	138.7	63
Sakhalin O.	1975	274.1	83
Sverdlovsk O.	1975	156.5	85
Kuybyshev O.	1975	148.1	78
Chita O.	1975	159.8	63
Bryansk O.	1975	147.8	57
Dnepropetrovsk O.	1975	142.7	80
Ivano-Frankivsk O.	1975	118.2	35
Primorskiy Kray	1975	184.7	76
Kabardino-Balkavskiy ASSR	1975	130.5	57
Bashkir ASSR	1975	144.4	56
Karel'skaia ASSR	1975	176.2	76
Turkmenia	1973		49
Ashkhabad O.	1973	166.2	32
Krasnovodsk O.	1973	160.9	82
Mariynskaya O.	1973	157.4	33
Tavshauzkraya O.	1973	122.5	30
Chardzhouskaya O.	1973	142.0	46
Askhkabad (city)	1973	140.8	100

Sources: Statistical handbooks published by the various political sub-divisions.

III. Regional Differences in Incomes, Urban and Rural

Ideally, one would like to measure urban-rural income differences per worker and per capita in republics and smaller sub-units, especially those in the RSFSR. Since no data on urban/rural incomes per se are available, recourse must be had to data in respect to incomes in the non-agricultural branches and in agriculture. As shown in Table 4, taken from the 1970 Soviet census, however, substantial percentages of all persons engaged in non-agricultural pursuits reside in rural areas, and the shares vary considerably among branches and republics. For example, in education, science, art and health, 29 percent of the total gainfully employed were classified as rural residents; conversely, 7 percent of those engaged in agriculture and forestry were urban residents. In industry, construction, transport and communication the proportion of rural residents ranged from 15 percent of the total in Armenia and Turkmenia to 30 percent in Moldavia. Urban-rural earnings patterns would be heavily influenced by differences in the structure of economic activity in non-agricultural branches, as well as their share in total incomes, especially in rural areas. Urban-rural income differences also might be influenced by regional differences in the proportion of women in the total labor force. Such data are also given in Table 4; they reveal sizeable differences among republics in the shares of women in both the urban and the rural labor forces. Finally, such differences would be influenced by a urban/rural wage rate differentials built into basic wage and salary scales, differences in skill mixes within branches and variations in natural conditions affecting agriculture. The information base for sorting all these factors out is virtually non-existent.

As a surrogate, we shall have to rely on assorted indicators of regional differences in agricultural and non-agricultural activities. The word "indicators" is required, because available data do not permit satisfactory estimates of such differential incomes, either per worker or per capita. Since all republics except Kazakhstan now publish average earnings of state employees by branch of the economy, one can obtain reliable estimates of average non-agricultural wages and of wages in state agriculture by republic. Data for collective farmer earnings in the public sector can be calculated with reasonable accuracy for 11 republics from regularly published data. The results are given for 1975 in Table 5. As might be expected, regional differences are much narrower in non-agricultural activities than in agriculture. In 1975, average non-agricultural earnings ranged from 82 percent of the national average in Moldavia to 109 percent in Turkmenia. The range (and also the coefficient of variation) was wider in 1975 than in 1970 or even in 1960, but one should remember that the on-going wage reform, being carried out gradually by geographic area and sector, was, not completed. All the same, the differentials continued to widen in 1976-78, as measured by average earnings for the state sector as a whole.

In the post-Stalin period the USSR has been implementing a policy of narrowing differentials between non-agricultural wages and those paid on state and collective farms. Thus, in 1975 wages in state agriculture were 78 percent of those in industry, compared with 72 percent in 1965. Comparable figures for earnings of collective farmers in the socialized sector were 62 percent and 49 percent, respectively. A similar reduction of differentials has been taking place in most of the republics, but evidently at uneven rates. In respect to state agriculture, average earnings failed to keep pace with those in industry in four republics, while in the others (for which data are available in both years) the gaps were reduced at varying rates.

Table 4
Percentage Distribution of the Labor Force by Branch of the Economy, Urban and Rural in 1970 (excluding private plots)

	Total Labor Force		Industry Construction Transportation and Communication		Agriculture and Forestry		Trade Procurement & Material Technical Supply		Education Science Art and Health		Housing-Communal, Economy, Credit and Administration	
	U	R	U	R	U	R	U	R	U	R	U	R
USSR	62	38	82	18	7	93	75	25	71	29	84	16
RSFSR	67	33	84	16	7	93	77	23	74	26	84	16
Ukraine	58	42	82	18	8	92	74	26	71	29	86	14
Belorussia	49	51	77	73	4	96	71	29	61	39	81	19
Uzbekistan	41	59	78	22	4	96	66	34	59	41	74	26
Kazakhstan	57	43	84	16	5	95	66	34	60	40	80	20
Georgia	49	51	76	24	7	93	75	35	67	33	80	20
Azerbaidjan	56	44	85	15	11	89	80	20	69	31	86	14
Lithuania	56	44	79	21	5	95	81	19	72	28	87	13
Moldavia	33	67	70	30	5	95	64	36	53	47	82	18
Latvia	68	32	82	18	6	94-	84	16	77	33	90	10
Kirgizia	44	56	71	29	5	95	61	39	53	47	70	30
Tadjikistan	43	57	79	21	8	92	72	28	62	38	77	23
Armenia	63	37	85	15	10	90	83	17	76	24	87	13
Turkmenia	52	48	85	15	6	94	80	20	69	31	89	11
Estonia	70	30	82	18	11	89	82	18	77	23	89	11
Percent Women												
USSR	50	50	41	33	40	51	76	66	72	70	48	40
RSFSR	51	49	42	36	37	48	79	72	72	75	50	43
Ukraine	50	52	40	31	47	54	76	66	73	71	47	39
Belorussia	51	51	44	31	35	54	77	68	74	70	41	34
Uzbekistan	46	49	37	20	44	55	52	29	69	47	43	28
Kazakhstan	47	47	35	33	37	42	74	64	75	70	48	44
Georgia	47	49	38	24	39	54	50	42	71	66	36	25
Azerbaidjan	42	47	32	12	46	54	50	23	68	49	39	17
Lithuania	49	47	41	26	29	50	74	72	74	73	47	52
Moldavia	51	52	42	31	46	53	68	57	71	71	45	34
Latvia	51	48	42	31	34	51	78	81	75	73	49	48
Kirgizia	49	48	39	31	39	50	68	46	72	64	46	37
Tadjikistan	46	45	37	13	41	52	50	13	67	33	45	17
Armenia	45	48	38	26	37	52	55	47	68	64	37	25
Turkmenia	42	48	33	25	26	53	59	24	66	41	42	20
Estonia	51	47	42	30	27	48	82	82	77	80	50	40

Source: 1970 Soviet Census, Vol. V, pp.124-204.

Data provided in plan fulfillment reports for the USSR and the republics indicate that differentials were reduced further during 1976-78, at least between the pay of collective farmers and that of the state labor forces as a whole. In 1975, the latest year for which reasonably complete data are available (see Table 5), average earnings in state agriculture ranged from 37 percent below the all-union average in Georgia to 39 percent above the average in Turkmenia. The incomplete data in respect to average annual wages from the socialized sector on collective farms (for 11 republics) show Georgia to be lowest with 16 percent below the national average and Estonia to be highest with annual earnings 86 percent above the average. In that republic, agricultural wages were higher than non-agricultural wages. A Soviet source has provided similar data for 1973 for the 10 economic regions of the RSFSR and for 24 oblasts, krays and ASSR's.[5] In that

Table 5
Average Annual Money Wages in Agricultural and Non-Agricultural Activities, by Republic in 1975

	Rubles			Percentages		
	Non-Agricultural Branches	State Farms	Collective Farms	Non-Agricultural Branches	State Farms	Collective Farms
USSR	1775	1522	1099	100	100	100
RSFSR	1860	1615	1200	105	106	109
Ukraine	1619	1202	970	91	79	88
Belorussia	1563	1149		88	75	
Uzbekistan	1677	1462	1211	94-	96	110
Kazakhstan	1792	1741		101	114	
Georgia	1510	953	919	85	63	84
Azerbaidjan	1558	1196	1128	88	79	103
Lithuania	1741	1400	1368	98	92	124-
Moldavia	1457	1192		82	78	
Latvia	1778	1540	1423	100	101	129
Kirgizia	1651	1386	1191	93	91	108
Tadjikistan	1684	1330	1138	95	87	104
Armenia	1724	1217	1399	97	80	127
Turkmenia	1926	2108		109	139	
Estonia	1909	2000	2041	108	131	186

Sources: Calculated from data given in republic annual statistical handbooks and annual reports on plan fulfillment. In the case of Turkmenia, the wages in state farms were calculated on the assumption that the differentials in 1975 were the same as reported for 1974. Estimates for Kazakhstan were calculated as a residual. The data for state and collective farms pertain to work in the socialized sector only and for the latter they include some income in kind (about 5 percent of the total in the USSR as a whole).

year, average annual pay of collective farmers ranged from 86 percent of the USSR average in the Volga-Vyatka region to 57 percent above the average in the Far East. Among the 24 sub-units, earnings ranged from 69 percent of the national average in Chubashskaya ASSR to 82 percent above that average in Moscow Oblast. Similar differences also exist in respect to occupations. Thus, in 1970, average monthly wages of collective farm chairmen ranged from 71 percent of the USSR average in Georgia to 56 percent above the average in Turkmenia; for tractor drivers the corresponding figures are 70 and 69.[6]

Both collective farmers and state farmers supplement their incomes with sizeable earnings from private agricultural activities, including income in kind as well as cash from sales of produce. From official Soviet data on budgets of collective farm families it can be determined that in 1977 income from private plots amounted to 55 percent of incomes received from work in the public sector; in 1970 the figure was 79 percent.[7] Comparable data are not available in respect to state farm families. A Soviet source reports that in 1970, one fifth of total family income of state farm families came from private activities.[8] Since the author evidently included payments from social funds in his definition of income, private plot income amounted to perhaps about 30 percent of state wages. Clearly, incomes from private agricultural pursuits must be taken into account in any assessment of urban-rural income differences. Unfortunately, the requisite data are meager indeed. Aside from those cited above, giving the share of the private subsidiary economy in total family incomes of collective farmers (and also of workers in industry), there are no officially published data on private plot incomes; moreover, the family budget data are available only occasionally for a republic and may be unrepresentative. To provide an idea of regional variations in incomes from private plots, one has to rely on studies by two Soviet economists (Sidorova and Teriaeva) pertaining to 1970 and earlier.[9] Apparently, these studies are based on detailed results of family budget surveys made available to the authors. According to data provided by Sidorova, the relative importance of private plots in family incomes differs greatly among the republics. In 1970, it exceeded income from the public sector in Georgia and was about equal to public sector wages paid for farm work in Moldavia and Belorussia.[10] In Turkmenia, in contrast, private plot incomes were only 27 percent of incomes received from work in the socialized sector. These relationships vary from year to year, with a strong trend toward a decreased share for private plots. In addition to differences in the contribution of private sector incomes to total family incomes, their relative size varies regionally and from year to year as a result of differences in the kinds of activity carried out in the private sector, weather and other natural factors affecting output, and prices. The data with which to sort all this out are not at hand. Moreover, it has even proved impossible to develop a reliable employment measure for the private sector by region.

In the absence of a reliable composite measure, Table 6 assembles several indicators of differences in agricultural and non-agricultural incomes in the republics in 1970, the year for which the information is most complete. The first two columns in Table 6 pertain to the state labor force. Differences among the republics in respect to non-agricultural incomes are narrow, ranging from 14 percent below the national average in Moldavia to 11 percent above it in Estonia. Differences in incomes of state agricultural workers are somewhat wider, with three republics having incomes one-fifth less than the national average and one republic having incomes nearly one-fifth higher than that average. Columns 3 and 4 give the results of the author's attempt to estimate "earned incomes" of collective farmers from relatives representing total incomes per family given by Sidorova.[11] The latter include incomes from "social consumption funds", 1.e. pensions, aid, education, health and other services provided from state and collective farm funds. The principal elements of 'earned income' are earnings in money and in kind from work for the collective farms and on private plots. Differentials in collective farmer incomes among the republics are much wider than for other incomes. When measured per family, they ranged from 12 percent below the national average in the Ukraine to 77 percent above the average in Turkmenia. The average size of family, however, differs greatly. According to the same Soviet source, the average family had 3.5 members in the USSR, but it had 5.6 members in Tadjikistan and only 2.1 in Estonia.[12] As a result, earned income differences per capita are very wide, ranging from one-third below the national average in Tadjikistan to more than double that average in Estonia.

The last three columns in Table 6 provide evidence on the extent to which regional differences are reduced, when payments and benefits from social consumption funds are taken into account for the respective groups of workers. Soviet statisticians routinely include these additional sums when calculating real incomes per capita. For the state labor force as a whole, these payments and benefits added nearly 37 percent to the income of the average worker in 1977.[13] Benefits are much larger for urban residents than for rural residents (among other things, they include the urban housing subsidy and reflect the substantially greater quantity of medical care provided in cities). For this and other reasons, their addition to money incomes of the state labor force does not significantly reduce regional differentials. In respect to collective farm families, however, the addition of benefits from social consumption funds to family incomes appreciably narrows differentials among regions. As would be expected, inter-republic differences are much wider, when incomes are calculated per capita. The data in Table 6 show clearly how the relative position of the Central Asian republics is worsened on this measure, while the relative positions of the Baltic republics are improved.

IV. Regional Differences in Real Incomes

Substantial differences in the cost of living exist among the USSR's republics, but especially among the economic regions, oblasts and krays of the RSFSR. These differences exist, first because there are zonal differences in prices of most food products and some non-food products, and second, because there are substantial differences in expenditures related to climatic differences, e.g. for housing (heat), heavy clothing and more calories in Siberia and the Far North. The information available on these important matters is meager. Neither the USSR nor the republics publish data on relative prices. We know that prices of food on collective farm markets differ substantially among cities. We also know that state retail prices for basic foods are differentiated by zones. Three zones apply to most foods, two zones to fish products, and four zones to wine and champagne. According to a recent source, prices for basic foods are 8 percent higher in Zone II than in Zone I and 14 percent higher in Zone III than in Zone I.[14] Basically, the foods affected are: flour, bread and bakery goods; meat and dairy products (except canned goods); sugar and confectionery product; fats; and eggs. The zonal differentials differ greatly by product. The areas in Zone I are: the Baltics, Ukraine, Moldavia, Belorussia (for some items), Kazakhstan, Central Asia, West Siberia and several other areas of the Western RSFSR. Zone II prices apply to Transcaucasia, Belorussia (for some items), the Urals, East Siberia, the industrial Center and Northwest parts of the RSFSR, the Far East (for some items) and Chita Oblast (for some items). Zone III prices affect the Far East and Kemerovo Oblast (for some items) and nine northern oblasts and other units of the RSFSR, including Tyumen' Oblast. In addition to differences in prices of goods, the prices of services (if available) vary widely among regions.

Some fragmentary information on regional differences in the cost of living is given in works by individual Soviet economists; their data seem to be based on surveys made in the late 1960's They pertain to urban workers, are for from complete, and do not always agree. Perhaps the best idea of how the cost of living differs among regions is afforded by a study made by the Institute of Labor of the State Committee for Labor and Wages and published in 1972.[15] This study compares the cost of a market basket of goods and services in 1968 in 14 geographic areas with its cost in the central oblasts of the RSFSR. The results of the study are reproduced in Table 7. In the regions studied, the lowest cost areas relative to the central oblasts are the Ukraines, Central Asia and Kazakhstan, all of which are in Zone I in respect to food prices. Conversely, the highest cost areas are in areas far from the supply sources such as Sakhalin, Magadan, Murmansk oblasts and in Yakutsk ASSR, where Zone III prices apply and where living conditions are arduous. The prices for some foods were reduced to Zone II in the latter areas as of January 1, 1970.

Table 6
Indicators of Regional Differences in Agricultural and Non-Agricultural Income, 1970

	Average Annual Non-Agricultural Wages	Average Annual Earned Incomes in State Agriculture	Earned Incomes on Collective Farms Per Family	Per Family Members	Average Annual "Social Wages" of State Employees	Total Incomes on Collective Farmers Per Family	Per Family Member
	(1)	(2)	(3)	(4)	(5)	(6)	(7)
USSR	100	100	100	100	100	100	100
RSFSR	105	102	100	109	104	102	109
Ukraine	95	96	88	106	96	80	92
Belorussia	91	80	93	105	88	84	94
Uzbekistan	97	97	133	80	97	188	69
Kazakhstan	103	111	125	95	103	148	110
Georgia	89	80	122	112	87	105	94
Azerbaidjan	94	83	101	65	94	92	58
Lithuania	100	95	134	164	96	122	150
Moldavia	86	91	97	97	82	85	84
Latvia	104	103	134	195	106	115	162
Kirgizia	96	89	104	74	94	93	68
Tadjikistan	101	80	107	62	98	95	55
Armenia	104	90	122	73	110	117	76
Turkmenia	107	117	177	107	94	153	90
Estonia	111	119	124	217	112	122	205

Sources: Col. 1. Calculated from data in annual statistical handbooks of the republics. Col. 2. *Ibid.* In addition to wages, the figures include estimates of incomes from private plots, calculated as explained in Gertrude E. Schroeder, *ACES Bulletin,* XVI, 2, (Fall 1974), p. 14.

Col. 3 and 4. *Ibid*, pp. 13-15. Earned income includes earnings in both the socialized and private sectors. The underlying data on incomes were calculated from percentage relatives of various kinds, and also size of families, given in M.I. Sidorova, *Vozmeshchenie neobkhodimykh zatrat i formirovanie fonda vosproizvodstva rabochev sily v kolkhozakh,* (Moscow, 1972), pp. 100-137.

Col. 5. Same sources as for Col. 1. Includes money wages plus pro-rata payments and benefits from social consumption funds.

Col. 6 and 7. M.I. Sidorova, *op. cit.,* pp. 108, 123. Total income includes incomes from all sources, including private plots and pro-rata shares of payments and benefits from social consumption funds.

Table 7
The Cost of Budget Market Baskets*
(In Percent of Central Oblasts)

	Single Worker		Family of Four	
	Excl. Taxes	Inc. Taxes	Excl. Taxes	Incl. Taxes
Central Oblasts	100.0	100.0	100.0	100.0
Bashkirskaya ASSR	102.5	103.2	99.8	99.8
Urals	113.1	115.7	102.7	102.8
Western Siberia	105.6	107.9	102.7	102.8
Eastern Siberia	118.2	121.2	115.8	116.5
City of Braksk**	148.5	153.6	140.6	142.3
Far East	127.1	130.7	124.7	125.7
Sakhalinskaya Oblast**	158.7	164.5	148.8	150.9
Arkhangel'skaya Oblast	128.8	132.6	126.9	128.0
Murmanskaya Oblast	158.7	164.5	148.8	150.9
Magadanskaya Oblast	180.0	187.2	166.4	169.1
Yakutskaya ASSR	172.0	178.8	158.0	160.4
Ukrainian SSR	97.6	92.1	91.4	93.9
Central Asia	93.2	88.4	90.7	90.3
Kazakh SSR	100.5	100.9	97.7	97.7

*Excluding kolkhoz-market prices, in 1968 prices.
**With the use of the market basket for the Far North.

Source: *Ekonomicheskie nauki,* 1. (1972), p. 53.

From this and other evidence, it is clear that the cost of living differs substantially among geographic areas in the USSR. The system of regional wage coefficients, of course, is designed to compensate for regional differences in the cost of living. In many cases, they do, but there are evidently many anomalies. For instance, wage coefficients of 10 to 20 percent apply to Central Asia and Kazakhstan even though they are assigned to Zone I in respect to food prices. The reverse is true in other cases. One author states that wages approximately compensate for the cost of living in the Far East, but that such is not the case in the Urals and Siberia.[16] In some cases, wage coefficients differ among industries in the same area. All of these factors contribute to high labor turnover and hamper the USSR's efforts to attract and retain workers in the Eastern and Northern regions, where large development projects are underway or planned.

V. Conclusions

For years, Soviet policy proclaimed the intent to narrow differences in incomes among the USSR's diverse regions. The author's earlier investigation suggested that little change in differentials occurred in the

1960's. Since 1972, the objective of reducing differentials has not been touted, Brezhnev having declared that the aim had been "basically achieved".[17] The wage reforms of the 1970's have widened wage differentials among the republics. However, the ultimate result may be to reduce differences in real incomes, taking account of price differences and differences in climatic conditions. The pre-reform arrangements evidently were replete with inequities and anomalies that were inimical to the government's desires in respect to territorial redistribution of employment. This conclusion must necessarily be tentative, since we lack detailed knowledge of the new regional wage coefficients, and data on regional differences in the cost of living are scarce.

Although we did not succeed in producing estimates of urban and rural incomes by region, the various substitute indicators reveal much wider regional differences in agricultural incomes than in non-agricultural incomes. Within each category, inter-republic differences have widened in the 1970's. However, for the USSR as a whole and in most of the republics for which data are available, the differentials between farm and non-farm money incomes have been continuously and significantly reduced in the 1970's, as they were throughout the 1960's. Earnings from private agriculture add substantially to incomes of both state and collective farmers. If these earnings could be taken into account fully, total incomes of agricultural workers from both sources might now be nearly equal to those of non-agricultural workers, both in the USSR as a whole and in many of the republics. In respect to the overall standard of living, however, the relative position of farmers would be worsened by lower levels of payments and benefits from social consumption and by the much fewer amenities available in rural areas. A recent Soviet source states that real income of collective farm families rose from 75 percent of those of families of workers and employees in 1965 to 87 percent in 1977 and will be 'essentially equalized' by 1980.[18] Probably, essential equality has already been achieved in respect to a comparison of non-agricultural incomes with those in state agriculture, when private plot incomes are taken into account. In Estonia, and perhaps Turkmenia, agricultural incomes already exceed those in non-agricultural pursuits. Differences are being rapidly reduced in other republics.

Footnotes

1. Alastair McAuley, *Economic Welfare in the Soviet Union,* (Madison, 1979), Chapters 5-7 (this source was not available to the author when the draft of this paper was being written and therefore could not be fully taken into account. His findings confirm those in this paper on many counts); Gertrude E. Schroeder, "Regional Differences in Incomes and Levels of Living in the USSR", in V.N. Bandera and Z. Lew Melnyk (eds.), *The Soviet Economy in Regional Perspective,* (New York, 1973), pp. 167-195; "Soviet Wage and Income Policies in Regional Perspective", *ACES Bulletin,* XVI, 2, (Fall 1974), pp. 3-20; "Soviet Regional Development Policies in Perspective", in NATO, Economic Directorate (ed.), *The USSR in the 1980's Economic Growth and the Role of Foreign Trade,* (Brussels, 1978), pp. 125-142; Karl-

Eugen Wädekin, "Income Distribution in Soviet Agriculture", *Soviet Studies,* XXXVII, 1 (January 1975), pp. 3-26.

2. I.F. Mizhenskaia, *Lichnye potrebnosti pri sctsialisme,* (Moscow, 1973), p. 94.
3. Schroeder, *supra.*
4. *Planovoe khoziaistvo,* 1 (1975), p 57.
5. V.V. Dyukov, *Sovershenstvovanie material'nykh uslovii vosproizvodstva rabochei sily v kolkhozakh,* (Kazan', 1977), pp. 58, 70.
6. *Spavochnik po oplata truda v kolkhozakh,* (Moscow, 1973), p. 9.
7. *Narodnoe khoziaistvo SSSR v 1977 god=,* p. 410.
8. S.L. Siniavskiy, *Izmenenie v sotsialno= strikture sovetskogo obshchestva,* (Moscow, 1973), p. 269.
9. A. Teriaeva, *Voprosy ekonomiki,* 5, (1972), pp. 66-77; M.I. Sidorova, *Obshchestvennye fondy potreblenia i dokhody kolkhoznikov,* (Moscow, 1969); Sidorova, *Vozmeshchenie neobkhodimykh zatrat i formirovanie fonds vosproizvodstva rabochei sily v kolkhozakh,* (Moscow, 1972).
10. Sidorova, *Vozmeshchenie,* pp. 100-102.
11. *Ibid.,* p. 108.
12. *Ibid.,* p. 136.
13. *Narodnoe khoziaistvo v 1977 godu,* p. 385.
14. M.V. Kokorev, *Tseny na tovary narodnogo potreblenia,* (Moscow, 1978), pp.184-190.
15. *Ekonomicheskie nauki,* 1, (1972), pp. 45-58.
16. L.P. Kuprienko, *Vlianie urovnia zhizni na raspredelenie trudovykh resursov,* (Moscow, 1976), p. 93. See also *Ekonomicheskie nauki,* 2, (1979), p. 64.
17. *Pravda,* December 22, 1972.
18. *Kommunist,* 12, (1978), p. 16.

Dr. Alastair McAuley

Current position:
Lecturer in Economics
University of Essex
Wivenhoe Park
Colchester
Essex CO4 3SQ
England

Main field of work:
Wages, income distribution, social security and labour in USSR

Publications during the last two years
Economic Welfare in the Soviet Union 1979. Madison Wisconsin, and London.

"The Distribution of Earnings and incomes in the Soviet Union'', Soviet Studies XXIX, 2 (1977), 214-237.

'Women's Work and Wages in the USSR'', Ost Europa Wirtschaft, (1979).

"Soviet Anti-Poverty Policy, 1955-75'' Institute for Research on Poverty, University of Wisconsin, Madison, (Discussion paper no. 402-77)

Other remarks:
In the process of writing up a study on the position of women in the Soviet labour force, the earnings they receive, the jobs they do and the reasons for continuing sexual inequality.

Together with Dr. Ann Helgeson, a study of regional aspects of Soviet manpower policy is underway. They intend to examine both economic aspects of regional variations in the demand and supply of labor and also the evolution of institutional mechanisms for the regional direction of labor.

Regional Living Standards
Personal Income in the USSR Republican Variations in 1974

Alastair McAuley

This note provides an estimate of the disparity in living standards between the fifteen constituent republics of the USSR in 1974. Figures are given for the republican population as a whole and separately for kolkhozniki and state employees. I also attempt a tentative estimate of the range of variations in the living standards of collective farm households within the RSFSR. The figures given here continue the series to be found in my book (McAuley, 1979) to which the reader is referred for a more extended discussion of both methodological issues and substantive implications of regional inequality in the Soviet Union.

Data given below show that the Soviet population as a whole and the population of individual republics benefited from a rapid increase in nominal personal income in the period 1970-1974. But, on the measure used here, inter-republican disparities widened. The figures also suggest that in Central Asia and parts of the Transcaucasus there was widespread poverty, urban as well as rural. Of course, the Soviet family income supplement (for details of which, see McAuley, 1979, p. 282) was not introduced until November 1974, and it is to be expected that this will have raised living standards in these areas, but the estimates given here suggest that income growth in these areas has been offset to a considerable extent by rapid population expansion. It is probable that this pattern has continued since 1974 (and will continue for the next five or ten years as well).

Before presenting my estimates of the variation in republican living standards, it is desirable to comment on the indicator used. As I have argued elsewhere, neither per-capita national income nor real wages constitute an adequate measure of popular living standards in the USSR. The first is unsuitable because it includes components that do not add to personal welfare and the second is inadequate because it excludes such components. In McAuley, 1979, p. 9-13, I suggest three alternative measures and it is one of those that is used in this note. Personal income is defined to include the value of all claims on resources that enter directly into the family's budget. For purposes of estimation it is derived as the sum of wages and salaries in the state sector, payments (in cash and kind) for labor by collective farms, transfers, receipts from the financial system and the proceeds of private subsidiary activity. The largest component of this last category is the output of private agricultural holdings, whether consumed by the producing household or sold on the so-called kolkhoz market. But the data derive ultimately from Soviet family-budget statistics and, in so far as they include other forms of private activity, these will be reflected in our estimates. Although payments for labor in kind by kolkhozy now account for a relatively small proportion of the collective farm wage bill, approximately half of the output of private agriculture is consumed by its producers; personal income is therefore a more accurate indicator of popular living standards than money income would be.

The Soviet government, like the governments of other industrial states, provides its citizens with a range of free or subsidized services (education, medical care, subsidized housing and so on). These are all excluded from personal income; the figures given below thus understate the absolute levels of consumption attained in individual republics. Also, insofar as the provision of these services varies between republics and social groups, the estimates given here may understate the extent of regional inequality. In principle, it should prove possible to derive estimates of republican spending on individual services (and thus derive estimates of what I have called total per-capita income) but the necessary Soviet data were not readily available for all republics. Also, I felt it undesirable to overburden this short note with statistics.

The sources and methods whereby estimates of republican per-capita personal incomes were obtained are set out in Appendix Tables A1-A8 and will not be repeated here. But two comments are in order. First, in the figures given below, no allowance has been made for direct taxes. Such figures do exist for particular years, but I was unable to locate ones relating to 1974. Since the Soviet tax schedule is almost proportional and since both marginal rates and average liability are modest, the use of gross rather than net personal income should not be the source of any considerable bias in general comparisons. On the other hand, there are substantial differences in liability between kolkhozniki and state employees (the latter pay more of the tax); the figures given here thus overstate disparities in material wellbeing between social groups.

Second, no attempt has been made to adjust the figures given here for differences in prices; I report nominal rather than real per-capita personal income for each republic. This will affect conclusions in two ways. It will result in an overstatement of income growth. (For the USSR as a whole, the cost of living rose by some 5.5% between 1970 and 1974 (Schroeder and Severin, 1976, p. 652) but I have no idea whether there were extensive variations around that figure.) Since the expenditure patterns of kolkhoznik and state employee households differ, comparisons of the improvement in living standards enjoyed by the two social groups will also be affected. The other consequence of this neglect of price differences is to bias inter-republican comparisons in 1974. Implicitly, it is assumed below that a ruble has the same value throughout the USSR. This is false; it is known that there are substantial regional variations in the cost of living. Although, for the most part, these are confined to the RSFSR, in 1968, prices were lower in both the Ukraine and Central Asia than in the central provinces and it is to be presumed that these differences have persisted. (See McAuley, 1979, pp. 115-118 for further discussion.) Thus, the figures given below probably overstate regional disparities in living standards and underestimate the real incomes of those living in Central Asia.

Table 1
Per-Capita Personal Income:
USSR and Republics, 1970, 1974

| | Per-Capita Personal Income (Rubles Per Year | Indexes of Personal Income | | |
		In 1970 USSR = 100	In 1794 USSR = 100	(Income in 1970 = 100
USSR	951.43	100.0	100.0	119.1
RSFSR	1,051.08	108.0	110.5	121.8
Ukraine	897.66	97.1	94.3	115.6
Byelorussia	940.97	93.8	98.9	125.6
Uzbekistan	661.06	74.2	69.5	111.5
Kazakhstan	860.03	87.5	90.4	123.0
Georgia	807.96	89.4	84.9	113.1
Azerbaijan	579.86	66.0	60.9	109.9
Lithuania	1,072.95	117.7	112.8	114.1
Moldavia	808.08	86.0	84.9	117.6
Latvia	1,131.39	125.1	118.9	113.2
Kirgizia	662.06	72.5	69.6	114.3
Tadjikistan	570.31	63.0	59.9	113.2
Armenia	776.57	87.1	81.6	111.6
Turkmenistan	729.74	78.8	76.7	115.9
Estonia	1,192.42	133.2	125.3	112.0

Sources: Tables A1, A8 and McAuley 1979, p. 109.

Table 1 contains estimates of gross nominal per-capita personal income in 1974 for the USSR as a whole and for each of the fifteen Soviet republics. Figures for 1970 are also given. These show that over the four-year period income growth was rapid, despite economic problems. For the USSR as a whole, incomes grew by some nineteen percent; in Byelorussia, where improvement was greatest, living standards improved by more than a quarter; even in Azerbaijan, the republic that recorded the least improvement, the growth was almost ten percent.

In 1974, per-capita personal income in Estonia (the leading republic) was almost 1200 rubles per year. This is a third above the All-Union average and more than double the income received in Tadjikistan, the poorest republic. It is difficult to give an idea of what these figures imply about living standards in the USSR in comparison with those in other countries but, in 1976, the official rate of exchange stood at $1.35 to the ruble. Alternatively, in 1967 the Soviet government published a report which put the official poverty line at 50.00 rubles per month per capita in 1965. Allowing for increases in the cost of living between 1965 and 1974, an equivalent standard would require an income of 694 rubles per capita per year at the later date. In terms of this standard, then, average incomes in Estonia were somewhat less than twice the poverty level; in the USSR as a whole, they were approximately forty percent above it; but in Azerbaijan and three of the four Central Asian republics *average* per-capita incomes were less than 700 rubles per year (and in Turkmenistan, the remaining Central Asian republic, per-capita income was a mere five percent above the poverty line). In all these areas, then, deprivation must be widespread.

Table 2
Per-Capita Personal Income:
State Employees and Kolkhozniki:
USSR and Republics, 1974.

	State Employees		Kolkhozniki	
	Personal Income 1974 (Rubles per Year)	Personal Income 1970 (Rubles per Year)	Personal Income 1974 (Rubles per Year)	Personal Income 1970 (Rubles per Year)
USSR	1,002.86	834	726.26	659
RSFSR	1,089.87	884	785.53	716
Ukraine	958.77	821	749.37	676
Byelorussia	978.06	773	840.51	688
Uzbekistan	730.20	654	530.70	499
Kazakhstan	872.81	704	684.15	624
Georgia	821.51	723	773.26	696
Azerbaijan	641.67	568	410.29	424
Lithuania	901.75	903	1,122.33	1,069
Moldavia	916.74	772	665.44	606
Latvia	1,114.47	979	1,246.06	1,123
Kirgizia	699.11	622	544.76	473
Tadjikistan	626.40	597	481.40	396
Armenia	840.59	746	491.09	516
Turkmenistan	773.04	618	665.32	645
Estonia	1,161.81	1,035	1,525.00	1,333

Table 2 presents estimates of the per-capita personal income received by kolkhoznik and state employee households in each of the republics. Traditionally, it was possible to identify kolkhozniki and their dependents with the peasantry, but the extensive conversion of collective farms into state farms during the 1960's makes that identification less apt. However, since the national populations of the non-Russian republics are predominantly rural, figures on kolkhoznik living standards may be taken to represent a measure of the material wellbeing they enjoy. Figures for state employees, on the other hand, include a substantial urban component (and, in the non-Russian republics may be more typical of immigrant Slav populations).

The figures in Table 2 show that state employee families enjoyed a substantial rise in living standards between 1970 and 1974. For the USSR as a whole, personal income grew by twenty percent; in Byelorussia it grew by more than a quarter as it did in Turkmenistan and Kazakhstan. Only in Lithuania was no growth recorded, although improvement was modest in Tadjikistan too. On the other hand, the level of income attained in several republics was still low. In Azerbaijan and three of the four Central Asian republics it was less than five percent above the adjusted poverty standard described above.

Kolkhoznik families enjoyed a far slower rate of increase in their living standards in the period 1970-1974 than did state employees; growth in kolkhoznik wellbeing was also considerably slower than it had been in the preceding decade. In Azerbaijan and Armenia, personal income even falls. In part, this relatively poor performance must be a consequence of the agricultural difficulties experienced in the USSR at this time, but I suspect that it also reflects central government policy since towards the end of the 1960's differentials had become somewhat compressed.

The figures in Table 2 also bring out the wide disparities in living standards that exist both between kolkhozniki in different republics and between state employees and collective farmers in individual republics. The table shows that kolkhozniki in Estonia enjoyed personal incomes that were almost four times as large as those received by collective farmers in Azerbaijan. More generally, kolkhoznik incomes were below the adjusted poverty line throughout Central Asia, in most of the Transcaucasus, in Kazakhstan and Moldavia. Indeed, for the USSR as a whole, personal per-capita income for collective farmers was barely five percent above the poverty line. Unless the incomes of state-farm households are substantially above those of kolkhozniki, these figures suggest that there is widespread rural poverty in the Soviet Union. If sovkhoznik incomes do approximate those of other state employees. Table 2 suggests that there is still little room for complacency on the part of the Soviet leadership.

It is only in the three Baltic republics that collective farm living standards rise appreciably above poverty levels. And here they even exceed the standards attained by state employees. This result may well strike Soviet specialists as counter-intuitive. It is certainly not a freak of the figures for 1974 but has been true for much of the preceding decade to decade and a half. It is examined in some detail in McAuley, 1979, pp. 134-138. It is due, basically, to the productivity of private agriculture in those republics (mainly livestock farming, the keeping of pigs and chickens) and the small size of collective farm families. (Table A8 indicates that this was less than three persons in all the Baltic republics whereas in Central Asia it was almost six persons.) There is also some evidence to suggest that the Baltic peasants work extremely hard. Figures in Churakov, 1977, p. 23 appear to imply that when due allowance is made for work on

Table 3
Republican Variations in Living Standards, 1960-1974

Coefficient of Variations of Per-Capita Personal Income Among:

	State Employees	Kolkhozniki	Total Population
1960	5.1	15.8	11.2
1970	6.3	20.8	12.4
1974	12.5	18.4	14.8

Sources and Notes: Rows (1) - (2) McAuley, 1979, p. 111, 141, 362; Row (3) calculated from Tables 1 - 2. In calculating the variance in per-capita income for each social group, income was weighted by republican population shares.

the private plot, the average number of days worked by kolkhozniki in the three Baltic republics in 1974 exceeded 350; in none of the Central Asian republics did it exceed 280. (In Georgia, by the way, Churakov implies that the total number of days worked, collective and private, was little as 215.)

For the USSR as a whole, Table 2 suggests that collective farm living standards were approximately 70-75% of those enjoyed by state employees. This is somewhat less than the gap reported by Rusanov for 1966 (Rusanov, 1971, p. 83) but rather more than that discovered by myself for 1970 - 79%. (McAuley, 1979, p. 128, 139.)

So far, discussion has concentrated on the levels of welfare achieved by the different social groups in each of the Soviet republics. The treatment of inequality has been heuristic. But Table 3 attempts a more formal measurement of its extent. It reports the coefficient of variation (standard deviations divided by the mean) for each of the distributions given in Tables 1 and 2. It also gives analogous figures for 1950 and 1970. The figures in Table 3 show that for all three series, the coefficient of variation was higher in 1974 than it had been in 1960 - and thus, according to this measure, regional inequality had increased. Although inequality among kolkhozniki is greater than it is among state employees, according to Table 3, it has declined since 1970. On the other hand, inequality among state employees has almost doubled since 1970.

For the population as a whole, the coefficient of variation of per-capita personal incomes by republic in 1974 was 14.8%. This is approximately equal to the value for the United Kingdom reported by Williamson in the mid 1960's. It is rather greater than he found for countries such as Australia and New Zealand, but less than that for Japan, the USA or France (Williamson, 1968, pp. 99-158). Thus, disturbing as these trends must be, in view of the Soviet government's stated objective of reducing regional disparities in living standards, it is as well to keep the scale of inequality in perspective.

It is possible that the low value of the coefficient of variation reported for the USSR is a consequence of the peculiar regionalization implied by the use of the Soviet republics - where the RSFSR accounts for from one third to one half of the total. The figures in Table 4 were produced to test this. For the distribution as recorded, the calculated coefficient of variation was 6.95%, whereas using a figure for the RSFSR as a whole it was 13%. Thus the hypothesis advanced above is refuted - at least on these data.

But the figures in the Table are of some intrinsic interest (although I am somewhat sceptical of their reliability, since I am not sure that I have properly understood what Churakov's index refers to: but at all events I have attempted to produce analogous figures for other republics). Two things stand out: first, with the exception of the Far Eastern Region, there is remarkably little variation in this index of welfare within the RSFSR. And the Far East can be neglected since it contains a very small proportion of the population and, more than most, is affected by variations in the price level. Second, the use of the family rather than the individual as the unit of distribution both reduces overall inequality and changes the ranking of individual republics. For example, Turkmenistan and not Estonia emerges as the best-off republic and the Ukraine rather than Azerbaijan would appear to be the worst-off. But, as I have argued elsewhere, the family is an inappropriate unit of analysis when dealing with inequality and I see little point in discussing the results of Table 4 in more detail.

There is much more that could be said about the income estimates given in this paper, but perhaps such discussion is better left to another time.

Table 4
Personal Income per family of Kolkhozniki:
USSR, Republics and Regions of the RSFSR, 1974

	Personal Income per Family: USSR = 100		Personal Income per Family USSR = 100
RSFSR		Kazakhstan	126.8
including		Georgia	118.4
North West	102.1	Azerbaijan	89.3
Central	103.5	Lithuania	126.6
Volgo-vyatskii	100.4	Moldavia	93.8
Central Black-Earth	101.5	Latvia	120.5
Povolzhskii	94.9	Kirgizia	100.9
N. Caucasus	98.5	Tadjikistan	116.3
Urals	96.7	Armenia	114.8
W. Siberian	106.2	Turkmenistan	155.5
E. Siberian	97.0	Estonia	122.8
Far Eastern	119.3		
Ukraine	87.5		
Byelorussia	105.0	USSR (Rubles	2,482.6
Uzbekistan	124.0	per year)	

Sources: Tables A6, A8; Churakov, p. 29.

Table A1
Personal Income: USSR and Republics, 1974

Million Rubles

	Personal Income	Wages & Salaries	Earnings from Kolkhozy	Private Subsidiary Activity	Transfer Payments	Other Receipts
USSR	239,823	157,370	17,100	18,848	43,074	3,431
RSFSR	140,137	98,179	6,600	7,213	26,095	2,050
Ukraine	43,688	25,746	5,022	4,447	7,831	642
Byelorussia	8,751	4,767	1,091	1,325	1,446	122
Uzbekistan	8,917	4,757	1,250	1,450	1,375	85
Kazakhstan	12,085	8,574	394	836	2,120	161
Georgia	3,959	2,144	299	807	646	63
Azerbaijan	3,224	1,974	217	414	580	39
Lithuania	3,515	1,987	344	612	508	64
Moldavia	3,061	1,527	525	545	431	33
Latvia	2,790	1,765	196	281	505	43
Kirgizia	2,157	1,332	230	219	351	25
Tadjikistan	1,902	1,070	308	232	271	21
Armenia	2,141	1,462	106	179	355	39
Turkmenistan	1,801	964	413	149	258	17
Estonia	1,698	1,122	105	139	303	29

Notes and Sources: Col. (3) Table A2; Col. (4) Table A3; Col. (5) Table A4; Col. (6) Table A5; Col. (7) calculated as the sum of interest at 2% on savings deposits (NK SSSR '74 p. 606) Net loans to Housing Co-operatives (NK SSSR '74 p. 609) and an arbitrary 1.05% of the wage bill.

Table A2
Average Monthly earnings:
USSR and Republics, State Sector 1974

	Average Monthly Money Earnings of State Employees in Rubles		
USSR	141.1	Lithuania	137.5
RSFSR	147.7	Moldavia	114.1
Ukraine	128.5	Latvia	142.5
Byelorussia	122.2	Kirgizia	131.7
Uzbekistan	134.0	Tadjikistan	134.1
Kazakhstan	146.0	Armenia	135.7
Georgia	115.6	Turkmenistan	156.0
Azerbaijan	121.2	Estonia	154.0

Notes and Sources: Earnings data from NK SSR '74 p. 561; NK RSFSR '74 p. 387; NK. Uk. SSR '74, p. 416; NK B SSR '76 p. 157; NK Uz SSR '75 p. 288; NK Ka SSR '76 p. 143; NK M SSR '74 p. 133; NK La SSR '75 p. 305; NK Ki SSR '74 p. 222; NK Ta SSR '74 p. 181; NK Ar. SSR '74 p. 154; *Bolshaia Sovetskaia Entsiklopediia, Ezhegodnik,* 1975 various pages.

Total Wages and Salaries were calculated as the product of average annual employment in the state sector (NK SSR '74 p. 553) and average annual earnings (monthly pay x 12). The resultant figure was divided between wages and salaries proper (col. (1) in Table A2) and holiday pay (included in transfers). Holiday pay calculated as 6.85% of the wage and salary bill. (See NK SSSR '74 p. 561).

Table A3
Earnings (in cash and kind) from
Collective Farm Employment USSR and Republics, 1974

	Average Annual No. of Kolkhozniki Participating in Collective Work ('000)	Average No. of Days Worked per Year	Average Pay per Man-Day (Rubles)	Total Paid Out for Labour (Million Rubles)
USSR	15,697	242	4.50	17,100
RSFSR	5,665	253	4.60	6,600
Ukraine	5,190	234	4.13	5,022
Byelorussia	958	244	(4.67)	1,091
Uzbekistan	1,047	253	4.72	1,250
Kazakhstan	281	209	(6.71)	394
Georgia	380	150	(5.24)	299
Azerbaijan	296	182	4.03	217
Lithuania	279	220	5.60	344
Moldavia	558	226	4.16	525
Latvia	143	239	5.74	196
Kirgizia	213	196	5.51	230
Tadjikistan	262	251	4.69	308
Armenia	89	255	4.64	106
Turkmenistan	283	210	6.95	413
Estonia	53	275	7.20	105

Notes and Sources: Col. (2) NK. SSSR '74 p. 449; full information for Cols. (3) - (5) for the following republics: NK SSSR '74 p. 422; NK RSFSR '74 p. 315; NK Uk SSR '74 p. 293; NK Uz SSR '75 p. 205; NK M SSR '74 p. 80; NK La SSR '75 p. 300; NK Ta SSR '74 p. 120; NK Ar SSR '74 p. 154. Data on Col. (5) NK Ki SSR '74 p. 143. Data on Col. (4) for Estonia, *Bolshaia Sovetskaia Entsiklopediia* 1975. For other entries in Col. (3) Churakov 1977 p. 23. Residual allocated between B.SSR, Ka SSR, G SSR and day rates interpolated; day rate for Tu SSR extrapolated according to All-Union growth rate 1970-74.

Table 4A
Private Subsidiary Agricultural Activity: USSR 1974

Source		Million Rubles
NK SSSR '74 p. 422	Total Kolkhoz Pay	17,100
ibid. p. 606	But Kolkhoz Pay accounts for 44.2% of Total Income; therefore Total Kolkhoznik income	38,687.8
ibid.	But Kolkhoznik private receipts amount to 26.6% of Total Income; therefore Kolkhoznik private receipts	10,291.0
	But Kolkhozniki occupy 54.6% of privately farmed land; on assumption that yields per acre are the same for all social groups, Total private agricultural output	18,848

The All-Union total for kolkhozniki was distributed between republics according to their shares in 1970 adjusted for the change in the number of kolkhoznik households in the intervening four years; (for 1970 receipts, see McAuley 1979, p. 538) republican kolkhoznik values were used to generate an estimate of state employee receipts on the assumption that, republic by republic, yields per hectare in private agriculture were the same. (Land-tenure data from NK. SSSR '74 p. 338) This latter series was adjusted proportionately to sum to the all-union total.

Table A5
Transfer Payment: USSR and Republics, 1974

Million Rubles

	Holiday Pay	Stipends	Pensions	Allowances	Total Transfers
USSR	11,574	2,100	22,100	7,300	43,074
RSFSR	7,195	1,200	13,200	4,500	26,095
Ukraine	1,912	399	4,462	1,058	7,831
Byelorussia	351	76	827	192	1,446
Uzbekistan	350	81	603	341	1,375
Kazakhstan	637	102	841	540	2,120
Georgia	158	35	382	71	646
Azerbaijan	145	42	325	68	580
Lithuania	146	26	241	95	508
Moldavia	112	26	210	83	431
Latvia	130	17	273	85	505
Kirgizia	98	23	168	62	351
Tadjikistan	79	22	125	45	271
Armenia	108	26	162	59	355
Turkmenistan	71	15	120	52	258
Estonia	82	10	161	50	303

Notes and Sources: Col. (2) calculated as 6.85% of the wage and salary bill (see Table A2). Full information on cols. (3) - (5): NK SSSR '74 p. 578; NK. RSFSR '74 p. 29; NK Uz SSR '75 p. 304; NK MSSR '74 p. 139; NK La SSR '75 p. 307; NK Ki SSR '74 p. 250 (excluding stipends and allowances); NK Ta SSR '74 p. 183 (excluding stipends and allowances); NK Ar SSR '74 p. 167; Total Social Consumption for the following republics: Ka SSR, G. SSR Li SSR and ESSR from *Bolshaia Sovetskaia Entsiklopediia, Ezhegodnik,* 1975 various pages; allocated as follows Ka SSR according to 1975 proportions. NK Ka SSR '76 p. 155; G SSR, 1973 proportions NK GSSR '73 p. 204; Li SSR, 1972 proportions. EK Li SSR '72 p. 313; ESSR, according to 1972 proportions *Eesti NSV Rahvamajandus* 1972, p. 222. Pensions only B.SSR, NK BSSR '74 p. 171.

Missing data were estimated as follows:

Pensions - residual allocated in proportion to number of pensioners NK SSSR '74 p. 614

Stipends - residual allocated in proportion to the number of students in post-secondary educational establishments NK SSSR '74 p. 691-692

Allowances - residual allocated in proportion to the number of children in pre-school child-care facilities. NK SSSR '74 p. 613.

Table A6
Personal Income: Kolkhozniki and Dependents:
USSR and Republics 1974

Million Rubles

	Earnings from Employment		Private Subsidiary Activity	Transfers	Other Receipts	Personal Income
	on Kolkhozy	in the State Sector				
USSR	17,100	3,018	10,291	3,018	580	34,007
RSFSR	6,600	948	3,114	1,215	206	12,083
Ukraine	5,022	1,056	3,448	936	182	10,644
Byelorussia	1,091	100	706	175	36	2,108
Uzbekistan	1,250	217	795	177	42	2,481
Kazakhstan	394	32	132	70	11	639
Georgia	299	166	506	75	18	1,064
Azerbaijan	217	99	190	58	10	574
Lithuania	344	31	339	62	13	789
Moldavia	525	83	391	72	19	1,090
Latvia	196	27	134	31	7	395
Kirgizia	230	35	113	41	7	426
Tadjikistan	308	100	158	44	11	621
Armenia	106	54	62	22	4	248
Turkmenistan	413	60	149	27	11	660
Estonia	105	8	54	13	3	183

Notes and Sources: Col. (2) from Table A3 Col. (4) from Table A4; Col. (3) from McAuley 1979 p. 340 adjusted for changes in republican wage rates and the size of the kolkhoznik population; the resultant series was adjusted to sum to the USSR total (see NK SSSR '74 p. 606) Col. (5) USSR total from NK SSSR '74 p. 606; allocated amound republics in proportion to the numbers receiving pensions under the Kolkhoz Pension Law (NK SSSR '74 p. 614) Col. (6) calculated as 1.7% of total personal income (cf. NK SSSR '74 p. 606).

Table A7
Personal Income: State Employees and Dependents; USSR and Republics 1974

Million Rubles

	Wages and Salaries	Private Activity	Transfer Payments	Other Receipts	Personal Income
USSR	154,342	8,577	40,056	2,851	205,826
RSFSR	97,231	4,099	24,880	1,844	128,054
Ukraine	24,690	999	6,895	460	33,044
Byelorussia	4,667	619	1,271	86	6,643
Uzbekistan	4,540	655	1,198	43	6,436
Kazakhstan	8,542	704	2,050	150	11,446
Georgia	1,978	301	571	45	2,895
Azerbaijan	1,875	244	522	29	2,670
Lithuania	1,956	273	446	51	2,726
Moldavia	1,444	154	359	14	1,971
Latvia	1,738	147	474	36	2,395
Kirgizia	1,297	106	310	18	1,731
Takjikistan	970	74	227	10	1,281
Armenia	1,408	117	333	35	1,893
Turkmenistan	904	n.a.	231	6	1,141
Estonia	1,114	85	290	26	1,515

Notes and Sources: Col. (2), (4) and (5) from Tables Al and A6; Col. (3) from Table A4.

Table A8
Social Composition of the Soviet Population:
USSR and Republics 1974

Millions

	Kolkhozniki		Kolkhozniki and Dependents	State Employees and Dependents	Total Population (mid-year)
	Kolkhoznik Families ('000)	Average Family Size (1969			
USSR	13,698	3.42	46,825	205,240	252,065
RSFSR	4,807	3.2	15,382	117,495	133,327
Ukraine	4,898	2.9	14,204	34,465	48,669
Byelorussia	809	3.1	2,508	6,792	9,300
Uzbekistan	806	5.8	4,675	8,814	13,489
Kazakhstan	203	4.6	934	13,114	14,048
Georgia	362	3.8	1,376	3,524	4,900
Azerbaijan	259	5.4	1,399	4,161	5,560
Lithuania	251	2.8	703	3,023	3,276
Moldavia	468	3.5	1,638	2,150	3,788
Latvia	132	2.4	317	2,149	2,466
Kirgizia	170	4.6	782	2,476	3,258
Tadjikistan	215	6.0	1,290	2,045	3,335
Armenia	87	5.8	505	2,252	2,757
Turkmenistan	171	5.8	992	1,476	2,468
Estonia	60	2.0	120	1,304	1,424

Notes and Sources: Col. (2) NK SSR '74 p. 426. Col. (3) Sidorova, 1972 p. 115 (with corrections) Col. (6) calculated as simple average of January population in 1974 and 1975, NK SSSR '73 p. 9 NK SSSR '74 p. 9.

Table A9
Reconciliation of McAuley and Schroeder-Severin
Estimates of Personal Income in 1974
Million Rubles

| | McAuley | | Schroeder-Severin |
	Personal	Money	
Wages & Salaries	157,370	157,370	168,980
Kolkhoz Earnings	17,100	16,245	16,240
Private Receipts	18,848	9,411	9,700
Transfers	43,047	43,047	33,470
of which:			
Pensions	22,100	22,100	22,100
Allowances	7,300	7,300	7,070
Stipends	2,100	2,100	2,100
Holiday Pay	11,574	11,574	-
Insurance	-	-	2,200
Other Receipts	3,431	3,431	2,950
Military Pay etc.	-	-	3,600
Total Income	239,823	229,504	234,940
Income per capita			
(rubles per year)	951.43	910.50	932.06
Income per capita			
inc. military pay		924.78	

Notes and Sources: Col. (4) from Schroeder and Severin, 1976, p. 653. The major differences between the estimates are: the omission of income in kind both private and collective-farm sources from Schroeder. Military pay and allowances were deliberately omitted since I have no idea how they are distributed between republics. If they are added to money income as calculated above, the difference between the two estimates is 0.787 percent. The derivation of estimated receipts from the sale of private agricultural produce is set out in Table A10.

Table A10
Private Receipts from the Sale of Agricultural Output: 1974

Product	State Purchases m. rubles	Share of Population %	Receipts by Population m. rubles
Potatoes & Vegetables	3,284	18	591
Cattle & Poultry	24,464	13	3,180
Milk	11,418	5	571
Eggs	2,864	7	200
Wool	2,306	16	369
Total Receipts From State			4,911
CFM Sales			4,500
Total Value of Private Sales			9,411

Sources: Rows (1) - (5) *NK SSSR '74,* p. 320-21; Row (7) *ibid.,* p. 621.

Dr. Heinrich Vogel

Current position:
Director of Bundesinstitut fur ostwissenschaftlich und internationale Studien
Lindenbornstrasse 22
5ooo Köln 30
Germany

Main field of work:
Consumption and social policy in the USSR
Transfer of technology, West-East

Publications during the last two years:

(with J. Slama) ''Comparative Analysis of Research and Innovation Processes in East and West'', in C.T. Saunders (ed.), East-West European Economic Interaction-Workshop papers, vol. 3, Wien-New York 1977.

(with P. Hanson) ''Technology transfer between East and West: A review of the issues'', in Osteuropa-Wirtschaft, 2 (1978).

''Les tendances demographiques en Bulgarie'', in Revue d'Etudes Est-Ouest, IX, 2 (1978).

Regional Differences in Living Standards: Efficiency of the Distribution Network

Dr. Heinrich Vogel

I. Living Standards and the Distribution Network

The development of living standards in the USSR is discussed less as an aim in itself but rather as an issue closely related with the most pressing problems hindering the growth of the Soviet economy. It is in this context that the population's aspiration for higher levels of consumption is no longer a delicate deviation from the narrow path of building socialist society. Rather, it is now considered as an integral part of growth-oriented policy by stimulating the growth in labor productivity. In negative terms, a higher level of consumption is to reduce the impact of notorious phenomena like bad working discipline, unplanned fluctuations and migration of labor.

Soviet consumers identify a higher living standard no longer with rising monetary incomes but rather with the availability of goods and services for private use. Poor labor discipline and a low interest in the quality of production, therefore, can be interpreted as the reflection of insufficient supply of goods and services to buy: "The existence of a sufficient quantity of goods in the market, the expansion of the assortment and the appearing of new goods increase the working people's interest in raising their personal incomes."[1] It goes without saying that the standard of living of any population is not just a matter of private consumption of goods and services. The volume and structure of public services distributed in the network of education, medicare, social and cultural institutions are of no less importance for the level of social welfare. Soviet literature duly stresses this argument and refers to a considerable and constantly growing amount of services for the population.[2] Problems in the distribution of goods and services of private consumption meet with far greater concern. No doubt, the Soviet consumer is beginning to lose his notorious patience. At the moment his reaction in the sphere of daily work has reached an extent which may well be characterized in the terminology of Western labor disputes: "slow down" or "work to rule."

There is much concern in Soviet literature about the persisting neglect of private consumption on the side of planners and producers. Brezhnev's reprimand at the Central Committee Plenary Session in November 1978 for those "who consider production of Group B (consumer goods) as a balancing-pole" is worth reading. No less under attack is the distribution process in the official network of trade and services (*sfera obsluzhivaniia*). Complaints about the frustrating discontinuity of supplies refer to mismanagement and lack of interest on the part of shop attendants. Resolutions of Party and State organs like the joint decree of Central Committee of the CPSU and Council of Ministers of the USSR of July 1977[3] induce big campaigns urging voluntary commitments of the collectives; sometimes they cause changes among the leading cadres. The effects of such public actions, however, fade away and leave the consumer dissatisfied and in an even more aggressive mood: the recent discussion published in *Literaturnaya gazeta* of August 23, 1978 ("Deficit and queue: whom to blame?") is quite instructive. Losses in economic terms (with regard to overall labor supply) and in social terms (spare time for the citizens) are considerable: the total annual time spent by the population for shopping is estimated to reach 35 billion hours, equivalent to the working time of 18 million people. Twenty-five percent or 8.7 billion hours (4.5 million working people) are spent for queueing at the counter and-- separately still in the majority of retail trade-shops--the cash desk.[4] According to a different survey in Riga from 1972 the time spent on queueing amounted to 18 percent of the weekly total time for shopping.[5]

Organizational measures, more inputs of capital and labor are recommended, queues are condemned as "lack of trading-culture." But all this is not new. In addition, the on-going quarrels as well as poor statistical data on private consumption and trade show little if any improvement on the macro-level of information.

II. The Regional Aspect

The vast territorial expanse of the USSR (22 million square kms.) adds further problems. Large sections of republics and economic regions are underdeveloped in terms of industrialization and in what is called in contemporary Soviet literature "social infrastructure."[6] Equalization of differences in living standards for the entire population is a major issue for both propagandists and analytical writers. "The solution of this problem is not only of social but also of enormous economic significance because it creates most favourable conditions for the effective use of labour and other productive resources and for an equally effective economic development."[7]

Scholarly discussion on regional differences in living standards and the strategies towards an equalization of social infrastructure is not new. The aggravated problems in recent years of bringing labor into remote and underdeveloped areas with hard geographic conditions has stimulated further discussions and has resulted in significant efforts in sociological and

Table 1
Demographic and Economic Data (1977)
(Indices USSR = 100)

Republic	Demographic Data (Indices: USSR = 100)		Volume of Savings in per Inhabitant (Rubles) per Inhabitant	Produced National Income 1970 USSR =
	Inhabitants per km²	Share of Urban Population		
USSR	100	100	100	100
RSFSR	68	113	113	112
Ukrainskaia SSR	701	98	112	97
Belorusskaia SSR	390	89	108	92
Uzbekskaia SSR	284	65	37	61
Kazakhskaia SSR	46	89	69	81
Gruzinskaia SSR	617	82	107	73
Azerbaidshanskaia SSR	579	84	46	61
Litovskaia SSR	44:	95	165	112
Moldavskaia SSR	992	63	61	81
Latviiskaia SSR	339	108	124	132
Kirgizskaia SSR	151	63	47	67
Tadzhikskaia SSR	221	56	35	56
Armyanskaia SSR	846	105	118	78
Turkenskaia SSR	43	74	44	74
Estonskaia SSR	277	111	147	133

Sources: Calculated from Table AI, *Narodnoe khoziaistvo SSSR v 1977 godu*. (Moscow, 1978); G.V. Gorlanov, "Territorial'nyi aspekt ekonomicheskogo oboshchestvleniia-obosobleniia proizvodstva pri sotsializme," *Vestnik Leningradskogo Universiteta, [Seria ekonomika, filosofiia, pravo]*, 1 (1977).

economic research. Reports indicate that the annual turnover of labor due to unplanned migration is estimated at 14-15 million people.[8] One of the leading centers in regional studies is the Novosibirsk "Institute for Economics and Organization of the Industrial Production." A chapter of a recent impressive publication concisely summarizes the trends and problems of this region.[9] A regression analysis from the same institute of factors for the outflow of population from newly developed urban settlements shows a close relationship with factors of housing, water supply, sewage and social-cultural infrastructure in general.[10]

An equally important aspect of regional analysis is the difference of living standards and efficiency of the distribution network between urban and rural areas. Monetary incomes in rural areas are now rising at a faster rate than those of the urban workers and employees. Yet, at the same time, the network supplying goods and services from the urban centers to the country seems to expand rather slowly.

In spite of the considerable analytical and programmatic literature on regional differences in living standards the stock of published statistical data is still fragmentary with the general disadvantages of high levels of aggregation. Data on capital investment and on very important aspects (regional distribution of light industries, transport radius of major categories of consumer goods, the stock of special technical equipment such as cold-storage and transport, regional price differences in retail trade, etc.) are extremely scarce. But such are the usual handicaps for external analysis of any aspect of Soviet society. As a result, those figures that analysts do have support the general suspicion that the lack of data indicates zones of low propagandistic returns.

Table 2
Density and Capacity of Network (1977)
(Indices: USSR = 100)

Republic	Shops per 10,000 Inhabitants		Selling Space in Trade (1000m²)	Number of Seats in Catering
	Retail Trade	Public Catering		
USSR	100	100	100	100
RSFSR	96	100	106	104
Ukrainskaia SSR	111	100	106	107
Belorusskaia SSR	96	109	110	105
Uzbekskaia SSR	81	82	68	76
Kazakhskaia SSR	104	91	96	75
Gruzinskaia SSR	118	127	94	97
Azerbaidzhanskaia SSR	107	127	64	87
Litovskaia SSR	77	82	93	110
Moldavskaia SSR	96	91	83	91
Latviiskaia SSR	104	109	109	154
Kirgizskaia SSR	85	82	67	62
Tadzhikskaia SSR	70	100	63	63
Armyanskaia SSR	74	127	91	109
Turkmenskaia SSR	81	100	73	66
Estonskaia SSR	100	127	107	148

Sources: Calculated from Tables A2 - A5

Basic data on the distribution network in the USSR in 1977 are presented in the Appendix. In the preceding and following tables the regional differences among the republics and among three selected oblasts of the RSFSR are measured against the All-Union average.

The results are not surprising: if on the level of Republics we take the volume of retail trade, public catering and services per inhabitant as the main criteria, then the "richest" republics are Latvia, Estonia, Lithuania and the RSFSR with scores mostly above the average. The "poorest" are Azerbaidzhan, Tadzhikistan, Turkmenistan, and Kirgizistan. With regard to the density of the network Georgia is best off, quite ahead of

Azerbaidzhan, Estonia and the Ukraine (with Tadzhikistan, Lithuania, and Uzbekistan at the end). In network capacities, Latvia leads Estonia, Belorussia, Ukraine, and the RSFSR (with Tadzhikistan, Kirgizistan, Uzbekistan and Turkmenistan at the end). This corresponds fairly well with the ranking order according to national income produced or volumes of per capita-savings in bank-deposits (Table 1). Usually the volume of savings deposits is regarded as an indicator for growing wealth of the population. Some authors, however, interpret its higher rate of growth compared to that of retail trade-turnover as unsatisfied monetary demand (up to 75 percent of savings).[11] The discrepancy between density/capacity levels and performance in Georgia, Armenia and the Ukraine is extremely difficult to explain.

Table 3
Performance of the Network (Indices; USSR = 100)

Republic	Volumes of Retail and Public Catering			Volumes of Services	
	per Shop (1000 Rb) 1977	per Inhabitant (Rubles) 1970	1977	per Shop (1000 Rb) 1977	per Inhabitant (Rubles) 1977
USSR	100	100	100	100	100
RSFSR	111	110	110	101	105
Belorusskaia SSR	97	91	98	77	107
Ukrainskaia SSR	85	91	92	78	106
Belorusskaia SSR	97	91	98	77	107
Uzbekskaia SSR	71	55	63	45	62
Kazakhskaia SSR	84	87	85	66	86
Gruzinskaia SSR	66	77	80	40	96
Azerbaidzhanskaia SSR	52	52	59	36	59
Litovskaia SSR	144	110	113	89	127
Moldavaskaia SSR	88	76	83	67	102
Latviiskaia SSR	137	148	142	132	187
Kirgizskaia SSR	84	73	70	73	74
Tadzhikskaia SSR	73	62	58	51	66
Armyanskaia SSR	81	79	81	50	82
Turkmenskaia SSR	78	73	69	50	66
Estonskaia SSR	133	150	144	99	162

Sources: Calculated from Table 4

Differences from one republic to the other as well as on regional levels below (rayon, oblast') are discussed quite extensively in Soviet literature. The factors influencing the per capita-levels of retail trade, public catering and services are numerous: the size (selling space), form of organization (self-service) and technical equipment are mentioned in a 1976 programmatic article by Politbureau member K. Mazurov.[12] The population may spend less on goods and services due to an underdeveloped

Table 4
Differences Among Selected Oblasts of the RSFSR (1977)

Oblasts	Demographic Data		Density of Network (Shops per 1,000 Inhabitants)			Performance of Network			
	Inhabitants per km²	Proportion of Urban Population	Retail Trade	Public Catering	Services	Volume of Retail Trade per Shop (1,000 Rb.)	Volume of Retail Trade per Inh. (Rubles)	Volume of Services per Shop (1,000 Rb.)	Volume of Services per Inh. (Rubles)
1. Moscow (city) (absolute fig.)	300.8	100	13	10	6	1506	1938	77	39
USSR = 100	2570	161	48	91	6,000	640	218	267	162
RSFSR = 100	3760	143	50	91	7,500	575	198	266	154
2. Kamchatskaia Obl. (absol. figures)	.8	83	24	9	10	585		44	44
USSR = 100	7	134	89	82	10,000	249	160	153	182
RSFSR = 100	10	119	92	82	12,500	223	145	152	174
Moscow (city) = 100	.3	-	185	90	167	39	74	57	112
3. Belgorodskaia Obl. (absol. figures)	47.3	52	30	10	7	261	731	32	22
USSR = 100	404	84	111	91	7,000	111	82	111	91
RSFSR = 100	591	74	115	91	87,500	100	75	100	87
Moscow (city) = 100	16	-	231	100	117	17	38	42	56

Sources: *Nardone khoziaistvo SSSR v 1977 g.* (Moscow, 1978); *Narodnoe khoziastvo RSFSR v 1977 g.* (Moscow, 1978)

network of shops as shown for the Kemerovskii oblast' by Vitkin and Kocherga.[13] The level of wages dependant upon the production and share of population in working age.[14] Other authors refer to consuming age, average size of families, density of population,[15] climatic conditions and traditions in nutrition.[16] None of the surveys, it should be noted, is covering a statistically representative sample.

It is particularly difficult to interpret data on retail trade-turnover which are biased by differences in retail prices between various parts of the USSR and also differences in the population's propensity to spend. "The population of Siberia consumes less or puts the money aside (for vacation, etc.)."[17] Such a statement is of little help for a closer look at differences in the relevant data for individual parts of the RSFSR down to the oblast' level. In most areas of Siberia and the Far East higher retail prices amount to a large extent for above average levels of retail trade-turnover. Generally the working population earns much more and is also served in shops which enjoy preferential supplies. For two oblasts the factors of income and costs of living can be quantified for the year 1975 (USSR = 100):

Region	Average Monthly Wages	Cost of Budget Market Baskets (incl. Taxes)	Retail Trade Turnover incl. Public Catering per Inhabitant
Magadanskaia Oblast'	239	169	190
Sakhalinskaia Oblast'	188	155	155

Sources: G. Schroeder, Tables 3 and 7 in her paper printed in this volume and RSFSR *Narodnoe khoziaistvo 1977 g.*

Obviously savings will be above average, too, with substantial sums earmarked for laying the foundation of a better life elsewhere. A careful study of all aspects including consumption and additional monetary incomes from private farming[18] indicates the following ranking order of economic regions in the RSFSR regarding correspondence of actual levels of consumption with patterns planned in a long-term perspective. Patterns are based on "scientific norms" of consumption:[19]

Total Turnover	Food	Industrial Goods
Kaliningrad Oblast'	Baltic	Central
Central	Central	North-West
North-West	North-West	North Caucasus
Far-East	Far-East	Baltic
Volga-Viatski	Volga-Viatski	Far-East
Siberia (East and West)	West Siberia	West Siberia
Volga	East Siberia	Central Black Soil
Urals	Urals	Volga
North Caucasus	Volga	East Siberia
Central Black Soil	Central Black Soil	
	North Caucasus	

With regard to urban-rural differences it is important to remember that rural population buys a substantial amount of goods in urban shops. According to surveys the kolkhoz families in the RSFSR buy 38 percent of all non-food sales in urban shops. The shift from urban to rural consumption is considerable in rural areas surrounding the cities. At the same time tensions build up between the two population groups as can be observed in the big department stores of Moscow, Leningrad and other places. Table 5 ought to be corrected by this kind of urban/rural redistribution; the relevant data, however, are missing. At any rate: the extraordinarily high level of sales in rural shops of Kazakhstan (cf. Table 5) demands further interpretation. High priority of this region in grain production and the low density of population may serve as a working hypothesis. Nevertheless, it is clear that rural living standards are generally below those of urban levels. Results of a survey in the Volgograd oblast' from 1972-73 indicate that low levels of services including the cultural sphere are responsible for the outflow of population from the countryside: 39.6 percent of interviewees under age thirty and 38.1 of those over thirty left the village for this reason.[20]

III. Trends

Investment directed into the trade network since 1961 (data unfortunately also include enterprises of forestry and wood procurement) is considerable in absolute terms: 21.6 billion rubles or 3 percent of total investment in the RSFSR. Average selling space in newly installed shops rose from 79 m^2 to 235.5 m^2. Yet, differences in trade performance as measured by retail trade turnover per inhabitant remain practically the same over the entire period (cf. Table 3). It is instructive to calculate the range of Union-wide variations between maximum and minimum retail trade per capita by Union Republics (in case of the RSFSR down to economic regions) in absolute (Rubles) as well as in relative terms (maximum in percent of minimum level). Only between 1960 and 1965 does the range diminish; afterwards it widens considerably:[21]

The Range of Maximum and Minimum Retail Trade per Capita by Regions of the USSR				
	1960	1965	1970	1977
Rubles	296	379	560	896
Index (Minimum Level = 100)	231	229	241	274

Sources: See Footnote 21

On the other hand there are reports which indicate a narrowing of discrepancies, as in the article by Pyatakova and Lysenko.[22] The authors' Lorenz-curve indeed shows a clear reduction in differences of per capita trade-turnover for the Ukraine according to oblast' levels.[23]

A study of future trends for the entire USSR indicates a less than optimistic situation: "Since today there are very significant differences of levels, particularly in a comparison of economic regions and republics, a fundamental solution by equalizing them can be found only in a sufficiently long stretch of time (15-20 years)."[24] The current Five-Year Plan provides higher rates of growth in trade-turnover for the republics of Central Asia and Transcaucasia, in the raions of Siberia, Far East and the Non-Blackearth zone.[25] Equalization over the entire vast territory of the USSR, however, will certainly take more time than 15-20 years and the necessity of speeding up the development of the regions rich in resources especially energy will result in a continued policy of setting priorities at the expense of less important regions.

Table 5

Urban / Rural Retail Trade (State and Cooperative) Per Inhabitant and Share of Non-Food Goods (1977)

| Republic | Volume per Inhabitant | | | | Level of Rural Trade (Urban volume per capita = 100) | Share of Non-Food Goods in per capita Trade (Percent) | |
| | Urban | | Rural | | | | |
	Rubles	USSR = 100	Rubles	USSR = 100		Urban	Rural
USSR	1129	100	499	100	44	48	47
RSFSR	1128	100	648	130	57	45	44
Ukrainskaia SSR	1091	97	393	79	36	50	50
Belorusskaia SSR	1247	110	435	87	35	49	45
Uzbekskaia SSR	876	78	350	70	40	53	55
Kazakhskaia SSR	918	81	564	113	61	49	49
Gruzinskaia SSR	1141	102	265	53	23	53	54
Azerbaidvanskaia SSR	835	74	198	40	24	51	52
Litovskaia SSR	1465	130	361	72	25	50	42
Moldavskaia SSR	1360	120	358	72	26	57	55
Latviiskia SSR	1634	145	510	102	31	52	47
Kirgizskaia SSR	952	84	421	84	44	50	53
Tadzhikskaia SSR	983	87	263	53	27	55	55
Armyanskaia SSR	942	83	313	63	33	50	46
Turkmenskaia SSR	911	81	335	67	37	52	58
Estonskaia SSR	1601	142	588	118	37	50	43

Source: *Nar. khoz. 1977 g.*

Table A1
Basic Demographic Data 1977

Republic	Population (1000)	Inhabitants per km²	Share of urban population (percent)
USSR	260 040	11.7	62
RSFSR	136 546	8.0	70
Ukrainskaia SSR	49 478	82.0	61
Belorusskaia SSR	9 468	45.6	55
Uzbekskaia SSR	14 839	33.2	40
Kazakhskaia SSR	14 671	5.4	55
Gruzinskaia SSR	5 030	72.2	51
Azerbaidzh. SSR	5 865	67.7	52
Litovskaia SSR	3 366	51.6	59
Moldavskaia SSR	3 914	116.1	39
Latviiskaia SSR	2 529	39.7	67
Kirgizskaia SSR	3 511	17.7	39
Tadzhikskaia SSR	3691	25.8	35
Armyanskaia SSR	2 950	99.0	65
Turkmenskaia SSR	2 722	5.6	49
Estonskaia SSR	1 460	32.4	69

Source: *Narodnoe khoziaistvo SSR v 1977 g.*

Table A2
Retail Trade and Public Catering Shops

Republic	Number of Retail Trade Shops State & Cooperative (1000)		Number of State and Cooperative) Public Catering Shops (1000)		Retail Trade Shops per 10,000 Inhabitants	Public Catering Shops per 10,000 Inhabitants
	1970	1977	1970	1977	1977	1977
USSR	682	696	237	286	27	11
RSFSR	357	360	127	149	26	11
Ukrainskaia SSR	148	147	48	55	30	11
Belorusskaia SSR	24	25	8	11	26	12
Uzbekskaia SSR	29	33	12	16	22	9
Kazakhskaia SSR	39	41	11	15	28	10
Gruzinskaia SSR	15	16	6	7	32	14
Azerbaidzh. SSR	16	17	6	8	29	14
Litovskaia SSR	7	7	3	3	21	9
Moldavskaia SSR	9	10	3	4	26	10
Latviiskaia SSR	7	7	3	3	28	12
Kirgizskaia SSR	7	8	2	3	23	9
Tadzhikskaia SSR	6	7	2	4	19	11
Armyanskaia SSR	7	7	3	4	20	14
Turkmenskaia SSR	5	6	2	3	22	11
Estonskaia SSR	4	4	2	2	27	14

Source: *Narodnoe khoziaistvo SSSR v 1977 g.*

Table A3
Capacity of Retail Trade and Public Catering Shops
Per 10,000 Inhabitants

Republic	Selling Space in Retail Trade Shops (1000m^2)		Number of Seats in Public Catering Shops	
	1970	1977	1970	1977
USSR	1290	1622	411	582
RSFSR	1357	1714	429	605
Ukrainskaia SSR	1351	1715	430	621
Belorusskaia SSR	1346	1784	369	614
Uzbekskaia SSR	867	1101	313	442
Kazakhskaia SSR	1280	1562	291	434
Gruzinskaia SSR	1172	1523	468	565
Azerbaidzh. SSR	820	1045	365	504
Litovskaia SSR	1222	1512	417	638
Moldavskaia SSR	964	1354	324	523
Latviiskaia SSR	1571	1763	712	897
Kirgizskaia SSR	833	1090	264	362
Tadzhikskaia SSR	872	1025	282	366
Armyanskaia SSR	1191	1483	433	635
Turkmenskaia SSR	896	1192	252	372
Estonskaia SSR	1528	1744	665	859

Source: *Narodnoe khoziaistvo SSSR v 1977 g.*

Table A4
Volumes of Retail-Trade
and Public Catering Turnover

Republic	Volume of Retail-Trade Turnover and Public Public Catering (Millions of Rubles)				Retail Trade-Turnover per Shop 1977 (1000 Rubles)	Retail Trade-Turnover and Public Catering per Inhabitant 1977 (Rubles, current prices)
	1970		1977			
USSR	155	208	230	641	235	891
RSFSR	91	250	133	539	262	981
Ukrainskaia SSR	27	548	40	410	200	818
Belorusskaia SSR	5	233	8	239	229	873
Uzbekskaia SSR	4	985	8	187	167	559
Kazakhskaia SSR	7	290	11	040	197	757
Gruzinskaia SSR	2	315	3	569	155	712
Azerbaidzh. SSR	2	051	3	084	123	530
Litovskaia SSR	2	209	3	391	339	1011
Moldavskaia SSR	1	752	2	896	207	743
Latviiskaia SSR	2	241	3	181	318	1262
Kirgizskaia SSR	1	382	2	183	198	628
Tadzhikskaia SSR	1	167	1	895	172	520
Armyanskaia SSR	1	276	2	100	191	719
Turkmenskaia SSR	1	020	1	650	183	614
Estonskaia SSR	1	305	1	871	312	1287

Source: *Narodnoe khoziaistvo SSSR v 1977 g.*

Table A5
Services

Republic	Number of Shops providing Services (1000)		Volume of Services 1977, Millions Rubles (Prices of 1976)	Volume of Services per Shop 1977 (1000 Rubles)	Volume of Services per Inhabitant 1977 Rubles, current prices
	1970	1977			
USSR	239	264	6278	28.8	24.1
RSFSR	113	119	3451	29.0	25.3
Ukrainskaia SSR	50	56	1263	22.6	25.5
Belorusskaia SSR	9	11	245	22.3	25.9
Uzbekskaia SSR	13	17	222	13.1	15.0
Kazakhskaia SSR	13	16	305	19.1	20.8
Gruzinskaia SSR	10	10	116	11.6	23.1
Azerbaidzh SSR	6	8	83	10.4	14.2
Litovskaia SSR	3	4	103	25.8	30.6
Moldavskaia SSR	4	5	96	19.2	24.5
Latviiskaia SSR	3	3	114	38.0	45.1
Kirgiziskaia SSR	3	3	63	21.0	17.9
Tadzhikskaia SSR	4	4	59	14.8	16.0
Armyanskaia SSR	4	4	58	14.5	19.7
Turkmenskaia SSR	2	3	43	14.3	15.8
Estonskaia SSR	2	2	57	28.5	39.0

Source: *Narodnoe khoziaistvo SSSR v 1977 g.* The increase in the number of shops in the USSR from 1970 to 1977 was 10.4% of 1.4% a year — a rather low rate of growth.

Footnotes

1. G. Sarkisian, "Pod'em blagosostoianiia narod na sovremennom etape", *Voprosy ekonomiki*, 10 (1976), 56.
2. H. Vogel, "Social Security and Medicare", in: NATO, Economic Directorate (ed.), *Economic Aspects of Life in the USSR*, (Brussels, 1975), pp. 207-234.
3. *Ekonomicheskaya gazeta*, No. 30. July 1977.
4. A. Novitskii, "Kak sberech vremia pokupatelyu", *Trud*, 15 May, 1975.
5. P.V. Gulian (ed.) *Balans vremeni naseleniia Latviiskoi SSR*, (Riga 1976), p. 238.
6. G. Mil'ner and E. Gilinskaia, "Mezhraionnoe regulirovanie urovnia zhizni naseleniia", *Planovoe khoziaistvo*, 1 (1975), 56-63.
7. S.S. Shatalin, "Tempy i proportsii ekonomicheskogo razvitiia i narodnoe blagosostoianie", *Vestnik Akademii nauk* [Seriia ekonomicheskaia] 4 (1976), 70.
8. A. Kocherga, *"Problemy territorial'nogo planirovaniia narodnogo blagosostoianiia"*, *Planovoe khoziaistvo*, 2 (1979), p 96.
9. .A.G. Aganbegian, (ed.), *Razvitie narodnogo khoziaistva Sibiri*, (Novosibirsk, 1978), p. 120.
10. V. Lysenko, "Sotsial'no-bytovaia infrastruktura i problema prizhivaemosti naseleniia", in: *Sotsial'no ekonomicheskie problemy truda i urovnia zhizni. Sbornik*

statei, F.M. Borodkin (ed.) (Novosibirsk, 1976), p. 32.

11. See the discussion in: E. Aleksandrova and E. Fedorovskaia, "Rost blagosostoianiia trudiashchikhsia i sberezheniia naseleniia", *Voprosy ekonomiki,* 10 (1978), 75; V.A. Orlov and A.N. Shokhin, "Nekotorye metodologicheskie voprosy issledovaniya denezhnykh dokhodov naseleniia", *Izvestiia Akademii Nauk* [Seriia ekonomika] 5 (1976), 98, who use the term "Forced saving".

12. K. Mazurov, "Neuklonno povyshat'narodnoe blagostoianie", *Kommunist,* 16 (1976), 47-49.

13. M. Vitkin, "Territorial'nye balansy denezhykh dokhodov i razkhodov naseleniia", *Planovoe khoziaistvo,* 12 (1976), 87; A.I. Kocherga, et al., "Osobennosti organizatsii i razmeshcheniia predpriiatii obshchestvennogo pitaniia v krupnykh gorodakh", in: *Sotsial'no-ekonomicheskie problemy razvitiia regionov,* Akademiia nauk USSR, Sovet po izucheniiu proizvoditel'nykh sil USSR (ed.), (Kiev 1976), p. 129.

14. I. Beliaevskii, "Sotsial'no-ekonomicheskie faktory razvitiia roznichnogo tovarooborota", *Voprosy ekonomiki,* 3 (1978), 66.

15. See V. Dmitriev, "Mezhregional'noe sopostavlenie razvitiia bytovogo obsluzhivaniia", *Vestnik statistiki,* 11 (1978), 40.

16. A. Soskiev, "Vosproizvodstvo rabochei sily", *Ekonomika sel'skogo khoziaistva,* 10 (1978), 70.

17. See O.A. Nekrasov, "Ekonomicheskie problemy khoziaistvennogo osvoeniya Sibiri i Dal'nego Vostoka", *Vestnik Moskovskogo Universiteta,* [seriia ekonomika] 6 (1978), 13-14.

18. L.V. Bondarenko, "Problemy regional'nogo vyravnivaniia razvitiia roznichnogo tovarooborota", in: Sovet po izucheniiu proizvoditel'nykh sil pri Gosplane SSSR (ed.), *Regional'nye aspekty razvitiia sfery obsluzhivaniia Sbornik statei,* (Moscow, 1974), p. 78.

19. See C. Beaucourt, "Les perspectives de la consommation en URSS", in: NATO, Economic Directorate (ed.), *The USSR in the 1980s,* (Brussels, 1978), p. 119.

20. T.V. Riabushkin, et al., *Sotsiologiia i problemy sotsial'nogo razvitiia",* (Moscow, 1978), p. 261.

21. Bondarenko, *op. cit.,* 64-5; USSR and RSFSR Yearbooks for 1977.

22. F.S. Piatakova and Iu. M. Lysenko, "Ekonomiko-statisticheskii analiz regional'nykh razlichii v razvitii roznichnogo tovarooborota Ukrainskoi SSR", in: *Sotsial'no-ekonomicheskie problemy razvitiia regionov. op. cit.,* p. 70.

23. See A.T. Gorbenko, et al., "Nektorye voprosy regional'nogo razvitiia i sovershenstvovaniia organizatsii bytovogo obsluzhivaniia i zhilishchnogo khoziaistva v Ukrainskoi SSR, in: *ibid.,* 75.

24. I.S. Khvatov, "Sfera obsluzhivaniia kak ob'ekt regional'nogo planirovaniia", in: *Regional'nye aspekty, op. cit.,* p. 13.

25. A. Aleshin and T. Koriagina, "Effektivnost' i kachestvo bytovykh uslug v desiatoi piatiletke", *Planovoe khoziaistvo,* 2 (1978), 67.

Comment

Mme. Chantal Beaucourt

L'évolution des revenus régionaux en U.R.S.S. va-t-elle dans le sens de l'égalisation des niveaux de vie qui est l'un des fondements de la politique soviétique ? Par ailleurs, la politique soviétique des revenus doit coopérer à une redistribution de la main-d'oeuvre entre branches et régions ; dans quelle mesure a-t-elle réellement affecté et pourrait-t-elle affecter les transferts de population active entre villes et campagnes ou entre régions ?

Les études entreprises par le Prof. Schroeder et le Dr. Vögel pour répondre à ces questions présentent un intérêt tout particulier à une étape du développement de l'U.R.S.S. où l'amélioration de la productivité du travail devient le facteur déterminant de la croissance et où le consommateur risque d'être frustré dans ses espérances par un ralentissement de cette croissance. Par ailleurs, leurs approches se complètent heureusement. L'égalisation des niveaux de vie doit, en effet, s'apprécier d'abord en termes de revenus et de besoins, et c'est là la démarche fondamentale du Prof. Schroeder dans son analyse des niveaux régionaux des revenus et dans leur appréciation en fonction des divergences territoriales du coût de la vie en U.R.S.S. ; cette égalisation doit s'apprécier également en termes de biens et services offerts à la population et de la couverture des besoins. L'analyse des ventes du commerce de détail, entreprise par le Dr. Vögel apporte donc un éclairage complémentaire très appréciable pour y répondre.

Le sujet est intéressant mais difficile à traiter : aborder l'étude d'un problème soviétique sous son aspect régional est toujours une entreprise courageuse : les données — et souvent les démarches — sont à multiplier par 15 ou 18, et délicate vu la rareté des statistiques régionales. On retrouvera cette difficulté tout au long d'un colloque consacré à l'économie régionale mais le problème se pose avec particulièrement d'acuité lorsqu'on cherche à évaluer les revenus réels de la population, même si l'on fait abstraction des ressources subsidiaires que procure le travail "gris" ou "noir" dont on sait qu'il est très important, et des biens et services que ce travail procure à la population. On ne peut que regretter sans le reprocher à leurs auteurs que leurs estimations ne puissent atteindre le niveau des grandes régions économiques.

Mais l'un des grands mérites de l'étude du Prof. Schroeder est de nas pas avoir esquivé aucun des aspects de ce problème.

Le problème est par ailleurs complexe. D'une part, en effet, comme le note G. Schroeder, un accroissement des écarts des revenus salariaux peut très bien réduire les divergences des niveaux de vie de la population, si l'ontient compte des différences régionales de prix mais aussi des conditions de vie. D'autre part, il peut se manifester une certaine contradiction entre la réalisation de l'objectif d'une égalisation systématique du niveau de vie (plutôt que des revenus) et celle d'une politique des revenus, en tant qu'instrument d'une redistribution de la main-d'oeuvre. La politique des revenus peut, en effet, être amenée à favoriser les branches et les régions, où, selon le planificateur, la main-d'oeuvre peut être utilisée avec le plus d'efficacité pour l'économie nationale, et où les besoins de population active sont les plus pressants, en y offrant des salaires et autres avantages, supérieurs à ceux que justifierait le coût de la vie relatif de ces régions, et, en même temps, à restreindre le niveau relatif des revenus dans les régions où les ressources d'emploi sont nombreuses et même excédentaires mais vers lesquelles la population active tend à se rendre.

Ces considérations sont en effet prises en compte (ou devraient l'être) par le planificateur lorsqu'il établit les coefficients régionaux de saliares et les prix de zone. Mais il est, dès lors, difficile d'apprécier si les évolutions des écarts régionaux de revenus répond à l'objectif d'une égalisation des niveaux de vie, -vu notamment l'imprécision des données du coût de la vie ou si la politique de redistribution de la main-d'oeuvre est prioritaire. Plutôt qu'une critique qui ne saurait trouver d'objet dans les rapports très fouillés et intéressants qui nous ont été présentés, on s'attachera à en tirer quelques enseignements complémentaires sur les facteurs explicatifs des écarts des niveaux de revenus régionaux qui ont été constatés ; les propositions qui seront faites se présentent davatage d'ailleurs comme des questions posées aux rapporteurs.

1. Et tout d'abord, en ce qui concerne les revenus salariaux du secteur d'état, deux facteurs semblent peser fortement sur les niveaux régionaux de ces revenus : le degré de développement de la région et la structure de la production industriel le.

Une observation très intéressante ressort, en effet des évaluations faites par le Prof. Schroeder : dans le républiques où le niveau de salaire moyen est le plus élevé, il l'est pratiquement dans tous les secteurs ; et inversement dans celles où ce niveau est le plus bas, il l'est également dans l'ensemble des secteurs. Or on trouve aux deux bouts de la chaîne, les républiques Baltes et celles d'Asie Centrale, c'est-à-dire celles qui sont le plus ou le moins développées. L'égalisation des niveaux de vie passe par celle des conditions économiques de la production qui, si elles sont bonnes permettent d'accroître le productivité du travailleur, et l'analyse des potentiels économiques régionaux apportera sans doute des compléments intéressants sur ce point.

Par ailleurs, à l'échelle de l'U.R.S.S., les écarts salariaux entre branches industrielles sont considérables et souvent supérieurs aux divergences des salaries entre secteurs ; récemment encore les coefficients régionaux de salaires concernaient exclusivement les branches de l'industrie lourde. Peut-on expliquer par là, la position très élevée de la Turkménie dans l'échelle des salaires industriels ?

2. Les facteurs explicatifs des divergences régionales entre les revenus urbains et ruraux sont encore plus nombreux et difficiles à cerner. Le type de culture et la qualité des sols sont, certes, des éléments importants des écarts des revenus agricoles mais le planificateur devrait l'avoir pris en compte dans l'établissement des prix par produits et par zones.

La prédominance du système d'exploitation agricole, — étatique ou collectif — pourrait également expliquer les divergences entre certaines républiques qui disposent à peu près des mêmes conditions naturelles et économiques : les écarts des revenus sont en effet plus grands dans les kolkhoz que dans les sovkhoz (tableaux 5 et 6 de G. Schroeder), que l'on prenne ou non en compte les revenus provenant des lopins. Ce pourrait être par exemple, une explication de la différence des revenus agricoles de la Turkménie et de l'Uzbékie, tous deux producteurs de coton : La Turkménie qui compte plus des 2/3 du nombre des Kolkhoz de l'Uzbekie (avec la même surface par kolkhoz) ne comprend que 13% des sovkhoz.

De même les taux d'activité de la population et le nombre d'heures travaillées par personne active, dans les différentes républiques et régions traduisent des écarts beaucoup plus importants que ceux des rémunérations régionales les heures de travail (voir V. la. Churakov, *Aktualnie problemy ispolzovania trudovykh resursov sela,* (M. 1972)) le nombre d'heures de travail par kolkhozien actif va de 81% du niveaux moyen de l'U.R.S.S. en Géorgie à 145% en Estonie. On aurait pu penser qu'il y avait une certaine compensation avec le nombre d'heures de travail sur les lopins, il n'en rest rien. Mis à part la Géorgie, c'est en Transcaucasie que le travail sur les lopins est le moins élevé et les R.S.S. Baltes, la R.S.F.S.R. et l'Ukraine qui réalisent le plus grand nombre d'heures de travail collectif, consacrent également davantage de temps sur les lopins. (tableau 6).

En même temps, le ''cas'' géorgien pourrait être le reflet de la forte rentabilité des travailleurs sur les lot sindividuels : le niveau de vie est apparemment élevé, les salaires sont bas. Mais les heures travaillées sur les lopins forment plus de la motié des revenus. Ainsi le parallélisme entre le nombre d'heures travaillées et les revenus est assez proche dans la plupart des R.S.S. Mais il faudrait pourvoir y ajouter le travail des jeunes et des retraités. Or selon Churakov, il est plus élevé dans les régions de la R.S.F.S.R. où il y a relativement plus de main d'oeuvre rurale. Il faudrait également tenir compte de l'impact de l'emploi saisonnier, relativement mal payé : la rémunération ateint 70 à 73% de celle de l'emploi permanent ; plus il est abondant, plus le niveau moyen des rémunérations est donc concerné. Enfin les fonds sociaux de consommation sont également assez différents dans les kolkhoz et dans les sovkhoz, et en partie payés sur les revenus des kolkhoz.

3. Les écarts des revenus réels de la population.

L'étude des revenus réels de la population est probablement la plus difficile à établir mais également celle qui présente le plus d'intérêt. On voudrait simplement rappeler à ce sujet que les transferts de revenus entre régions, par le biais de la taxe à la valeur ajoutée sont très importants (cf M. Mazanova) et favorisent les régions moins développées. Ces transferts coopèrent à l'égalisation des niveaux de vie en facilitant dans ces régions des investissements qui ne sont pas à la portée des finances locales : c'est ainsi que 100% de la T.C.A.

perçus en Uzbekie et au Kazakhstan demeure dans la R.S.S., mais 27% seulement en Ukraine et 26% en Lettonie, le reste étant versé au budget central.

Un autre type de transfert de revenus difficilement mesurable concerne les ventes sur le marché kolkhozien dans une autre république voisine. Il n'est pas négligeable si l'on se réfère aux chiffres d'Andrew pour le Kazakhstan.

Le problème de l'appréciation des niveaux de vie régionaux, est donc particulièrement complexe. En prévoir l'évolution est néanmoins trè important dans une vue prospective : les planificateurs appliqueront-ils, à la lettre le principe d'une égalisation des revenus entre régions ou, pour pallier une redistribution territoriale des travailleurs qui ne s'opère pas dans la direction souhaitable, feront-ils porter l'effort sur les revenus salariaux des régions où les besoins de main d'oeuvre se font plus pressants. Dans les conditions d'une évolution démographique peur favorable, on peut penser que cette deuxième tendance prévaudra. On pourra alors prévoir un accroissement des écarts régionaux des revenus des travailleurs. C'est, en effet sur les régions où les conditions climatiques et de travail sont les plus dures et donc les besoins de la population et le coût de la vie les plus élevés (les régions où les conditions de vie sont meilleures et le coût de la vie plus bas (Asie Centrale).

Or, dans la situation actuelle, et ce n'est pas l'un des moindres enseignements que l'on peut tirer de l'étude du Prof. Schroeder, dans le premier groupe de régions, les uppléments salariaux ne couvrent même pas la hausse du coût de la vie, alors que dans le 2ème groupe, le coût de la vie est moins élevé que dans l'ensemble du pays et les salaires néanmoins plus importants. On ne saurait plus, dès lors s'étonner de l'orientation des flux migratoires. Cependant les revenus réels de la population ne sont pas encore un indicateur suffisant de son niveau de vie dans la mesure où les dépenses et donc la consommation peuvent être freinées ou différées par suite d'une insuffisance de la quantité ou de la qualité des produits offerts. Et il est vrai que souvent l'insatisfaction du consommateur soviétique résulte davantage des défauts de l'approvisionnement que de l'évolution de ses revenus. Les ventes du commerce de détail pour lesquelles on dispose de données régionales détaillées et régulières, constituent donc un instrument important de l'étude des niveaux de vie et leur analyse par le Dr. Vögel apporte un éclairage complémentaire très appréciable à ce sujet.

On voudrait simplement, pour conclure, apporter des précisions sur trois points :

Lindice régional des dépôts en caisse d'épargne fourni par le Dr. Vögel est intéressant mais pour être significatif de l'inadéquation de l'offre à la demande, on aurait aimé pourvoir suivre l'évolution des dépôts, parallèlement à celle des revenus de la population, dans les différentes régions.

Les ventes du commerce de détail sont une base d'estimation des niveaux de consommation, particulièrement précieuse pour les produits non alimentaires puisque la quasi totalité de ces produits est écoulée par ce circuit. Elles sont beaucoup moins significatives des niveaux de consommation relatifs des villes et des campagnes lorsqu'on sait que 40% environ des achats de ces produits par les kolkhoziens se font dans les villes.

Enfin, parmi les facteurs qui expliquent la différenciation des revenus de la population, la taille des familles semble avoir un impact particulièrement important sur le volume du commerce de détail par habitant. Une analyse comparée du commerce de détail par habitant et du nombre d'enfants de moins de 16 ans dans les diverses R.S.S. publiées dans *Voprosy ekonomiki* montre en effet que si pour un accroissement des revenus monétaires par travailleur de 1%, le commerce de détail par habitant augmente en moyenne de 1,02%, l'accroissement du nombre d'enfants par 100 habitants diminue le volume de ce commerce de 0,57% en moyenne dans le pays.

Professor Elizabeth Clayton

Current Position:
Professor of Economics
University of Missouri
Columbia, Mo.

Main field of work:
Soviet economic development; Soviet agriculture

Other remarks:
Fellow of the Kennan Institute, Old Smithsonian Bldg, Washington, in 1978-79 working on an assessment of performance in the Soviet agricultural sector

Autarky and Regional Investment
Regional Self-Sufficiency
Dr.Elizabeth Clayton

Tr   rue self-sufficiency is possible only in an economy that is very small, quite simple, and even backward. In a modern industrialized economy, the large-scale technology that expands production also increases regional specialization and reduces self-sufficiency.[1] In an extreme, the self-sufficiency of all regions might contract until each region specialized in its best product and supplied it to all other regions, but this extreme is impossible because it requires transportation whose capacity is limited and because some products cannot be transported at all. Within the extremes of self-sufficiency and specialization is an optimal spatial organization of production where the gains from large-scale production and specialization offset the costs of transport.

One measure of self-sufficiency is the regional similarity in industrial structure. In the Soviet Union, industry has dispersed spatially as the economy has modernized. In a major study, Hans-Jurgen Wagener found that the structure of industry across regions and product categories has become more similar over time. The only exception occurs in those industries that require natural resources.[2] A Soviet scholar, A. G. Granberg, has confirmed this result in a regional input-output study.[3] Thus the Soviet economic regions are relatively self-sufficient in industrial products, and long-haul transport is reserved for products in natural resources.

This dispersion of industry is characteristic of large, modern economies.[4] Perhaps suprisingly, it reflects less a self-sufficiency of regional production than an integration of inter-regional trade. This apparent anomaly occurs because the categories that define an industry are delineated broadly and disguise the wide variety of products within the industry, e.g., the consumer goods (the "light") industry produces both textiles and televisions. While the production of consumer goods is well dispersed across regions, the production of textiles and televisions probably is not, and requires inter-regional trade.

The ability to integrate the regional economies and to expand inter-regional trade is one hallmark for an efficient economic system. In order to examine the ability of the Soviet system to attain this integration, this paper develops a case study in agricultural production. The reasons for choosing agriculture are two-fold. First, the dispersion of agriculture has been studied in many different economic systems and some well-grounded theoretical expectations concerning dispersion have been formed from these studies. Second, the product data necessary for empirical analysis are readily available.

The modernization of agriculture normally increases regional specialization and dissimilarity, and decreases self-sufficiency in individual products. One stimulus for specialization is the rising consumer income that generates a demand for more food, with a greater diversity that is satisfied by products from other regions and from abroad. A second stimulus for specialization is the comparative advantage generated in some regions by natural differences of soil and climate. Some regions specialize in agriculture, just as countries of Denmark and the United States specialize in agricultural products in international trade. Soviet geographic science distinguishes its concept of regionalization by its particular attention to these differences from nature.[5]

Soviet policymakers now have altered past priorities to invest more in agriculture. A first section of this paper outlines the symbiotic development of agriculture and industry that enhances and complements the natural factors of production. A second section examines the effect of the consumer demand for food diversity on the present balance between regional self-sufficiency and specialization in food products. A final section suggests the possible barriers to a spatial reorganization of agriculture that matches resources and demand.

A note on the definition of regions: since this paper relies on standard statistics that are collected by republic, the republic is the basic regional unit. Ideally, a demarcation between regions would sum up all the detail such as climate and soil, the level of poverty, and the ethnic composition, without regard to political borders.[6] The republic unit measure captures these differences only imperfectly, e.g., the ethnic composition of the Kazakh SSR includes many Russians as well as Kazakhs. In inter-regional comparisons, the Russian SSR (RFSFR) will be compared with the Baltic region (the SSRs of Latvia, Lithuania and Estonia); the central Asian region (the SSRs of Uzbekistan, Tadzhikistan, Turkmenistan, Kirgizia and Kazakhstan); or, more simply, the non-Russian (all but the RFSFR). A looser comparison is between north and south; a decade ago, Wagener labeled these as developed, or not; this study adopts the more neutral geographic nomenclature because the development itself is a topic.[7] Unless noted otherwise, all data are from the Soviet statistical handbooks (*Narodnoe khoziaistvo; Sel'skoe khoziaistvo*).

I. Regional Self-Sufficiency in Agricultural Production

The recent large investments in Soviet agriculture have increased output but left large disparities in agricultural development. One effect of these regional disparities is the income inequality between north and south, and between urban and rural families. These are the subjects of other papers in this collection. Another effect is the disparity in production methods, particularly the labor-intensiveness. This section outlines the relationship between industrial development and the modernization of agricultural production methods, drawing on the economic literature of growth strategies in agricultural development.

Soviet agriculture was displaced by industry as its workers were absorbed by factories and cities, and its product supported more people even as its workforce declined. As a share of the total labor force, agriculture declined from 42 percent in 1960 to 29 percent in 1974, and its number fell from 39 million to 37 million.[8] The well-being of consumers was improved as per capita retail sales doubled, and even the rural households increasingly purchased their food at the store instead of growing it at home.

However, the labor force declined only in the north and northwest republics: the RFSFR, the Ukrainian SSR, the Belorussian SSR, and the Baltic republics. In the south, particularly in central Asia, the agricultural labor force increased. While the age of migrants was young in both north and south, the sex composition of migrants in the north was balanced between men and women while that of the south was predominantly male. The migration of southern women from agriculture continues to be rare.[9] This implies that the workers in the north who re-locate are settled more permanently in their new urban environment than those in the south.

In the regions where the labor migration was larger and more balanced by sex, the average family income is higher, but this is related less to the migration than to the socio-economic advantages that typically accompany agricultural development. The higher per family income of the north can be attributed almost wholly to a higher participation rate in the labor force, and the higher per capita income to a smaller family size.[10] The opposite characteristics, of fewer working women and more children per family, are typical of the rural population of an underdeveloped economy. They disappear with economic development, particularly in agriculture.[11]

A lower labor force participation rate in a population reduces the production per capita in both industry and agriculture. Insofar as a Soviet republic does not import capital from outside, its agriculture fails to receive the manufactured inputs that make it more productive. Stated from another perspective, the north's better record in modernizing its agriculture and releasing its labor force occurred in part because its industry provided more and better inputs to its agriculture, so that output did not fall when its labor departed.

When agriculture is modernized, it replaces the traditional inputs of land and labor with industrial inputs, but the choice to replace land or labor will vary according to the factor endowment.[12] The best known path, named the "American model" after its progenitor, replaces farm labor with technology that is primarily mechanical, in areas where the land/labor ratio is relatively high. The strategy is labor-saving and the output per worker rises; the northern USSR has used this strategy with some success. An alternative strategy, called the "Japanese model" after its precursor, augments agricultural land. It is most appropriate where the land/labor ratio is relatively low. This strategy is land-saving, and the output per hectare rises; the Georgian SSR has used it with some success and it is appropriate for much of the southern USSR.

In an area where the population and labor force are growing, as in central Asia, a high priority is to increase the available land per worker. Except in the Kazakh SSR, central Asian agriculture occurs on irrigated land. In 1976, irrigated land composed 97 percent of sown area in Turkmen SSR, 73 percent in Uzbek SSR, 62 percent in Kirgiz SSR, and 60 percent in Tadzhik SSR. These contrast with the national average where 5 percent of the land is irrigated. An increasing share of agricultural investment has constructed irrigation networks, desalinized land, and pumped water to deserts in the arid south. However, the loss of irrigated land each year is very high; in some areas, over half of new land is allocated for replacement.

A necessary catalyst for using new technology is the education of workers. At all stages of production, modern technology requires workers who are literate, even sophisticated, and one-third of the gains in agricultural productivity can be attributed to this source. The Soviet north has more educated workers than the south, but not enough. Iakimov, a Soviet author, writes of the north that new capital equipment does not increase production on farms where fewer than eight percent of workers are in the skilled category, with one to two years of technical training and some experience.[13] In southern republics, less than five percent of agricultural workers have completed a middle-level education of eleven or more years.

To illustrate the nexus between agriculture, industry, and education, consider the use of chemical fertilizers, an important manufactured input in agricultural modernization. They increase soil fertility and are indispensable in growing some hybrids, where their use must be monitored carefully. Farmers in the south use less fertilizer, of lower nutritive quality, than those in the north. Most is applied to technical crops such as cotton. Two examples illustrate:

(1) Production costs of vegetables produced are lower in the north than in the south, but include more fertilizer. In 1970, on state farms in the Lithuanian SSR, the cost of vegetables was 82 rubles per ton, of which 7 was for fertilizer. In the Turkmen SSR, it was 146 rubles per ton, of which only 2 were for fertilizer. Other products for which cost data is available suggest a similar low use of fertilizer in the south, despite its need for a land-saving strategy of development. While other economic considerations affect the use of fertilizer, the education of workers increases their willingness and ability to acquire and use this modern input.[14]

(2) Fertilizer production occurs more often in the north, where workers are better educated, than in the south. In a recent study of Soviet investment policy, Donna Bahry found that high investment per capita precedes the acquisition of political power, and not the reverse, suggesting that investment decision-makers rely on information from users and their ministries.[15] Since better educated workers have greater access to technical information, they can better assert and press the claims of their republics for investment funds. The documentation of horizontal links between educated farmers and their industrial suppliers is weak at best, but some accumulated correlations lend credence to their presence, e.g., the deliveries of fertilizer in republics whose labor is better educated consistently yield more of their weight in usable nutrients.

The national migration of new graduates out of agriculture diminishes the effect of a regional investment in education. In 1974, agricultural graduates numbered 192,000, but the next year's increment to educated workers was only 170,000. Among tractor-machinists, fewer than ten percent of those trained for agriculture remain in that sector. However, the losses from migration are lower in the south than in the north. Collective farms, who subsidize students' stipends in exchange for the promise of their labor in the future, invest more in the south, where the workers are more likely to return, than in the north.[16]

While educated agricultural workers are few in number, they also are concentrated in institutes for research and teaching, and not on farms. The number of institutes is large, but their activity is concentrated in the north. Ivashchenko, an analyst from the Soviet planning agency (Gosplan), writes that 128 agricultural institutes for research can hybridize wheat, but only four of them supply the varieties sown most in production.[17] Both the concentration of educated workers and their small number will be slow to disappear. P. A. Oram, citing the Consultative Group on International Agricultural Research, estimates that to develop a sound research organization requires seven to ten years; to establish a capable college of agriculture requires 25 years.[18]

To summarize: Soviet regions are self-sufficient in agricultural development in that each region has invested most heavily in those resources that are most scarce. Regional self-sufficiency in output, where each region supplies its own food, is examined in the next section, along with the economic basis for specialization and integration by trade.

II.   Regional Self-Sufficiency in Agricultural Consumption

A region may be self-sufficient in agricultural products, but only at a subsistence level. As Soviet consumers receive more income, they want to diversify their diets with products from other regions. The FAO estimates that Soviet consumers, as their incomes rise, will want to include in their diets less grain and starchy vegetables, and more of meat, fruit, and vegetables.[19] To respond to this demand requires that Soviet agricultural producers develop regional specialties in products that they produce most efficiently, and that they produce a surplus to trade. This section examines the recent regional specialization of Soviet agriculture, the major administrative measures for encouraging specialization, and the achievements in meeting the new consumer demands. It focuses on fruits and vegetables, whose demands are growing most rapidly.

Producers in Soviet agriculture are limited by plans, by climate, and by transport capacity. To analyze the regional specialization in agricultural products that have been introduced by the plans, the limits of climate and transport define product categories. A product's category is not immutable and may change as new technology and investment remove a transportation barrier to regional specialization or add a regional adaptation to climate. In three groups, the product categories are:

(1) Products limited by climate to only a few regions and easily

transported, because the products are not perishable or fragile and the weight-volume is favorable. These include Soviet cotton, tea, and sugar beets. The expansion of production and the integration of trade depends on the opportunities to import from other regions the products that are substitutes in production, and to transport both products in trade.

(2) Products produced in all regions and easily transported, by reason of the same characteristics as in (1). This category includes Soviet grain: intra-grain trade, as between rye and rice may be in category (1) or (2). Some fruits and vegetables are in this category, but the number is limited to those that transport easily, and climate is an obvious barrier for citrus.

(3) Products produced in all regions but transported between them only with difficulty, and traded very little. This includes Soviet milk and egg production. Most fruits and vegetables are in this category, but the

Table 1
Concentration Coeffilcients, Selected Agricultural Products and Population, USSR, 1960 and 1975

Product	1960	1975	Specializing Region*
All crops (ruble value)	9.4	12.2	none
Specialized production (concentration coeffieient above 20.0):			
Sugar Beets	37.0	40.0	Ukraine
Fruits & Berries	39.6	34.6	Ukraine, Transcaucasus, Moldavia
Less specialized production (concentration coeficient below 20.0):			
Grain	14.8	11.8	Kazakhstan (1960 only)
Potatoes	15.1	19.3	Belorussia
Vegetables	14.0	10.2	Ukraine
All animal products (ruble value)			
	8.5	8.4	none
Meat	8.9	15.4	RSFSR (1975 only)
Milk	7.6	11.5	none
Eggs	7.7	12.8	Ukraine (1960 only) RSFSR (1975 only)

*A region is specialized if its share in production exceeds its share in population by 5% or more. Unless otherwise noted, specialization occurred in both 1960 and 1975.

Sources: *Narodnoe khoziaistvo v 1975 g.* for data
       Sel'skoe khoziaistvo for 1960 data

opportunities to move some products to category (2) are feasible.

(This paper omits two specializations that would complete the list: a category (4) to include products produced in no region and wholly imported from abroad, e.g., Soviet bananas and pineapple; a category (5) to include perverse regional specialization, where economic criteria would ban it from the region. The data are inadequate to study the last category.)

The measure of regional specialization chosen here is a concentration coefficient which compares a region's share of production with its share of population. The coefficients are shown in Table 1. Thus, in fruits and berries in 1975, Moldavia's share of population (1.5%) was subtracted from its share of national production (13.1%) for a difference of 11.6. The differences of each region were summed without regard for a sign to give a concentration coefficient that can be compared between products. A high coefficient indicates more regional specialization in that product than a lower one.

This table indicates that crop production moved away slightly from the populated regions, but that animal products continued to be produced where the people are located. (The grain coefficient is an anomaly, and increased in 1976; the reason is the poor crop in the Kazakh SSR in 1975.) Concentration coefficients in aggregates always display less specialization than those for narrower categories because of regional adaptations, and the Soviet coefficients are no exception, e.g., rye is more specialized by region than its aggregates of grain or of total crops. Similarly, the coefficients would be increased further if the geographical units were subdivided. The coefficients shown in the table indicate the concentration of production by major food groups, without regard to regional adaptations within the groups. For example, meat production is not disaggregated by product. If a region specializes in producing one variety of meat and does not ship it out or trade for other varieties, so that consumers have little choice among varieties of meat within the producing area, this would be shown only by separate concentration coefficients for beef, pork, and poultry.

According to the Heckscher-Ohlin theory of inter-regional trade, a region's specialization of production is optimal when its production reflects its resource endowment, so that a region that has a labor surplus and a land shortage should produce crops that use much labor but little land. By this accounting, the southern republics should shift the land that produces grain to vegetable production. As an example from state farm data for 1970, in Tadzhikistan and the Ukraine, this transfer would increase the total supply of both vegetables and grain, and increase even more the revenues in ruble value units. (A more detailed numerical example of such a shift is worked out later in this section.) However, the Heckscher-Ohlin theory assumes that transportation costs are negligible.[20] This assumption is untenable for the Soviet Union, and the specialization of production has been achieved not so much by regions as by farms.

The specialization in vegetable production more by farm organization than by region has been documented by Robert Stuart and F. M. Leversedge in a case study of potato and cabbage production in the Moscow oblast, 1966-71.[21] They show that specialization was concurrent with the conversion of collective farms into state farms. The supply of vegetables to consumers in Moscow increased. While the state farm has the ideological advantage of a superior form of socialist property, it also has greater access to capital equipment and pays higher wages, so that the shift to specialized production was accompanied by infusions of human and mechanical capital. Both yield and labor productivity increased along with the output.

Since the resource endowment differs between state and collective farms, as it does between regions, the same principle of specialization (Heckscher-Ohlin) that applied to regions is relevant for comparing organizations. Using Soviet data for 1970, published in their agricultural handbook, the following will illustrate the potential gain from a transfer of vegetable and potato production between all state and collective farms in the Ukrainian SSR:

(1) The average state farm produced one ton of vegetables with 8.4 days of labor, and one ton of potatoes with 6.9 days of labor. The average collective farm produced vegetables with 16.0 days of labor and potatoes with 6.6 days.

(2) If a state farm shifted 8.4 days of labor from potatoes to vegetables, it would lose 1.2 tons of potatoes but gain 1.0 ton of vegetables. If an average collective farm made the reverse shift of 16.0 days of labor from vegetables (losing 1.0 ton), it would gain 2.4 tons of potatoes. The net gain is 1.2 tons of potatoes, and no vegetable production would be lost.

(3) Valuing the product at the average national price for potatoes (114 rubles per ton) and vegetables (163 rubles per ton), the gain would be 25 rubles for the state farm and 111 rubles for the collective farm. For simplification, this analysis assumes that the supply of other inputs such as land can be adapted to the new use, and it illustrates clearly the potential for gain. It does not rely on national product prices, and point (3) is used only for illustration. In contrast to an inter-regional shift, a change in transport cost is negligible.

The gain from specialization by organization change is disappearing. Today, more than 90 percent of state farms are specialized, and 80 percent of collective farms. However, a farm is specialized if 50 percent of its receipts are received from one product, and most farms receive 60-65 percent.[22] The remaining diversification of agriculture appears to guarantee farm inputs, i.e., 10 percent of collective farms specialize in grain production and produce 28 percent of that sector's grain, but the specialists in other products produce most of the grain (72%). Most are meat and dairy farms that seek to guarantee animal feed supplies.

To summarize: Rising income has created new demands by Soviet consumers for fruits, vegetables, and meat. While one response to these new demands is the regional specialization of agricultural production, the Soviet response has been an organizational specialization within regions, which minimizes transport costs. Thus the Soviet consumer-producer nexus continues to be based on an agriculture that is self-sufficient, by products.

Any specialization by regions and trade integration is slow to develop.

III. Barriers to Regional Specialization

The hypothesis underlying this paper is that an optimal regional diversification of agricultural production would increase output and provide consumers with the products they most want, with resources left over for more. This section lists some barriers to a spatial reorganization of agriculture and the regional specialization of output:

(1) A primary barrier to diversification is the absence of adequate transportation, storage, and processing. The products whose demand is increasing the fastest are more perishable and fragile than the products whose demand is declining. The new demand impinges not only on producers but on the delivery infrastructure.[23]

(2) Since the labor force in the south is less educated and from a more traditional and conservative culture, it may be unwilling to adopt its commercial specialization.

(3) Prices of agricultual products have regional variations that counter resource endowments, so that the price received by a region with poor resources is higher than that received by a region with better resources. This reduces the internal incentives to push for regional diversification, and the external ability to plan for it.[24]

(4) Non-economic reasons may prevail, e.g., the dependence of the north on the south may not be desirable or feasible, or the equalization of incomes may have a higher priority than the goals hold here.[25] Dienes earlier found that the republics in the west had better economic justification for investment funds than those in the east (Siberia) who received them, but those economic criteria were ignored.[26]

(5) Intra-regional differences in republics may be more important than inter-regional, particularly with regard to large cities. While this paper examined regional development on the basis of the Heckscher-Ohlin theory of specialization and trade, the Soviet planners have used another model, locating agricultural production in self-sufficient, concentric rings around cities, rather than in disparate climatic regions. (This may be termed a "von Thunen" model.) Jackson notes that the urban agricultural regions have been defined for Moscow, Leningrad, the cities of the Urals, the Dnieper bend, and the Donbas.[27] While this policy diminishes the opportunity to diversify output, it minimizes the need for transportation.

Despite these barriers, some regional diversification in crops has occurred in recent years, demonstrating a willingness to provide consumers with the food they want through socialized agriculture and regional diversification. Agriculture requires extensive investment to overcome the barriers of resource endowments and transportation, and to integrate the economic regions. While self-sufficiency is an anachronism in a modern society, to intgegrate the disparate regional parts without strain to egalitarian or strategic goals is a task to rival industrialization.

Footnotes

*The co-rapporteur for this paper was Hans-Jurgen Wagener who contributed many helpful additions.

1. Stefan Valavanis, "Losch on Location",*Regional Economics*, ed. Harry W. Richardson, (New York, 1969), pp. 32-41.
2. Hans-Jurgen Wagener, "Rules of Location and the Concept of Rationality: the Case of the USSR", *The Soviet Economy in Regional Perspective*, ed. V.N.Bandera and Z.L. Melnyk, (New York, 1973), pp. 63-103.
3. A.G. Granberg, *Mezhotraslevye balansy v analize territorial'nykh proportsii SSSR,* (Novosibirsk, 1975). See also, the same author, "The Construction of Spatial Models of the National Economy", *Regional Development and Planning: International Perspectives,* ed. Antoni R. Kuklinski, (Leyden, 1975), pp. 189-200. (I am indebted to James Gillula for these references.)
4. Edgar Hoover, *Regional Economics*, (New York, 1971), p. 210.
5. W.A.D. Jackson, "The Problem of Soviet Agricultural Regionalization", *Slavic Review,* XX, 4 (1961), 656-78.
6., R.S. Mathiesen, "The Soviet Contribution to Regional Science: A Review Article", *Journal of Regional Science,* 7, 1 (1969), 125-40.
7. Wagener, *op. cit.*
8. Stephen Rapawy, *Estimates and Projections of the Labor Force and Civilian Employment in the USSR 1950 to 1990,* Foreign Economic Report #10, (Washington, 1976).
9. P.P. Litviakov, *Demograficheskie problemy zaniatosti*, (Moscow, 1969).
10. Elizabeth Clayton, "Regional Consumption Expenditures in the Soviet Union", *ACES Bulletin*, XVII, 2-3 (1975), 27-46.
11. Bruce F. Johnson and Peter Kilby, *Agriculture and Structural Transformation*, (New York, 1975).
12. Yujiro Hayami and Vernon Ruttan, *Agricultural Development: An International Perspective*, (Baltimore, 1971).
13. V.N. Iakimov, *Tekhnicheskii progress i vosproizvodstvo rabochei sily v kolkhozakh*, (Moscow, 1976).
14. Adequate supplies of water are necessary for the proper application of mineral fertilizers. Almost all agricultural land in Turkmenistan is irrigated.
15. Donna Bahry, "Distributive Politics and Soviet Elite Mobility: Two Models", Paper presented at the 1978 meeting of the American Political Science Association, New York City.
16. L.P. Kuprienko, *Vliianie urovnia zhizni na raspredelenie trudovykh resursov,* (Moscow, 1976).
17. V. Ivashchenko, "Pervoocherednye zadachi sel'skokhoziaistvennoi nauki", *Planovoe Khoziaistvo,* 10 (1977), 77-83.
18. P.A. Oram, "Comment", *Distortions of Agricultural Incentives*, ed. Theodore W. Schultz, (Bloomington, 1978), p.37.
19. FAO, *Agricultural Commodity Projections, 1970-80,* Volume 2, (Rome, 1971), p. 282.
20. Erling Olsen, "Regional Income Differences within a Common Market", *Regional Economics,* ed. Harry W. Richardson, (New York, 1969), pp. 107-114. These differences for agriculture are examined in Karl A. Fox, "Toward a Policy Model of World Economic Development with Special Attention to the Agricultural Sector", *The Role of Agriculture in Economic Development*, ed. Erik Thorbecke, (New York, 1969), pp. 95-126.
21. R.C. Stuart and F.M. Leversedge, "Soviet Agricultural Restructure and Urban Markets", *Canadian Geographer*, 19, 1 (1975), 73-93.
22. V. Balashova, *et al.*, "Nekotorye voprosy izucheniia spetsializatsii kolkhozov", *Vestnik Statistiki*, 2 (1978), 8-17.
23. V. Kotelianets, "Transportnyi faktor i kontsentratsiia proizvodstva", *Ekonomika sel'skogo khoziaistva*, 12 (1978), 34-9.
24. Morris Bornstein, "Soviet Price Policy in the 1970's", *Soviet Economy in a New Perspective*, ed. John Hardt and the Joint Economic Committee, (Washington, 1976),

pp. 34-45.
25. Hans-Jurgen Wagener has emphasized the impostance of income distribution goals in in Soviet regional policy (*op. cit.*).
26. Leslie Dienes, "Investment Pricrities in Soviet Regions", *Annals* [of the American Geographers], 62, (1972), 437-54.
27. Jackson, *op. cit.*, p. 660.

Dr. Alan Abouchar

Current Position:
Professor of Economics,
University of Toronto
Toronto, Ontario
Canada

Main field of work:
Soviet economy, transportation
economics and planning and urban
economic analysis

**Publications during
the last two years:**
Transportation Economics and Public
Policy
Economic Evolution of Soviet
Socialism
Soviet Planning and Spatial Efficiency

Other remarks:
Professor Abouchar has served as
consultant to public sector agencies
in Brazil, Canada, Iraq,
Yugoslavia, and West Africa in the
fields of transportation, urban
planning, and regional economics. He
was, for nine years, editor of Matekon
and is currently editor of the Eastern
Economic Journal. His academic
degrees include Ph.D. (economics)
and M.A. (statistics) form the
University of California at Berkeley,
A.M. and B.A. degrees (economics)
New York University, and M.A.
(pure mathematics) from York
University (Toronto).

Autarky and Regional Investment
Regional Industrial Policies in the USSR the 1970's
Professor Alan Abouchar

I. Introduction

Why are we interested in regional economic policy? If we know the basic motivations conditioning development patterns today we can say something about what is to happen in the next few years, which in turn may help us to say something about the basic international political/economic/ strategic and domestic economic/political intentions of the Soviet government. But analysis of Soviet regional industrial development policies may be most successful if we do not start with stated policies but, rather, start by determining what has taken place and try to infer policies from the events. This is because policies which are stated to support one or another action may fail to be realized for either of two reasons: (1) they were never intended to be put into effect but were stated in the first place for domestic or external political and military (or economic) reasons, or (2) stated policies, however earnestly intended, may simply be incapable of fulfilment owing to bureaucratic inertia, economic obstacles, and so on (compare the policy of limiting growth of the largest Soviet cities). The problem is especially severe at the macro level since basic industrial development policies are rarely stated and are especially difficult to infer or reconstruct from general statements of policy. In general, the national/economic program is rarely couched explicitly in terms of military strategy, income distribution, and potential nationalities problems. The verbiage that usually accompanies plan indicators provides little of value because it is all things to all people, expressing the sincere desire of the leaders to accelerate the rate of growth of the whole economy and of individual regions in a timely and even manner, ensuring that capital and human resources are used most productively, and aiming to achieve an even more improved level of well-being and consumption for all the people....

Not that it is easy to infer policies from events themselves. The main problem is the fact that there is not a one-to-one relationship between policy motivations and realizations. Two types of problem arise in this regard: (1) logical confusion, and (2) the problem of disentanglement of different motives. Concerning the first, we should consider the attainment of greater income equality as a policy objective. If it is successful, more equal income distribution is the result. But certain international strategic/

93

political policy motivations may also promote income equalization. Thus one term can refer both to a motivation and a realization of that motivation, but to the realization of other policy objectives besides, and there is a tendency to associate that event or realization with the motivation of the same name. As long as we are careful to recognize the danger we may be able to avoid it.

The other problem is more difficult to consider. Since policies cannot be classified into a set of stimuli to mutually exclusive events, and while a stated policy may help to set the wheels in motion, the economic event or phenomenon that is observed is usually the result of many desires, objectives, and concerns. This certainly applies to specific micro policies, such as the decision to undertake the Ural Kuznetsk Kombinat (although it is something of an understatement to call this a micro policy!), and probably even more to macro policies. Thus, while a host of considerations at times impinged on the UKK decision--including questions of short-term military strategy, cost effectiveness, maximization of long-term rate of growth, long term political considerations undoubtedly including fear of secession--it is really not possible to trace the decision to one single factor.

Let us look a little closer at the definitional problems. Most of us would agree on what is meant by, and the difference between, military motives and economic motives, or on what is meant by military and political considerations where foreign relations are concerned. We would probably also agree that questions of the growth rate of the economy or of the preferential development of heavy industry are economic considerations. But I would also wish to include under the rubric "economic," policies which are concerned with income distribution, achieving greater equality even though it leads to a lower rate of growth (which it might but need not necessarily do), even though there is a tendency to associate the rate of growth of the economy or an industry exclusively with economic policies and objectives. Thus, the division between political and economic motives and policies becomes blurred: decreasing inequality in income distribution might be regarded as an attempt to achieve a political goal-- satisfying the economic aspirations of ethnic-national minorities--or it may be regarded as an economic goal if one is thinking within the context of national welfare maximization.

Accordingly, we set out to determine what have been the main industrial development trends in the 1970's and then attempt to infer policies which are compatible with them. A classification of regional development patterns and the main policies compatible with them is given in Table 1. We distinguish four different types of regional industrialization patterns: (1) a more or less stable distribution of production; (2) a shift in regional production shares in regions which are already well populated; (3) a shift of production shares in the direction of sparsely settled regions; and (4) a shift in production to select regions bordering potential foreign adversaries. We indicate which of these are compatible with three broad categories of policy objectives: (a) international relations (military and political; (b) economic growth objectives; and (c) economic equity considerations. We stress that often a policy designed for one objective has implications for another objective so that the policy instruments designed explicitly for one kind of objective may have even more important consequences in regard to another objective.

Table 1
Correspondence Between Observable Economic
Phenomena and Major Policy Objectives

Observable Phenomenon	These Policies are Consistent with this Phenomenon
a) No shift in regional production shares	Maximization of long term rate of growth (?). Maximization of short term rate of growth.
b) Shift of production shares in favor of economically less industrialized but already well established regions	More equal income distribution (i.e. distribution of consumption). Maximum long term rate of growth subject this income distribution constraint (as compared with production in industrialized regions and shipping to less industrialized regions).
c) Shift in production shares to select sparse regions in east	Maximization of long term rate of growth (?). National defense vs. China.
d) Shift in production shares to select less industrialized but already well established regions (those bordering potential adversaries), e.g., Moldavia	Foreign Military and political considerations.

The main relationships between observable phenomena and policy which emerge are, first, that shifts in production to populous but backward regions imply more equal income distribution and, also, probably the highest rate of growth subject to the distribution constraint;[1] (2) the maximum long term rate of growth may be achieved under observable behavior (a) or (c) (no shift or shift to sparse regions), depending on the aboundance and quality of the resources in the sparse regions. With observable behavior (c), however, a lower short term rate of growth would be observed. Finally, "shifts to sparse regions" is probably most consistent with national defense, which we may regard as the principal external political-military concern.[2]

By convention, we use the expression "income equality" or "income distribution" although frequently what we are really interested in is the degree of equality or inequality of consumption. If we are talking about real income, there is usually no problem, except insofar as consumption of goods and services, such as education and health, which are provided in ways not directly related to income are concerned. The problem also arises of determining the relationship between welfare and consumption: does 20% more goods imply 20% higher welfare? To the extent that consumption is related to the income earning process, clearly there is some ambiguity. This second problem is probably less consequential at earlier levels of development.[3]

The first problem, however, would require analysis of the known wage-related components of consumption. A more difficult problem, and one which is especially related to Soviet statistical practice, is the fact that there is really no series on total wage-related consumption. Production by sectors A and B does not conform perfectly to the distinction between producer goods and consumer goods, since sector A includes a very large amount of durables production. This problem is known elsewhere (e.g., automobile purchases are treated as investment in Brazil), but it is potentially more serious in the Soviet Union since the statistics are not published in sufficient detail to break out the durable goods items (as cars can be broken out of Brazilian statistics). On the other hand, since durables consumption is still relatively low in the USSR, the problem, although quite serious potentially, may in fact not be terribly consequential[4] at present.

II. A Look at the Record

Unfortunately, Soviet statistics at the economy-wide level appear with a two year time lag (the 1978 statistics will be in the 1979 yearbook which will reach North American shores in mid 1980). Regional handbooks lag a year or two behind national yearbooks. Moreover, statistics are incomplete in many important respects, e.g. relative republic average wage levels are not included.

So what have we? First, we do have data on output as far as 1977 by major industrial sector (A and B) from the yearbooks and for total industry for 1978 from *Pravda*. We also have planned total industrial growth by republic for the rest of the decade, with no sub-industry breakdown. The same is true for agriculture. Finally, we have little in the way of measures of income or consumption. We do have statistics on rate of growth of average wages and of average real income by republic, but nothing on inter-republic comparisons. Thus, we must accept as a proxy for income inequality a social indicator such as level of urbanization. The problems in making welfare interpretations of personal income figures because of regional price variation and differences in regional consumption mixes (e.g. Shroeder's paper) and other considerations which suggest that urbanization itself might be a good index of welfare levels (e.g. Vogel's paper) hearten us in our choice of this measure for our purposes. Republic urbanization ratios are shown on Table 2.

Table 2
Urban Population as Percentage of Total Population
All-Union and Individual Republics; Selected Years

	Region	1966	1970	1975	1976	1977	1978
0.	USSR	53	56	60	61	62	62
1.	RSFSR	59	62	67	68	69	70
2.	Ukrainian SSR	51	55	59	60	61	61
3.	Belorussian SSR	39	43	51	52	53	55
4.	Uzbek SSR	36	37	38	39	39	40
5.	Kazakh SSR	47	50	53	54	54	55
6.	Georgian SSR	46	48	50	51	51	51
7.	Azerbaidzhan SSR	50	50	51	52	52	52
8.	Lithuanian SSR	45	50	56	57	58	59
9.	Moldavian SSR	28	32	36	37	38	39
10.	Latvian SSR	60	62	65	66	67	67
11.	Kirgiz SSR	37	37	38	39	39	39
12.	Tadzhik SSR	36	37	38	37	36	35
13.	Armenian SSR	56	59	63	64	64	65
14.	Turkmen SSR	48	48	49	49	48	49
15.	Estonian SSR	63	65	68	68	69	69

Source: *Narodnoe Khoziaistvo SSSR,* various years

To simplify the following exposition we use the conventions and notation as follows: ρ will denote an attained geometric rate of total industrial growth, with subscripts A and B referring to sectoral growth rates and subscripts 1, 2, 3, 4, 5 referring respectively to the periods 1966-70, 1971-75, 1976-80, 1976-77, and 1977-78. an apostrophe or "prime" sign indicates a planned rate.

One final reservation. Clearly, we should want any analysis of regional patterns to go down below the republic level, especially for the two largest republics, Kazakh SSR and RSFSR, but only fragmentary statistics are published (attained growth for major RSFSR regions). This is especially necessary for us to say something about observable phenomenon (c) and to try to analyze further the issues of growth and foreign political and military relations.

We have looked at the republic growth rates since 1965. The calculated growth rates together with the necessary Soviet primary (handbook and newspaper) statistical data and explanations are contained in Tables 2 and 3.

Economy-wide industrial growth achievements and plans have all fallen off since 1966. This shows up, first, in the dynamics of the attained growth rate, falling from 8.5% to 7.4% between 1966-70 and 1971-75 and averaging 5.3% in the first three years of the 10th FYP. Also, the planned

Table 3

Compound Rates of Growth of Gross Industrial Output: All-Industry, Group A and Group B. All-Union and Individual Republics, Attained and Planned Rates, Various Years

	Region	1966-1970			1971-1975			1976			1977			1978	19	1976-80	
		P_1	P_{1A}	P_{1B}	P_2	P_{2A}	P_{2B}	P_4	P_{4A}	P_{4B}	P_5	P_{5A}	P_{5B}	P_6	P_2	P
0.	USSR	8.5	8.6	8.4	7.4	7.6	6.5	4.9	5.5	2.9	6.0	5.8	5.7	4.8	8.0	6.3
1.	RSFSR	8.2	8.4	7.7	7.3	7.7	6.2	4.9	4.8	2.2	5.4	5.9	4.3	4.5	8.0	6.5
2.	Ukrainian SSR	8.4	8.2	9.2	7.1	7.4	6.0	4.2	5.5	1.5	6.0	5.9	5.9	4.4	7.4	5.7
3.	Belorussian SSR	12.3	13.0	11.4	10.4	11.6	8.3	6.7	8.1	4.7	8.0	9.0	7.7	7.6	9.6	7.1
4.	Uzbek SSR	6.3	6.0	7.3	8.5	8.6	8.3	5.3	5.3	7.4	5.0	4.4	8.1	5.3	8.6	6.5
5.	Kazakh SSR	9.3	9.2	9.7	6.9	7.6	6.6	2.8	4.2	0.0	4.8	3.3	5.8	4.1	9.7	7.1
6.	Georgian SSR	8.9	8.4	9.6	6.8	6.8	6.6	5.0	6.5	4.3	6.8	7.4	6.2	7.4	7.6	6.5
7.	Azerbaidzhan SSR	6.5	5.9	8.3	8.5	8.1	8.7	8.0	6.7	11.2	7.4	6.9	8.9	8.0	7.8	6.8
8.	Lithuanian SSR	11.7	12.8	10.3	8.3	9.2	7.0	5.4	6.4	4.2	5.1	6.1	3.4	5.6	8.3	6.0
9.	Moldavian SSR	9.4	8.9	10.0	9.3	11.6	6.3	4.5	6.9	1.5	6.8	5.4	8.0	3.6	10.1	8.0
10.	Latvian SSR	9.4	11.0	7.9	6.4	7.6	5.1	5.1	5.6	3.9	4.2*	3.8	3.8	3.1	7.0	4.7
11.	Kirgiz SSR	13.0	15.4	8.6	8.7	8.9	7.5	4.6	5.8	4.2	3.8*	3.6	2.7	7.2	9.2	6.2
12.	Tadzhik SSR	8.1	6.8	12.0	6.8	7.1	6.0	2.9	2.8	3.7	5.6	3.4	10.0	5.5	6.6	7.3
13.	Armenian SSR	11.4	10.9	12.8	7.7	7.6	7.9	9.0	8.3	9.6	7.6	8.3	6.3	7.7	10.4	7.7
14.	Turkmen SSR	8.4	8.6	7.4	9.0	9.6	7.0	1.3	0.6	5.0	2.6	1.2	5.4	3.6	10.4	6.0
15.	Estonian SSR	8.6	8.6	8.6	7.1	7.9	5.9	5.7	6.8	6.0	3.4	3.8	2.1	3.1	6.6	4.4

Sources: Calculated from data in *Narodnoe khoziaistvo SSR* and individual republics, various years; *Ekonomicheskaia gazeta*, 1976, nos. 11, 47; *Pravda* 20/1/79; *Gosudarstvennya plan razvitiia narodnogo khoziastva SSR na 1971-75 gody*, Moscow, Izdat. politcheskoi literatury, 1972.

*Rates calculated correctly from inconsistend data in source. Note * refers to indicated rates only.

growth rate fell from 8.0% in 1971-75 to 6.5% in 1976-80. It is probably worthy of note, incidentally, that, while in the 1971-75 period the group A rate of growth was below that of group B, lip service at least was paid to a faster rate of growth of B during the ninth and tenth plans. Moreover, the planned rates of growth of group B in the two five-year plans of the 1970's were .3 and 1.5 percentage points higher than the rate of group A.

This period has been marked by wide variation in the individual republic industrial growth rates, as may be seen in Table 3. This refers to all three growth rates (total, A, and B). There has also been wide variation in the planned total growth rates (also shown in Table 3); unfortunately, data are not published on the respective planned growth rates of A and B at the republic level. Evidently, very few republics had higher A rates of growth than B.

Can we find any patterns behind the positive and negative deviations between republic rates and the all-union rate? First of all, since there is so much variation in growth rates, and since so many republic growth rates exceed the national average, it is clear that many and diverse forces msut be at work and that production shares are shifting. How much of this shift can be attributable to long-term growth maximization as opposed to foreign military/political concerns cannot be judged. It must certainly be true, though, that the high all-industry growth rates observed in recent years in the Far East and in Siberia reflect both long term growth hopes and political and military fears.

To explore the hypothesis that planned and attained growth rates may have been influenced by income distribution considerations we examined the rank correlation coefficients between the republic urbanization ratios, as a proxy for real personal income and consumption as noted previously, and the rank of republic growth rates. The Spearman rank correlation coefficient was calculated for seven time intervals and its level and dynamics provide an interesting insight into what is taking place. The details are shown in Table 4.

First we observe that the only statistically significant value is the correlation coefficient for the 1976-80 period: its level and sign indicate a strong inverse relationship between real income and welfare levels (as measured by our urbanization ratio proxy) and growth, suggesting a strong income distribution objective. But this is best approached within the entire context so let us look first at the others.

We note first that ranks are assigned in such a way that a positive correlation coefficient r_s implies that relatively faster growth is associated with lower urbanization ratios and negative values of r_s with higher growth rates for republics with higher urbanization ratios. Thus, a positive correlation coefficient implies a positive association between the rate of industrial growth and poverty, as indicated by the urbanization proxy.

We must, of course, avoid mechanical interpretation of the results, an effort aided, to be sure, by the fact that very little emerges which is statistically significant at conventional levels (5 percent or less). The 1971-75 attained rate suggests that, on the whole, inter-republic welfare differentials

Table 4
Spearman Rank Correlation Coefficient Between
Urban Ratio and Rate of Growth of Total Industrial
Production, Various Time Intervals

Time Interval and Measure of Growth	r_s	t	Prob 't' $>$ t
1966-70: attained rate	.013	.413	$>$.6
1971-75: attained rate	.47	1.927	$>$.05
1971-75: planned rate	-.32	-1.28	$>$.2
1976-80: planned rate	.70	3.55	$>$.002
1975-76: attained rate	-.35	-1.344	$>$.2
1976-77: attained rate	.5	2.08	$>$.05
1977-78: attained rate	.2	.74	$>$.4

$$r_s = 1 - \frac{6\Sigma d_i^2}{n(n^2-1)} \quad ; \quad t_{n-2} = r_s\sqrt{\frac{n-2}{1-r_s^2}} \quad , \quad i = 1,\ldots 15; \ n = 15_i$$

$$t_{.025,13} = 2.160 \qquad\qquad t_{.05,13} = 1.771$$

Note: Ranks are assigned in such a way that a positive r implies that relatively faster growth is associated with lower urbanization ratios: and negative values of r associate higher growth rates with higher urbanization ratios.

were reduced. The really interesting thing, though, is that this r_s was observed.

What happened? The rank correlation for planned growth was seriously affected by the change in the rank of a few key republics: Moldavia (planned rank 11, attained rank 2); Turkmen SSR (planned rank 15, attained rank 3); and Armenia (planned rank 1, attained rank 8). The much higher attained than planned growth for the first two may have reflected the increasingly tense relations between the Soviet Union and the adjacent foreign countries, Moldavia adjacent to Rumania and Turkmenia next to Iran and Afghanistan, but growth in the latter also reflected the rapid development of the Turkmen oil based industries.[5] Thus, while the much greater attained than planned rate for these two republics may well have been prompted by foreign policy and growth maximization concerns, it also worked in the direction of more equitable income distribution.

When we come to the 10th FYP, however, we observe a striking pattern of planned republic growth rates and urbanization levels. The high correlation coefficient--and the correspondingly high value of t--would occur purely by chance only with very low probability, less than once out of every five hundred times that such an experiment was conducted. While, as we have seen, it is possible for some republics to be both strategically situated and have low urbanization ratios, it is also possible for some to be strategically located and not (Armenia for example). Thus, while a policy of satisfying strategic concerns might also have salubrious effects on income distribution, as it appears to have had in the previous quinquennium, as noted, a correlation coefficient as high as the one observed for the 10th FYP would seem to be more directly related to a conscious pattern of developing the poorer regions.[6] But satisfying strategic concerns may also work against welfare equalization, as indeed seems to be the case in the pattern of planned growth rates for 1976-80, with a high rate of industrial growth being planned for Armenia, a republic with the fourth highest urbanization ratio. Incidentally, a greater concern with the human side in the 10th FYP also shows up in the planned growth rate for group B--1.5 percentage points higher than that of group A.

Regarding the attained growth rates, however, the picture is rather different, the rank correlation coefficients for the first three years of the 10th FYP being, respectively .35, .5, and .2. While the last two coefficients (those for 1977 and 1978) are at least positive, they are so low as not to be inconsistent with a pattern of industrial growth which is random in relation to the urbanization ration, while in the first (that for 1976) the pattern of republic growth rates actually runs counter to urbanization patterns and, hence, works against the equalization of welfare levels.

It is interesting to examine the individual republic records of attained growth and urbanization which caused the rank correlation coefficients for attained growth to differ so sharply from that for planned growth in the 10th FYP and to explore the hypothesis that strategic considerations may have intervened to cause a pattern of growth rates which was inconsistent with promotion of welfare equalization. The most dramatic difference is observed in the shift from the significant and positive coefficient of the plan to the negative coefficient for 1975-76. Armenia did have a high attained rate, as in the plan although not actually equal to the planned rate, but the rates for a number of other republics changed drastically. Moldavia, so favored earlier in the plan and in the previous quinquennium, slipped to 11th place; this would seem to conflict with the hypothesis of strategic necessity until it is noted that its 10th FYP projected rate of growth of agriculture, the highest in the country, is 6.5% per year, over 50% higher than the republic next on the list, Armenia. Agriculture is probably capable of producing faster short term effects on living standards. On the other hand, a number of other strategically situated republics with high industrial growth plans--most notably all five Central Asian Republics-- slipped sharply between their planned and attained growth rates. It is not that their planned rates were overly ambitious--except perhaps for the Kazakh Republic; the others were close to or less than their attained rates for 1971-75. It may simply be that, while in principle the government still would like to bolster these republics to levels projected in the plans, the enormous expenditure of resources further east is simply too much to support and still achieve planned growth rates elsewhere.

III. Conclusions and Prospects

In this paper we have attempted to detect the main forces behind the pattern of attained and planned industrial growth rates since 1965. No single broad social or economic policy emerges, and, indeed, we scarcely expected that one would. Indeed, I am surprised that there was as much coherence as has been observed--an apparent concern with reducing inequalities in real welfare levels being observed during the 10th FYP. To say this, of course, is not to suggest that the regime in 1975 was inherently socially conscious; we must allow for the possibility of recognition on the leaders' part that the best way to minimize the threat of subversion and ensure that far-flung republics adhere to the national structure may be by putting bread on their tables. Nor does recognition of this basic tendency require that income distribution explicitly or implicitly be the only concern of national policy-making or that some investment may take place which undoes some of the equality which might otherwise be attained.

What does this general pattern as well as the specific developments of recent years presage for the future? As noted earlier, the rates of industrial growth are falling in almost all republics, suggesting that there may be real problems at hand. Part of it may be due to overcommitment and grandiose ambitions in the east and we must await the completion of same before there is a resurgence elsewhere (recall the tremendous share of investment in the Ural Kuznetsk Kombinat--25-40% of the total investment in industry and transportation).

Footnotes

Note: * refers to indicated rates only.

1. It is conceivable but not likely that a higher rate of growth subject to the income distribution constraint could be achieved with no shift in production. This might be possible if the scale economies in the production of consumer goods were very great. For most consumer goods, this is not the case. In a higher consumption economy, with a greater role being played by consumer durables, this consideration could not be ruled out so easily. However, if this were the situation a mechanism would have to be found to transfer the consumption to the under-developed region, a role normally played by wages, which, if production is not to increase in the region, could not be called upon for this function.

2. We note here that maximizing the short term and long term rate of growth of the economy is consistent with other foreign policy objectives, such as extension of influence in Africa. Such policies would in turn have an ambiguous effect upon the economy, and so we may neglect them here.

3. For an analysis of this issue in a developed economy, see Abouchar, Alan, "Regional Welfare and Measured Income Differentials in Canada," *Review of Income and Wealth,* (December 1971).

4. Although standard Soviet statistical sources do not break consumer goods produced by sector A out of the total production of sector A, there does exist some fragmentary information. According to E. A. Ivanov, in 1965 and 1970 the percentage of total consumer goods production produced by "branches of heavy industry" were 19.0% and 22.6% respectively, the total amount increasing by 74% between the

two years. (E. A. Ivanov, *XXIV Session of the CPSU on the Relationship between Groups A and B in Industry,* Moscow, Izdatel'stvo Ekonomika, 1972, p. 31.

5. A good summary of this development is given by Ann Sheehy in "Industrial Growth Lags in Turkmenistan," Radio Liberty Research memorandum, RL 5/79, 3 Jan. 1979.

6. It should be noted that in using the rank correlation analysis rather than an analysis of the cardinal values themselves we have done two things: 1) given equal weight to each region so that, to the extent that the authorities would like to have conclusions drawn from lists of 15 republics and to the extent that people think in terms of the distribution of republic welfare levels when they think about equality, we have built their intentions into the computations; and 2) eliminated the effect of extreme observations which might have a disproportionate effect on the result.

Comment

Dr. Hans-Jurgen Wagener

Commenting on Dr. Clayton's paper puts me in a somehow indetermined situation which the author herself probably must have experienced, too. What did the organizers of the symposium have in mind when they invited a paper on regional self-sufficiency? What is the problem? Is there any problem? This is by no means evident. Before dealing with Dr. Clayton's interpretation of the question, namely regional disparities and specialization in agriculture, I shall briefly touch upon self-sufficiency in general.

What do we mean by regional self-sufficiency? How advanced is regional interdependence? How advanced is the national economic integration? Are there factors that impede such development?

To answer the questions we would need regional input-output tables and interregional trade flow matrices. As far as I know, there have been made attempts in the USSR to collect the necessary data, but the results are not available to us (cf. Gillula and Bond, 1977). Exact statements on integration are thus not possible.

Instead of autarky in every individual good and service we could also think of aggregate demand and supply when speaking about regional self-sufficiency. Here we do not need detailed input-output data but 'only' the regional balance of payments. Self-sufficiency in this context means that regions develop on the basis of their own financial means. If a region happens to be less developed than others and wants to catch up, it has to provide internally for the necessary savings. Wide interregional differentials in income are the consequence.

I have elsewhere (cf. Wagener, 1972 and 1973) formulated the hypothesis that Soviet economic policy with respect to the regions has opted for development of less developed regions and for as little income differentials as possible. The obvious consequence is no regional self-sufficiency in the aggregate sense but massive capital transfers. The highly centralized economic system of the USSR is functional for the implementation of these objectives. I have tried to corroborate the hypothesis with an estimate of capital transfers and a comparison of data on produced and used national income. It must be admitted, however, that the data base is rather weak and that the statistical problems are enormous.

Any statement on regional self-sufficiency or integration must take into account the foreign trade situation of the concerned country. Regions close to the more important foreign trade partners, such as the Western parts of the USSR, lend themselves much more to foreign trade production and international integration than others far away such as Transcaucasia or Central Asia. This is true only for trade in manufactured products. Since Soviet trade is still dominated by raw materials, the present regional distribution of foreign trade will not follow the indicated pattern. With the share of manufactured goods in foreign trade growing, the relative importance of the Western regions will also eventually increase.

By mentioning the issue of development we have already touched upon the next problem: why regional self-sufficiency? If national self-sufficiency or autarky may be a policy objective in itself for the sake of national independence and autonomy, this is much less obvious for regional self-sufficiency. All the more in a country where internal autonomy and self-determination receive a very low priority *vis-a-vis* a highly centralized political system and planning apparatus. Experiments with a more decentralized territorial planning and control system immediately yielded strong autarkic tendencies with rather disruptive consequences for national development.

Recognizing national economic integration as a major policy objective, regional self-sufficiency or tendencies in that direction can only be a by-product of other major objectives or the result of adverse circumstances, leaving aside purely non-economic reasons. Such an other objective might be seen in the formula for Soviet regional development: specialization and complex development. Dr. Clayton kindly refers to my earlier mentioned study where I tried to show that the policy of complex development resulted in a certain assimilation of industrial structures. However, structural convergence or structural similarities in terms of aggregate branches of industry need not embrace regional self-sufficiency. Let me remind you only of the structural similarities of highly industrialized economies and their international economic integration. As a result we are rather inclined to conclude that complex development is a precondition for integration and specialization on an equal footing.

As to the adverse circumstances, natural conditions (long distances between settlements and industrial centers, rivers, mountain chains, deserts, etc.) as well as historical conditions (low level of development of all kinds of infrastructure) may necessitate a certain degree of regional self-sufficiency. For the Soviet situation it is rather safe to assume great possibilities for improvement of the transport system and for lowering transport costs with the concommitant result of greater opportunities for national integration.

We may conclude that complex development is not equal to self-sufficiency or autarky. It means the creation of an industrial base for regional development and not that every region (however defined) must have its own coal mine and steel works. A completely undeveloped region cannot specialize except in bananas and the like, i.e., in its natural advantages. This is not very conducive for industrialization. So, if in the Soviet

Union, we can observe after a period of more complex development a certain trend towards specialization, this does not testify to a radical change in policy, as some people seem to imply, but rather to a new phase in the process of development. In the early phase, the setting up of basic capacities and the construction of the necessary infrastructure account for a certain structural imitation and autarkic trends. In international trade and development, this is called the 'infant industry phase' which legitimizes (autarkic) protective trade policies. With on-going industrialization and the improvement of the transport and communication systems, interregional trade will increase and possibilities for specialization will become more obvious.

Dr. Clayton concentrates her argument on agriculture. In this context we may ask the question whether there is a principle difference between industry and agriculture with respect to regional self-sufficiency or specialization. Motives for specialization are absolute advantages of different natural conditions, comparative advantages due to different factor endowments (capital, labor, qualification), scale factors. Its closer relation to nature makes primary production more dependent upon natural conditions than manufacturing where comparative advantages and scale factors may be of greater importance. As Dr. Clayton correctly states, many advantages of specialization can be reaped by organizational instead of regional specialization. This presupposes a high degree of interfirm (or interfarm) cooperation which Soviet agricultural policy is actively promoting.

The second difference can be seen in the product itself. On the whole, agricultural products are more perishable than industrial products. Together with long distances and transport problems this factor leads to regional self-sufficiency or agro-industrial cooperation. Von Thunen's circles which Dr. Clayton observed in the Soviet Union have existed in the West, too. They have been broken up by modern transportation, improvements in gross and retail trade and innovations like deep-freezing, etc. That all is still to come in the Soviet Union. On the other hand there is a regional specialization in Soviet agriculture based on agro-industrial cooperation (besides industrial crops there are canned meat, fruit and vegetables). Whether this is what the consumer wants or only a second best is open to discussion. The folklore will have it that even Soviet farmers must eat canned fruit and vegetables on occasion of a great feast.

In regard to factor endowments and comparative advantage, it is necessary to see that the textbook argument of Heckscher and Ohlin is a static one. In a dynamic context factor endowments are not invariable. On the contrary, the situation of an individual sector of the economy depends heavily on its own development and on the development of the other sectors (industrialization, labor qualification, accumulation, improvement of infrastructure). We conclude that agricultural specialization will have to respond more to natural conditions than industrial location policy but that the process of industrialization will have major repercussions upon agriculture's production conditions.

We come now to the central argument of Dr. Clayton, i.e., the hypothesis "that an optimal regional diversification of agricultural production would increase output and provide consumers with the products they most want," and that among other factors, the North-South difference in development is mainly responsible for a suboptimal diversification. The disparities between North and South are mainly seen in a lower land-labor ratio, a poorer supply of manufactured inputs, a lower stock of human capital: in short, a less developed technique in agriculture and consequently a lower productivity. We will have to take a closer look to see whether the hypothesis can be corroborated by the facts.

The lower land-labor ratio in the South is a fact if, in this case, we regard Kazakhstan as belonging to the North and if we disregard climatic and soil conditions. The poorer supply of manufactured inputs follows, according to Dr. Clayton, from a disparity in industrial development, which can hardly be disputed, and regional autarky in industry, which is less obvious as we have suggested.

As example she cites production and use of fertilizers. Here, I cannot quite follow her reasoning. There are regional differences in the utilization of fertilizers (cf. *Vestnik statistiki,* 3 (1979),71-74). However, they do not reflect a North-South contradiction but rather the natural conditions for the application of fertilizers. The application depends not only on supply and know-how but also on the necessary humidity which decreases from North-West to South-East with the exception of irrigated land. With respect to supply we see that the Southern republics produce fertilizers as they are used (cf. *Narodnoe Khoziaistvo SSR za 60 let,* (Moscow, 1978)214, 325. If the North (or rather the West) produced more fertilizer than it uses, this has also something to do with the above mentioned influence of foreign trade. Since the average distance of fertilizer transport by train (and all fertilizers are transported by train) is 1,053 km (*Ibid.,* pp. 392-3) it may, however, be argued that regional self-sufficiency could be improved. Scale factors in bulk chemical production rather than labor qualifications may contradict this argument.

The comparatively low level of labor qualification in South is seen by Dr. Clayton in the disproportionately high share of women in rural labor force. It is true that the share of women workers and employees is significantly lower in the Southern republics of the USSR whereas their participation in kolkhoz work (with the exception of Kazakhstan) shows very little regional differences. One should note, however, that women participation is lower on average in the kolkhoz sector than in the state sector of the economy; (cf. *Vestnik statistiki,* 1 (1979), 72). It does not follow herefrom, however, that Southern agriculture relies disproportionately on a female labor force.

Whe present situation of Soviet agriculture can be briefly depicted as follows: On a relatively low level of modernization in the whole country the South has an absolute disadvantage in land, for certain products an absolute advantage in natural conditions, and a relative abundance in labor. From this it follows that productivity gains could be reached by high investments (modernizations) which in the North should be rather labor saving and in the South land improving. The accumulation of physical capital must be accompanied by an appropriate accumulation of human capital. At the present state of development these two factors of production are rather complementary than substitutive. If this policy were followed in a planned and purposeful way, it should be possible to observe together with a falling land-labor ratio is rising capital-land ratio, a rising qualification-land ratio and finally also a rising output-land ratio. If there are no major technological barriers or disparities it should be possible to estimate cross-regionally an agricultural production function for the Soviet Union as a whole.

Table 1

Agricultural Input and Output Relations for the
Kolkhoz and Sovkhoz Sectors Only, 1971-1976

	Land-Labour Ratio 1	Capital-Land Ratio 2	Qualification-Land Ratio 3	Output-Land Ratio 4
USSR	8.13	0.73	3.09	0.543
Kazakhstan	22.58	0.36	1.45	0.210
RSFSR	10.95	0.64	2.72	0.443
Belorussia and Ukraine	4.87	1.00	4.27	0.886
Baltic republics	6.11	1.82	6.95	1.093
Moldavia	2.39	1.72	5.30	1.459
Central Asia	2.33	1.58	6.79	1.339
Transcaucasia	1.75	2.05	10.07	1.528

1) Arable hectares (ha) utilized per agricultural worker.

2) Million rubles fixed capital per arable 1000 ha utilized.

3) Number of specialists per arable 1000 ha utilized.

4) Million rubles gross production (average annual for 1971-75) per arable 1000 ha utilized.

Source: *Narodnoe khoziaistvo SSR za 60 let,* (Moscow, 1978), pp. 278 291, 293, 356, 371, 378, 380

Table 1 gives a rough indication of the present regional pattern of input-output relations in the kolkhoz and sovkhoz sectors of Soviet

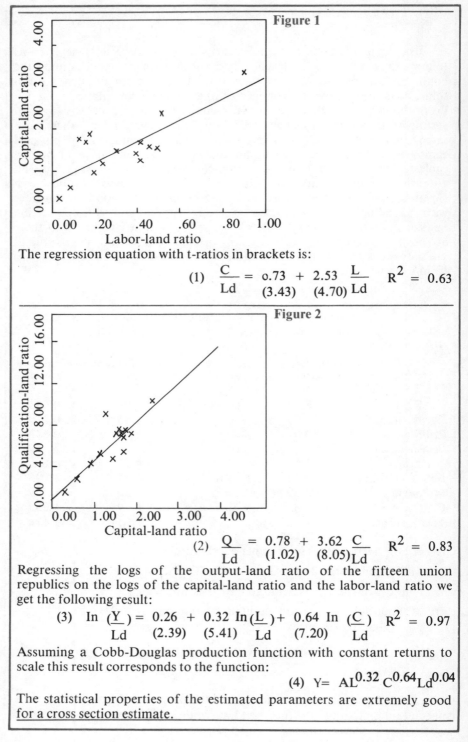

Figure 1

The regression equation with t-ratios in brackets is:

$$(1) \quad \frac{C}{Ld} = \underset{(3.43)}{0.73} + \underset{(4.70)}{2.53} \frac{L}{Ld} \qquad R^2 = 0.63$$

Figure 2

$$(2) \quad \frac{Q}{Ld} = \underset{(1.02)}{0.78} + \underset{(8.05)}{3.62} \frac{C}{Ld} \qquad R^2 = 0.83$$

Regressing the logs of the output-land ratio of the fifteen union republics on the logs of the capital-land ratio and the labor-land ratio we get the following result:

$$(3) \quad \ln\left(\frac{Y}{Ld}\right) = \underset{(2.39)}{0.26} + \underset{(5.41)}{0.32} \ln\left(\frac{L}{Ld}\right) + \underset{(7.20)}{0.64} \ln\left(\frac{C}{Ld}\right) \qquad R^2 = 0.97$$

Assuming a Cobb-Douglas production function with constant returns to scale this result corresponds to the function:

$$(4) \quad Y = AL^{0.32} C^{0.64} Ld^{0.04}$$

The statistical properties of the estimated parameters are extremely good for a cross section estimate.

agriculture. This pattern corresponds on the whole with our expectations. As to the input relations, figures 1 and 2 show a more detailed cross-sectional correlation for the fifteen individual union republics. In particular it can be seen that the capital-land and qualification-land ratios are directly proportionate, since the absolute term of equation (2) is not significantly different from zero.

We conclude that the role of land for Soviet agricultural output growth seems to be rather negligible. Therefore, we would hesitate to recommend the 'Japanese model' even only for the Southern regions. It is rather the 'European model' (relatively high labor and material input intensity) which could serve as an alternative. About two thirds of productivity differences can be ascribed to capital and correspondingly, as noted, the remaining third to labor. It is obvious that a policy to raise agricultural productivity must call for a big share of investment in agriculture, if labor is expected to decrease. Further we conclude that the regional input-output relations fit well into a regular functional form. We did not find indications for a technological gap between North and South or for regional self-sufficiency in agricultural development. The picture is rather one of deliberate planning and coordination in macro-economic terms on a nation-wide scale whereby differences in factor endowments have been taken into account.

A final observation on prices, incomes and planning is in order. Dr. Clayton suggests implicitly that labor incomes are more or less equal between regions and this fact corresponds with the already mentioned general objectives of Soviet regional policy. This is mainly due to a price policy which differentiates prices regionally. She criticizes regional price differentiation because it impedes specialization. That is true if specialization is determined by the price mechanism. Under the described conditions the price mechanism would counteract, however, the socialist objective of income equality, although in textbooks (and alas, only in textbooks) we find factor price equalization theorems based on the price mechanism.

The allocative situation depicted above together with labor income equality are the results of a certain amount of central planning which the price mechanism could hardly bring about. In this aspect specialization cannot be left to the price mechanism and regional self-determination, but it must also be centrally planned. With specialization, however, we leave the realm of macro-economic variables which lend themselves most to central planning. It must be expected, therefore, that centrally planned specialization will encounter difficulties.

References:
J.W. Gillula and D.L. Bond, "Development of Regional Input-Output Analysis in the Soviet Union," in V.G. Treml (ed.), *Studies in Soviet Input-Output Analysis,* (New York, 1977), pp. 282-307.

H.-J. Wagener, *Wirtschaftswachstum in unterentwickelten Gebieten, Ansatze zu einer Regionanalyse der Sowjetunion,* (Berlin, 1972).

H.-J. Wagener, "Rules of Location and the Concept of Rationality: The Case of the USSR," in V.N. Bandera and Z.L. Melnyk (eds.), *The Soviet Economy in Regional Perspective,* (New York, 1973), pp. 63-103.

Comment

Professor Zbigniew Fallenbuchl

The importance of foreign trade for the Soviet regional development depends on three factors: (1) the volume of foreign trade; (2) its geographic direction; and (3) its commodity composition. Dr. McAuley concentrates, to a great extent, on the first factor. The relative importance of foreign trade in the Soviet economy is limited, whether it is measured by the share of the world trade, as Dr. McAuley does, or as a percentage of national product. For example, when the Soviet GNP is calculated in accordance with the Western methodology and converted into U.S. dollars not by the official rate of exchange but by the average purchasing power ratio of the dollar to the ruble,[1] the ratio of trade (export plus import) to GNP was about 8% in both 1976 and 1977. Even keeping in mind the obvious limitations of such calculations and taking, therefore, into consideration a considerable safety margin, this is a small involvement in foreign trade for a modern industrial country.

However, foreign trade plays now a more important role than it was often the case in the past, although progress has been slow and uneven. Since 1960 Soviet trade has been growing less rapidly than the value of world trade. The share of Soviet import in total world import increased from 2.3% in 1950 to 4.2% in 1960 but declined to 3.6% in 1970 and 3.5% in 1977. The corresponding figures for the share of Soviet export in total world export were 2.9%, 4.3%, 4.2% and 4.0%.

Even when the total volume of import is small, its importance may be quite big. This is the so called supply multiplier, which is usuallly associated with the name of Professor F. D. Holzman.[2] The basic idea is that a removal of one small bottleneck can have a strong overall production effect. The multiplier may be particularly strong in the case of regional development. An entire region may be opened up for development as the result of imported special drilling or mining equipment, without which the extraction of oil or other raw materials would not be possible, or machinery for a particular plant, which could not be established otherwise. The new oil field, mine or industrial plant may stimulate a rapid development of the region, even when the value of imported equipment and machinery represents almost an insignificant proportion of GNP for the country as a whole. The importance of foreign trade for regional development cannot, therefore, be measured by the total value of foreign trade.

The involvement of the Soviet Union in foreign trade is at present sufficiently important to warrant some concern among the Soviet

113

planners about the distance between the location at which a given exportable commodity is produced, or import is utilized, and the point at the border at which export leaves, or import enters, the country. These distances are usually very long because of the geographic direction of Soviet trade and its commodity composition.

Trade with other CMEA countries represents about half of total Soviet trade (in 1977 it was 52.5%). The calculation of the CMEA share in total trade is distorted because the intra-bloc trade takes place at special prices which differ from the current world prices at which the rest of trade is calculated. In 1973-75 the CMEA share was considerably understated in all countries of the bloc. The distortion is now smaller but some understatement still exists.

Western Europe is the second largest group of Soviet trading partners. In 1977 it represented 21.3% of Soviet imports and 23.0% of exports. Together the CMEA countries and Western Europe amount to about 75% of Soviet foreign trade and probably not less than 80% of that trade crosses the western border of the country. However, a very large part of the production for export takes place in the eastern regions and the relative importance of those regions in the production of exportables rapidly increases.

This tendency is connected with the commodity composition of the Soviet exports. Manufactured goods represent a relatively small part of total exports. In 1977 machine and equipment represented 18.8% and manufactured consumption goods 2.7%, together 21.5%. Most of these commodities are exported from regions west of the Urals. On the other hand, fuels represented 35.1%, ores and concentrates 8.1% and wood and its products 5.1% (together 48.3%). Most of these commodities are produced east of the Urals. The remaining part of exports is products (18.2%). At least some of these exports are also produced in the eastern regions. Altogether, because of the commodity composition of export, a very large proportion of it originates in the eastern regions. This is particularly true in the case of trade with advanced western countries in which in 1977 mineral fuels represented 54.4% and crude materials 20.7% of Soviet exports to those countries.

Transportation over long distances is, therefore, a major problem. According to a Soviet source, the average distance that cargo for export must travel within the U.S.S.R. is from one and half to two times longer than the distance travelled by identical goods used domestically. Moreover, the average distance of the shipment of exports tends to increase as the result of the exhaustion of raw material sources in the western regions.[3]

On the import side the problem is less important, but it also exists. Most imports come from the western direction, from other CMEA countries and from Western Europe. Many of them are used in big industrial centres in the European Soviet Union and in the Urals. However, with a relative increase in the importance of CMEA deliveries for joint investment projects and western deliveries for the expansion of the production of fuels and raw materials in the eastern regions, the cost of transport is becoming more important in this field as well.

Until recently domestic transportation costs were apparently almost ignored in the calculation of the profitability of production for export and in the calculation of investment costs in various regions. However, with rising cost of fuel, transport cost is increasing and it is necessary to ship fuel over increasingly long distances to supply transport carriers. It is, therefore, not surprising to find now in the Soviet economic literature an interesting discussion concerning the regional effectiveness of foreign trade transportation.

A relatively simple analytical test has been devised in this connection in the form of the "regional coefficient of economic effectiveness of export and import." In the case of an exported commodity it is the ratio of revenue per unit of output (in foreign currency) to total production and transport cost per unit of output of the exported commodity.[4]

Apparently quite considerable differences in the value of coefficients for various regions have been observed for various commodities. In the case of coal, coke, iron ore, nitrogen fertilizers, grain and cotton fibre the differences between the maximum and the minimum value of the regional coefficients of effectiveness range up to 150%. This is a relatively narrow range and it suggests that the location of the production of these commodities is not too widely dispersed in geographic sense as otherwise there would be considerable variations int he cost of transportation. In the case of pig iron, lumber, and pulp and paper the difference is about 200% and in the case of oil, natural gas, cement and round timber it reaches 300%. The wide ranges suggest that better results could be achieved by concentrating all export production in the most efficient and less distant locations. With such big variations it is possible that production for export in some remote areas is unprofitable.

The objective of these calculations is to introduce a more rational selection of regions in which production for export should be located, to select regions which should specialize in production for export and to take the cost of exporting production from a given place into consideration whenever the location of new plants is decided.

The importance of regional effectiveness of production for export is not limited to mining and production of basic materials. The process of CMEA integration increases the degree to which various Soviet manufacturing industries are involved in specialization and cooperation agreements with industries in other CMEA countires. As large quantities of goods are imported and exported under these agreements, the cost of transportation is very important for the overall effectiveness of cooperation. The regional location of plants involved in specialization and cooperation should, therefore, be carefully examined. In some cases the cost of transportation may be so high that otherwise quite profitable cooperation agreements should not be undertaken.

It is expected that the proportion of the commodities produced under specialization and cooperation agreements in total export will grow within the next few years (for example, in the U.S.S.R. trade with Poland this share is expected to grow from 7% of total trade between these two countries in 1971-75 to 22% in 1976-80). The problem of "regional effectiveness" of export and import, taking into consideration full transportation costs, will, therefore, increase in importance.

In the Volga region an important complex is already emerging as an aggregate of production and transport facilities which work, to a considerable extent, for export to the CMEA countries and utilize import from that source on the basis of specialization and cooperation agreements. The Volga integrated system includes major enterprises of the oil-extraditing and petrochemical industry, iron and steel, non-ferrous metals and machine building in Volgograd, Kuibyshev, Saratov, Kazan, Toliatti, Ulianovsk and in the near future will also include the automotive complex in Naberezhnye Chelny. The work of these centres is characterized by continuous reciprocal deliveries of raw materials, supplies, parts and finished products to and from other CMEA countries. This is a new feature in the Soviet regional development.

The whole problem of the impact of the CMEA economic integration on regional development in the Soviet Union deserves perhaps a special paper. To the extent to which it involves greater Soviet export of fuels and raw materials it creates a greater need for the expansion of new sources of potential exports which are now available only in the eastern regions.[5] On the other hand, through the specialization and cooperation agreements the CMEA integration will tend to induce the location of manufacturing industries closer to the western borders of the U.S.S.R.

Another type of foreign trade of the Soviet Union, which should be more carefully examined from the point of view of its potential importance for regional development, are the buy-back and other compensation agreements with the West. The value of export form the already effected agreements is expected to grow from $830 million in 1977 to about $4 billion in 1985.[6] In this way a large part of Soviet debt is linked with future export deliveries and the size of the future exports guaranteed by these contracts often exceeds the debt repayment obligations of the project. The deals are, therefore, export expanding.[7] Their profitability from the Soviet point of view depends, therefore, not only on the cost of importing investment goods to the remote locations but also on the cost of exporting from those locations.

A list of compensation agreements, showing the location of plants, would be a very useful indicator of future expansion of exports from various regions. This would, however, require again another separate paper.

An interesting point is that, taking into consideration the location of fuels and other raw materials, present manufacturing capacities and centres of population, an optimal situation for the Soviet Union would probably be to expand exports of manufactured goods to the CMEA and West

European countries, including those produced in connection with specialization and cooperation agreements, while expanding the export of oil, natural gas and some other raw materials in the eastern direction to Japan and to the western coast of North American in exchange for investment goods from this direction for the development of Eastern regions.

Footnotes

1. National Foreign Assessment Center, *Handbook of Economic Statistics 1978*, (Washington, D.C., 1978), p. 19.
2. Franklyn D. Holzman, *Foreign Trade Under Central Planning,* (Cambridge, Mass., 1974), pp. 126-135.
3. L. Gramoteyeva, "Effektivnost rozmieshcheniia proizvoditielnikh sil", *Planovoe khoziaistvo,* 11, (1978).
4. L. Audeichev, I. Zaitsev, S. Moskalkov, "The Regional Development of the Economy of the USSR Under the Influence of Socialist Economic Integration", *Planovoe khoziaistvo,* 2, (1977).
5. N.N. Nekrasov, "Nauchniye osnovi generalnoi skhemi rozmieshcheniia proizvoditielnikh sil SSSR na period do 1980g", Polish translation in A. Kuklinski (ed.), *Planowanie rozwoju regionalnego w swietle doswiadczen miedzynarodowych,* (Warsaw, 1974), pp. 20-21.
6. Dennis J. Barclay, "USSR: The Role of Compensation Agreements with the West", in John Hardt (ed.), *The Soviet Economy in a Period of Transition,* (Washington, Joint Economic Committee, 1979).
7. Lawrence J. Brainard, "Foreign Economic Constraints on Soviet Economic Policy in the 1980's", in *Ibid.*

Warren W. Eason

Current position:
Professor of Economics
Ohio State University
1775 South College Road
Columbus, Ohio 43210

Main field of work:
Teaching and research on Soviet
Union and Eastern Europe population
and human resources

**Publications during
the last two years:**
"Demographic Problems: Fertility",
Joint Economic Committee (ed.),
Internal Determinants of Soviet
Foreign Policy (forthcoming)

Other remarks:
Project Director of Dynamic
Inventory of Soviet and East
European Studies in the United States,
for the American Association for the
Advancement of Slavic Studies
(1977-80)

Labor Force and Regional Raw Material Development
Demographic Divergences at Republic Level
Professor Warren Eason

I. Introduction

It is no longer news to students of Soviet affairs that the country is facing a population crisis—or, more precisely, a crisis in *labor supply* that has its roots in demographic variables affecting the growth and distribution of the population.

Perhaps calling it a crisis is to strong, because some of its manifestations, centering around a "scarcity" of labor, are exprienced by all countries to one degree or another at different stages of economic development. Neverthe less, the forces of scarcity in the Soviet case are gathering with unusual strength and speed. Even as this colloquium is taking place, a short but sharp transitional phase is underway shich will emerge in just a few years as a veritable new era in Soviet labor supply substantially and irrevocably different from that of the first half century of economic development (1928-78). Past experience suggests, moreover, that the system of planning and administration may not be able to cope effectively with the circumstances of the new era, even to the point of aggravating, perhaps seriously, the erosion in recent economic performance. It is these terms that the notion of "crisis" comes to mind, and Soviet leadership gives increasing indication of seeing it that way.

The basic nature of the problem—in both quantitative and institutional terms—is well known in the West, thanks largely to the prodigious efforts of Murray Feshbach, Stephen Rapawy and Godfrey Baldwin of the Foreign Demographic Analysis Division (FDAD) of the U.S. Department of Commerce.[2] The present paper perpetuates their involvement in the discussion by drawing from their published works and by utilizing, with their kind permission, some of their latest (unpublished) estimates and projections.

The overall dimensions of the problem are as follows:

1. Declining population fertililty over much of the country in recent years is leading to declining and even negative growth rates of the population of working ages, and to a corresponding slowdown in the rate of growth of the labor force.

2. As an integral and distinguishing feature of this overall trend, marked differences in fertility and, as a consequence, in population growth are manifest in different parts of the country. While fertility has persisted at extraordinarily high levels in Soviet Central Asia and parts of the Caucasus, in much of the rest of the country it has reached levels at or

below those necessary for population reproduction.

3. Regional differences in population growth project themselves into a potential aggravation of regional imbalances of labor that are already a feature of the Soviet economy.

4. The real problem, however, is not in the population and labor supply variables themselves, but in the *pressures* which they exert for planners, administrators and policy makers. If the declining rate of growth of the population of working-ages and the increasing imbalances in labor supply are not to be translated into a continued decline in the rate of growth of production, major accomodations and reforms will have to be introduced to reduce the imbalance and to increase the effectiveness with which human resources are developed and utilized in the production process. Largely in response to these pressures in labor supply already felt-- and to those perceived to be coming in the near future--Soviet plans now rely significantly more than ever before on increased *productivity* of labor to meet production targets.

The need to raise productivity has a note of urgency in the Soviet case-- given their ambitious economic objectives--because the changes in the population variables are of sufficient magnitude and their appearance is so timed, that they render the emerging pattern of labor supply fundamentally different from anything the Soviets have had to live with since the beginning of rapid industrialization in 1928. In a relatively short span of time, the Soviet Union is being transformed from a country where labor is the relatively abundant resource and labor policies and practices reflect this abundance, to one where labor is scarce and must be treated as such if economic performance is not to suffer.

The purpose of this paper is to examine the changes in the *population variables* that underlie the changes in labor supply, and in particular to examine their regional manifestations. The objective is to sharpen our understanding of the trends over time and the differences among regions, and thus clarify the implications for labor supply and its attending pressures.

The difficulties of working with Soviet regional data in any field do not have to be explained. The task is complicated in the population/labor field by the many instances in which data reported at the national level are reported with less frequency or not at all at the regional level. Particularly frustrating are the demographic data reported by republics but not by the regions within the largest republic, the RSFSR, leaving us without a regional breakdown within an area encompassing 76 percent of the territory and 53 percent of the population of the country.

A special effort was therefore made in preparing this paper to include a breakdown for the regions within the RSFSR whenever possible, along with the other 14 republics taken separately. An essential and invaluable point of departure for such an effort are the latest regional population projections of FDAD, kindly made available to the author, which are disaggregated to the level of "economic regions" within the RSFSR. The paper attempts a further disaggregation to the level of rural and urban areas within the respective regions, in order to provide a model of prospective regional labor supply which is more sensitive than the broader measures to the principal demographic factors of change.

II. Population Fertility and Mortality as Determinants of Labor Supply

Overall trends for the country as a whole

The decline (and subsequent recovery) in the rate of growth of the working-age population in the late 1950's and early 1960's, bringing with it the first serious threat of labor shortages, can be traced to the sharply lowered fertility and higher mortality rates of World War II. The more "permanent" decline in the rate of growth of the working-age population now underway has its roots in the decline in the birth rate which began in the early 1960's, the result of a decline in intrinsic fertility modified by the "echo" effect of both world wars on the size of the population of reproductive ages.

The curious if not surprising aspect of this sequence of events--a restriction of the flow of labor resources as the result of prior changes in fertility and mortality--is that it did not appear a good deal earlier in Soviet demographic history. By all logic--considering (a) the awesome population losses suffered during World War I and the Civil War, during the period of collectivization, and especially during World War II, as well as (b) the secular decline in fertility in both rural and urban areas that has been under-way in much of the country since the 1920's--labor should have begun to appear as a relatively scarce factor of production well before the 1960's and 1970's. The reason why it did not seems to lie with the timing or *periodization* of the relationship between changes in fertility and mortality and the rate of growth of the working-age population. Except for the mid-1960's, the potentially depressing effects on peacetime labor supply trends of both the *secular* and *episodic* changes in fertility and mortality that have taken place since the inception of the Soviet regime were effectively muted if not supplanted by equally strong effects in the opposite direction. As a result, except for the brief (but significant) decline during the 1960's, *the working-age population (in peacetime years) has maintained until this very moment a remarkably high rate of growth, of nearly 1.5 percent per year.* And even the period of lowered growth in the 1960's is preceded and followed by periods of equal length when growth rates reached 2 percent or more per year.

A diagramatic representation of the *periodization* which links the timing of births and deaths to the rate of growth of the working-age population, from 1900 to 1975 with projections to 2000, is set forth in Graph 1.[3] By tracing the main relationships pictured in Graph 1 we may see why the growth of Soviet labor supply until recently has remained essentially immune to the effect of declining fertility and higher mortality:

1. The reason why the *secular* decline in fertility (indicated by the crude birth rate) did not lead directly in time to a decline in the rate of growth of the working-age population is the parallel decline in the peace-

Graph 1

PERIODIZATION OF SECULAR TRENDS AND MAJOR EPISODES IN FERTILITY AND MORTALITY
COMPARED TO THE RATE OF CHANGE IN THE WORKING-AGE POPULATION:
U.S.S.R., 1900 TO 1975, WITH PROJECTIONS TO 2000

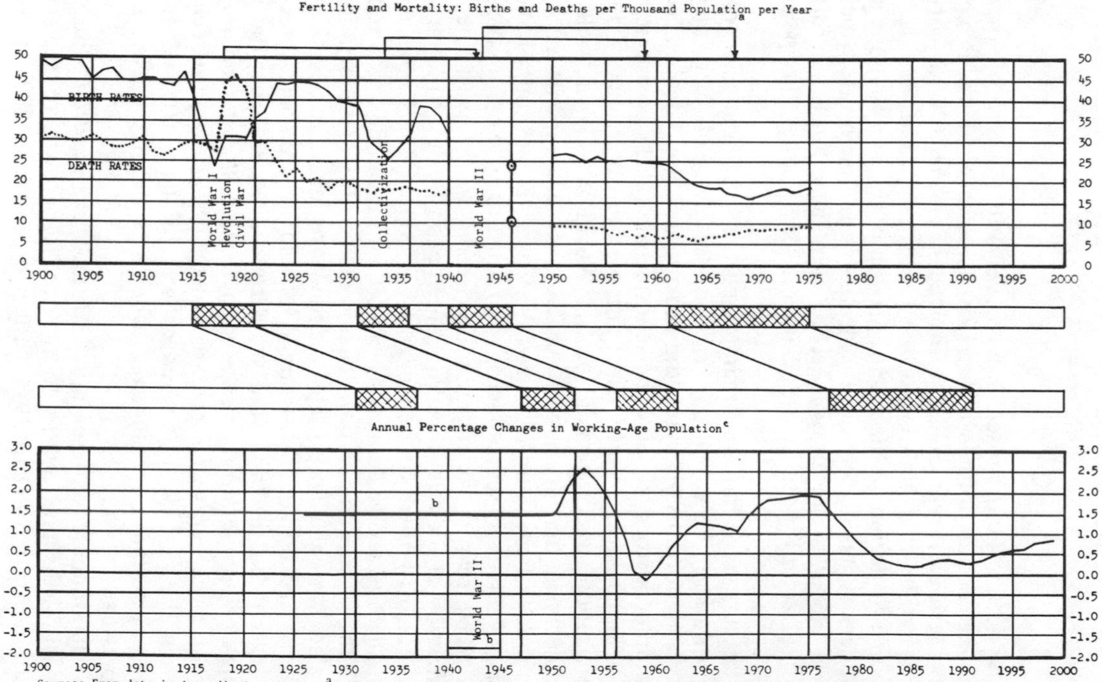

Fertility and Mortality: Births and Deaths per Thousand Population per Year[a]

Annual Percentage Changes in Working-Age Population[c]

BIRTH RATES

DEATH RATES

World War I
Revolution
Civil War

Collectivization

World War II

World War II

Source: From data in Appendix A. Notes: [a] Horizontal arrows indicate the time span of potential effect of low fertility during one episodic
period on reducing fertility approximately 25 years later.
[b] Horizontal lines indicate average annual percentage change over the given period.
[c] Working ages include males age 16-59 and females age 16-54 ("able-bodied population").

time mortality rate (indicated by the crude death rate) that has taken place through the 1950's. A large proportion of the decline in total mortality comprises infant mortality, which means that the number of infants born and *surviving* to adulthood from the 1920's to the 1950's declined by less (or even increased) in comparison with the birth rate. Thus it was not until that stage in the decline in fertility which began in the 1960's--when the crude death rate was stabilized at less than ten per thousand--that a rate of growth of the working-age population could be projected (after 1978) which drops significantly below the long-run average of about 1.5 percent per year, to less than 0.5 percent.

2. The reason why the successive *episodic* events had little or no generational effects on the rate of growth of the working-age population in peacetime lies with the coincidence of the events themselves. Thus:

> a. The effects of reduced fertility and increased mortality during the 1915-21 period sixteen years later, in 1931-37, were caught up in the turmoil attending collectivization. Furthermore, birth cohorts preceding and following those of 1915-21 were relatively large, which means that the average annual rate of growth of the working-age population during the whole period between the censuses, 1926 to 1939, was relatively high (1.5 percent).
>
> b. Similarly, the depressing effects of 1915-21 on the level of fertility some 25 years later--through reduction in the number of potential parents passing through the reproductive ages--fell squarely on the years affected by World War II (1940-46). The result was to aggravate the decline in fertility that took place during the war for other reasons, leading to perhaps 20 million less individuals born and surviving the decade of the 1940's than would have been the case without the war.[4]
>
> c. The direct effect of the large-scale losses among the adult population during the war, on the working-age population after the war, was "cushioned," so to speak, by the flow of individuals into the working ages from among the relatively large birth cohorts of most years from 1928 to 1941. The latter were also less affected by wartime hazards than other age cohorts. The result is an average rate of increase of the working-age population from 1946 to 1950 of about 1 5 percent per year, and estimated annual rates over the next five years as high as 2.5 percent.

All in all, therefore, during most peacetime years over almost three decades from 1928 to about 1956, the working-age population increased at sufficiently high rates (about 1.5 percent per year) to support a comfortable growth in labor supply.

The episodic events, of course, did succeed in reducing at once the *stock* of human resources--by up to 10 million in World War I and 25 million in World War II, and by 5 million or more during collectivization-- but the immediately depressing effect on labor supply was moderated, in effect, by the relatively large proportion of the population in rural areas. Conditions of "overpopulation," in other words, continued to exist well past World War II, and proved to be a resilient if declining force for filling the gaps created by successive demographic catastrophes. More on the role of the rural areas in labor supply below.

3. The first real curtailment in the rate of growth of the working-age population during peacetime covered the period from about 1957 to 1962. Caused by the coming of age of the depleted cohorts born during the war, the effect was short but sharp, and sent the shock wave of labor "scarcity" through the system for the first time. As with other "episodic" events that tended to depress labor supply, however, it was followed (and preceded) by periods of relatively high rates of growth.

4. Thus, from the early 1960's to the present--a period of almost 15 years--the working-age population has been increasing by one or two percent per year, as a result of (a) moderate and stable birth rates, at about 25 per thousand, during the 1950's, at the same time that infant mortality was declining to low levels, and (b) the fact that the number leaving the working ages at the upper end was relatively small.

5. It is therefore only from the present moment forward, as shown in Graph 1, that a serious and long-term slowdown in the peacetime rate of growth of the working-age population will begin to take place. The reasons are (a) the decline in the intrinsic fertility rates which accelerated in the 1960's and stabilized at levels near 1.0 (net reproduction rate) for much of the country,[5] and (b) the double "echo" effect on the population of prime reproductive ages (20-29) of cohorts born during World War I and II (see the arrows indicating this effect in Graph 1). Allowing for the number leaving the working ages at the upper end, the overall rate of growth of the working-age population is projected to decline from almost 2 percent in the 1970's to less than one-half of one percent from 1981 until the mid-1990's.

6. Thereafter, when individuals born in the 1980's begin to enter the working ages, as shown in Graph 1, an increased rate of growth to one percent per year or a bit more is projected. This "recovery" results from assuming a continuation of very recent trends in fertility, which have shown a slight reversal from their long-term downward movement.[5] Whether this represents a serious and permanent reversal remains to be seen, but the effect of recent trends in fertility is at least to stabilize--at positive but modest levels--the overall growth of Soviet labor supply going into the 21st century.

Regional trends

The relatively high rates of growth of the working-age population during most peacetime years in the past, described above, appear in virtually all parts of the country, although the rates in Central Asia, the Transcaucasus and some parts of the RSFSR historically have been above the average for the country as a whole. Even the sharp decline and recovery in the rate during the late 1950's and early 1960's, derived as it was from reduced fertility during World War II, shows up everywhere.

From this moment forward, however, regional growth rates of the working-age population become sharply divergent, reflecting the fact that after 1960 fertility rates remained very high in Central Asia, etc., while declining to one degree or another elsewhere.

A projection of the working-age population, developed by Murray Feshbach and Godfrey Baldwin, is reproduced in Table 1; it compares, by five-year intervals to the year 2000, (a) the RSFSR and other republics of "European Russia" with (b) Central Asia and the Transcaucasus. The comparison is startling. Even in the present five-year interval, 1976-80, the working-age population in the southern tier will have increased by 4,643,000, which is 44.6 percent of the increase for the entire country although only 25 percent of the population live there. During the next 15 years, however, from 1981 through 1995, while the working-age population in the southern tier will increase by 11,186,000, that of the rest of the country taken together will actually *decrease* by 1,649,000.

Table 1
Recent and Projected Changes in the
Working-Age Population: USSR Total
and Regions of High and Low Fertility
(in thousands)

Periods	Total	Regions of High Fertility	Regions of Low Fertility
1971-75	12,726	4,782	7,944
1976-80	10,408	4,643	5,765
1981-85	2,687	3,524	- 837
1986-90	2,830	3,469	- 639
1991-95	4,020	4,193	- 173
1996-2000	9,012	6,081	2,931
1981-95	9,537	11,186	-1,649

Source: From data in Feshbach and Rapawy, *op. cit.,* p. 129.
Notes: Regions of High Fertility include the republics of Central Asia plus Azerbaidzhan, Armenia and Georgia. Regions of Low Fertility include the rest of the country.

The crux of the labor supply problem in the coming decades is seen to lie with these figures, which project a picture of areas of rapidly developing deficit and surplus of labor supply. Policy options to forestall seriously depressing effects on economic performance include stepped-up migration from surplus to deficit areas--in spite of well-known resistance to such migration in the past--and increased flow of developmental capital to the labor surplus regions themselves.

The figures in Table 1 are serious and vexing for Soviet planners, but while the picture they present is correct enough as it stands, it tends to overstate the problem and thereby unduly restrict the policy options open to the planners. The reason is that, in calculating the figures, the RSFSR is treated as a whole, masking the fact that it encompasses within its borders considerable variations in regional labor-supply potential. When these variations are taken into account, the imbalance in labor supply appears less polarized than in Table 1, and as a consequence the policy options turn out to be less than exclusively focused on Central Asia.

The effect is partly in the differences in growth rates among the working-age population of the subregions of the RSFSR, but mostly in the prospects for drawing additional labor from agricultural occupations (and rural areas) to nonagricultural occupations (and urban areas). The RSFSR turns out to have certain "hidden reserves" of labor within its various subregions that may serve to ameliorate somewhat the crisis in labor supply as represented by the figures in Table 1. The remainder of the paper is devoted to identifying and interpreting the nature of these reserves and broadening the policy options that they imply.

III. Agricultural / Nonagricultural and Rural / Urban Determinants of Labor Supply

Overall trends for the country as a whole

Given the natural increases in the working-age population described above, the Soviet economy over the past half century has relied heavily on labor supplied from agriculture to meet the continuously growing demands of the nonagricultural sector for labor. The end result has been a shift in population distribution from one predominantly agricultural to one which is now (on the average) predominantly nonagricultural. In the course of this development, the functional relationship of supply has been transformed--from relatively large to relatively small numbers in agriculture from which supply for the nonagricultural sectors could be drawn.

The general rule underlying this functional relationship of supply may be stated as follows:[6] The higher the proportion of the labor force in agricultural occupations--for a given rate of growth of the total labor force and rate of change in the agricultural force--the greater can be the percentage increase in the nonagricultural labor force through the movement of labor from the one sector to the other. Thus, where the total labor force increases, for example, by 1.5 percent per year and the agricultural labor force remains constant (absolutely), the percentage increase in the nonagricultural labor force may be related to the agricultural labor force as a percentage of the total as follows:

Agricultural labor force as percentage of the total	Annual percentage increase in the nonagricultural labor force
85	10.0
50	3.0
15	1.7

Broadly speaking, this illustrates the Soviet case, as may be seen from the series depicted in Graph 2. The industrialization drive began in 1928 with about 85 percent of the labor force in agricultural occupations. From this high proportion in agriculture--while the total labor force was growing at an average of 1.5 to 2.0 percent per year (also shown in Graph 2)--it was relatively easy in the first decade to provide for an average annual increase of the nonagricultural labor force of almost 10 percent on the average, without seriously depleting agricultural labor resources.

As a matter of fact, if it had not been for the demographic effects of the collectivization drive, in which millions of adults lost their lives and millions of others fled to the urban areas, the planned rapid growth of the nonagricultural labor force during the early five-year plans could have taken place while the agricultural labor force remained unchanged or even increased. As it was, the agricultural labor force declined from about 70 million in the 1920's to less than 60 million in 1939--at which point, however, it was still almost 70 percent of the total (civilian) labor force.

Because the Soviet Union entered World War II with such a high percentage of its labor force in agriculture, it was able to sustain frightful losses in population, as described above, and still emerge with something more than half of the labor force in agriculture. The proportion of females in the surviving population was of course very high, but reliance on female labor in agriculture has always been a feature of the Soviet (and preSoviet) economy.

During the 1950's, as shown in Graph 2, the nonagricultural labor force increased by 3-4 percent per year, at the same time that the total labor force was increasing at historically high rates averaging in the vicinity of 2 percent due to the entry of the relatively large cohorts that had survived the war as young children. The net effect on the agricultural labor force in the 1950's was an average annual decline of only one-half of one percent per year. The percentage of the labor force in agriculture, however, had declined from 54 to 43, thereby passing through an important phase in the direction of the tightening of the labor supply from agriculture.

The brief but sharp drop in the rate of growth of the working-age population in the late 1950's and early 1960's, shown in Graph 1, caused an accelerated drain from the agricultural labor force in order to continue the growth of the nonagricultural sector. By the mid-1960's, therefore, the proportion of the labor force in agriculture had declined to the point (38 percent) where it required a 2.5 percent annual average decline in the agricultural labor force to release enough individuals to support a 3.5-4.0 percent increase in the nonagricultural, despite annual growth in the total of nearly 1.5 percent.

By the early 1970's, therefore, the agricultural labor force had declined to 30 percent of the total, and the real squeeze in labor supply began to show itself. In the seven years from 1970 to the present, although the total labor force increased by more than 1.5 percent per year, the *non*agricultural labor force was able to increase by less than 3 percent. Even that increase, the lowest in peacetime since 1928, required the agricultural labor force, by virtue of rural-urban migration, to decline by 1.5 percent per year.

From the present moment on, moreover, in terms of these average data for the country as a whole, the situation takes a major turn for the worse. If the recent 1.5 percent decrease in the agricultural labor force together with the projected lowered growth of the total labor force to 0.5 percent per year are projected into the 1990's (as in Graph 2), it means that the nonagricultural labor force will be able to grow by little more than 1 percent per year over the next 15 years.

After 1995, what might happen is less clear, because individuals who will enter the working ages then have not yet been born, and there is the usual uncertainty about future fertility trends. The recent stabilization of fertility rates, not to mention signs of possible increase, as noted above, may continue, in which case the constraints on labor supply may ease somewhat. But with the agricultural labor force less than 20 percent of the total, the rate of growth of the nonagricultural labor force can be at best only slightly greater than the rate of growth of the total, or in the vicinity of 1 percent per year going into the 21st century.[7]

What has been said up to this point about the agricultural/nonagricultural labor supply relationships refers to "average" conditions in the country as a whole, and depicts a substantial "drying-up" of resources in agriculture. What it really means for labor supply, however, cannot be completely indicated "on the average;" it requires examination of differences in the relationships by regions.

Regional trends

We would like to have a breakdown of the labor force by agricultural and nonagricultural occupations for the major regional subdivisions of the country, including those within the RSFSR, for enough years to establish the percentage distribution and respective rates of change up to the present. Unfortunately, we do not have such data, but we do have some useful "surrogate" measures that may serve the purpose, and even provide projections of trends over the next few decades.

In place of agricultural/nonagricultural data we can substitute rural/urban data; and in place of measures of the labor force we can substitute the population of working ages. The result is only approximate, but by utilizing

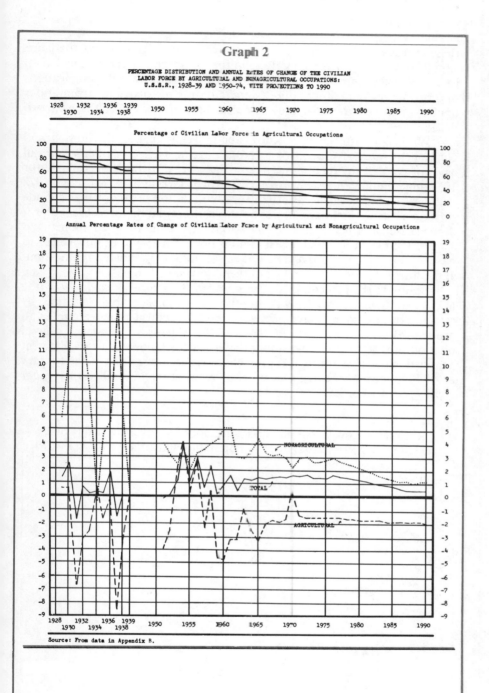

Graph 2

PERCENTAGE DISTRIBUTION AND ANNUAL RATES OF CHANGE OF THE CIVILIAN
LABOR FORCE BY AGRICULTURAL AND NONAGRICULTURAL OCCUPATIONS:
U.S.S.R., 1928-39 AND 1950-74, WITH PROJECTIONS TO 1990

Percentage of Civilian Labor Force in Agricultural Occupations

Annual Percentage Rates of Change of Civilian Labor Force by Agricultural and Nonagricultural Occupations

NONAGRICULTURAL

TOTAL

AGRICULTURAL

Source: From data in Appendix B.

129

these surrogates we are able to suggest orders of magnitude for the labor supply problem at a more or less uniform and consistent regional level throughout the country. In particular, we are able to trace the implications in terms of regional *labor supply potential* of some plausible assumptions about component rates of growth on an annual basis over the next two decades.

We begin with what we know about trends in the distribution and component rates of growth of the *total, urban and rural population* (all ages) of each of the republics. Data at this level of detail are available for 1959 and annually thereafter for 1961 through 1965 and 1967 through 1978 (January 1). Using this total-urban-rural-population breakdown as a crude surrogate for a total-agricultural-nonagricultural-labor-force breakdown, in the sense described above, we look to the trends in these components to suggest the extent to which given regions may or may not be considered to have a certain *labor supply potential* for ultimate transfer to the non-agricultural sectors of their own or other regions.

Scanning the percentage of the *population* in rural areas in 1978 (the latest year available at this writing) reveals considerable variation by regions--from over 60 percent in some of the Central Asian republics to around 20 percent in parts of the RSFSR. Having in mind the general relationships set forth above about the effect for labor supply of different proportions in agriculture, it is possible to group the regions of the country as of 1978 into *three* categories in terms of what may be called their *labor supply potential* or *LSP*.

Map 1

Regions of Low, Medium and High Labor Supply Potential (LSP),
According to the Percentage of the Population in Rural Areas: USSR 1978

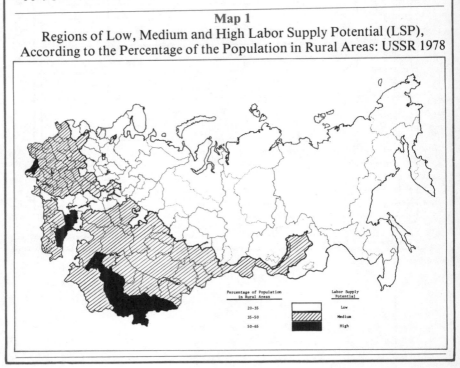

Percentage of Population in Rural Areas		Labor Supply Potential
20-35		Low
35-50		Medium
50-65		High

Those regions with 20-35 percent of the population in rural areas in 1978 are thus designated as regions of *low* LSP; those with 35-50, *medium* LSP; and those with 50-65, *high* LSP. The results of this designation are pictured in Map 1.

It will be noted that the region of low LSP, except for the Volga-Don territory, lies essentially north of the 45th parallel of latitude, including some of most industrialized and urbanized together with the least hospitable parts of the country. The region of medium LSP lies south of the 45th parallel, and encompasses within it the relatively small region of high LSP. The latter includes the Uzbek, Tadzhik, Kirgiz and Moldavian Republics, as well as the Dagestan and Checheno-Ingush autonomous republics of the RSFSR, most of which still have 60 percent or more of their population in rural areas. The Turkmen, Armenian and Azerbaidzhan republics, although displaying relatively high fertility rates and population growth through the recent past, nevertheless fall within the "medium" range of 35-50 percent of the population in rural areas.

Having defined the three regions of labor supply potential in terms of the rural population (all ages) as a percentage of the total, a surrogate for the unavailable data on the labor force within these regions is designated in terms of the population of *working ages*.

As a starting point toward quantification, absolute measures of the total, urban and rural population--all ages as well as working ages--may be derived for each of the three regions of LSP for 1959 and 1970, from regional census data reported in Volume II of the 1970 census. And from these date, in turn, it is possible to calculate the respective average annual percentage rates of change between the two censuses. The results, reproduced in Table 2, reveal the following growth patterns:

1. For each of the three regions taken as a whole, the *working-age* population increases by less than that of *all ages,* reflecting the decline and recovery in the rate of growth of the population of working ages that was already underway at the time of the 1959 census but continued to have its effect in the intercensal period.

2. The intercensal changes in the working-age population of the urban and rural areas separately reflect the different interrelationships in labor supply potential by which the regions are defined. *Regions of low LSP* show a relatively low rate of growth of the working-age population of urban areas (+1.6) as well as of the total (+0.7) and a relatively small decline in the rural (-1.1), while the rural working-age population as a percentage of the total declines from 34.6 to 28.4. *Regions of medium LSP,* on the other hand, with the same total growth (+0.7) as in the regions of low LSP but a higher percentage in the rural areas (56.8 in 1959 and 42.0 in 1970), show a much higher average rate of growth in the urban areas (+3.4). In *regions of high LSP,* an even greater increase in the working-age population of urban areas (+4.0) is coupled with an absolute *increase* in the rural areas (+0.6), a relationship that reflects not only the relatively high rate of growth of the total (+2.0) but the high percentage in rural areas (64.3 in 1959 and 56.7 in 1970).

Table 2
THE TOTAL, URBAN AND RURAL POPULATION, THE PERCENTAGE RURAL, AND AVERAGE ANNUAL INTERCENSAL RATES OF CHANGE, FOR REGIONS OF LOW, MEDIUM AND HIGH LABOR SUPPLY POTENTIAL: U.S.S.R., 1959 AND 1970

		1959	Annual Average Percentage Change	1970
	Region of Low Labor Supply Potential			
	Urban	32,667	+ 1.6	38,329
	Rural	17,301	− 1.1	15,290
Working Ages	Total	49,968	+ 0.7	53,819
	Percentage Rural	34.6		28.4
	Urban	51,304	+ 2.2	65,316
	Rural	32,369	− 1.4	27,735
All Ages	Total	83,673	+ 1.0	93,051
	Percentage Rural	38.7		29.7
	Region of Medium Labor Supply Potential			
	Urban	26,443	+ 3.4	38,321
	Rural	34,781	− 2.0	27,760
Working Ages	Total	61,224	+ 0.7	66,081
	Percentage Rural	56,8		42.0
	Urban	43,282	+ 3.3	61,967
	Rural	64,720	− 0.3	62,578
All Ages	Total	108,002	+ 1.3	124,545
	Percentage Rural	59.9		50.2
	Region of High Labor Supply Potential			
	Urban	3,078	+ 4.0	4,628
	Rural	5,552	+ 0.6	6,061
Working Ages	Total	8,630	+ 2.0	6,061
	Percentage Rural	64.3		56.7
	Urban	5,392	+ 4.6	4,708
	Rural	11,670	+ 2.5	15,416
All Ages	Total	17,152	+ 3.3	24,124
	Percentage Rural	68.0		63.9

Source: From data in TsSU, *Itogi vsesoiuznoi perepisi naseleniia 1970 goda,* Volume II, (Moscow, 1973), pp. 12-162, according to method described in text of paper.

Pending the publication of the results of the 1979 Census, in which (hopefully) will be found adequate data for another pivotal year, we can move forward from 1959-70 on the basis of two sets of data that are available: (a) the annual population (all ages) of rural and urban areas reported for most years since 1959 in sufficient detail that it can be recombined into the regions of low, medium and high LSP; and (b) single year estimates (1970-75) and projections (1976-2000) of the population--all ages and working ages--of each of the "economic regions" of the RSFSR and each of the 14 other republics prepared by Godfrey Baldwin of FDAD. With some minor assumptions to establish consistent territorial boundaries, it is possible to assemble the estimated and projected series also into the regions of low, medium and high LSP.

These available data leave us in the following position with respect to each of the three regions of labor supply potential: (a) we know the average interrelationships and annual rates of change for the total-urban-rural population of all ages and working ages for the intercensal period, 1959-70; (b) we can carry these changes forward to 1973 in terms of the total-urban-rural population of all ages; and (c) we can estimate (with Baldwin) the natural increase of the total population of all ages and working ages from 1970 to 1977, and we can project the same to 2000.

The question is this: How can we estimate the *working-age* population in the *urban* and *rural* areas *separately* for each of the three regions from 1970 to 1977, and project the same to 2000--in such a way that it will reflect a plausible, if not likely, pattern of growth rates in terms of their mutual implications for potential labor supply?

As far as estimates from 1970 to 1977 are concerned, the answer is that we can carry the 1959-70 average trends forward, modified by the changes that are suggested by the available series on the total-urban-rural population of all ages.

As far as projections to 2000 are concerned, we can extrapolate the trends of the recent past, given the projected total working-age population of each region, by setting the following limiting conditions:

Condition No. 1. *The rate of growth of the urban working-age population can be expected to decrease after the 1970's, but not to a level below +1.0 percent per year.* Maintaining such a minimal rate reflects what may very well turn out to be the intention of the planners, and it is a rate which is mutually supportable among the regions in terms of the other parameters of change that must be taken into account. A generally higher limit would require unrealistic assumptions about the prospects for the prospects for the release of labor from agricultural occupations and rural areas. A lower limit, or no growth at all would signify the failure of the system to capture the labor supply potential of the various parts of the country.

Condition No. 2. *The rural working-age population in the regions of*

Table 3

ANNUAL PERCENTAGE RATES OF CHANGE IN THE TOTAL, URBAN AND RURAL POPULATION OF ALL AGES AND WORKING AGES, FOR REGIONS OF LOW, MEDIUM AND HIGH LABOR SUPPLY POTENTIAL: U.S.S.R., 1959 AND 1970-77, WITH PROJECTIONS TO 2000

| Year | Region of Low Labor Supply Potential (LSP) | | | | | | | | | Region of Medium Labor Supply Potential (LSP) | | | | | | | | | Region of High Labor Supply Potential (LSP) | | | | | | | | |
| | All Ages | | | | Working Ages | | | | | All Ages | | | | Working Ages | | | | | All Ages | | | | Working Ages | | | | |
	Total	Urban	Rural	Per-cent Rural	Total	Urban	Rural	Per-cent Rural	Labor Supply Rural Deficit[a]	Total	Urban	Rural	Per-cent Rural	Total	Urban	Rural	Per-cent Rural	Labor Supply Rural Surplus[a]	Total	Urban	Rural	Per-cent Rural	Total	Urban	Rural	Per-cent Rural	Labor Supply Rural Surplus[a]
1959	+1.0	+2.2	-1.4	38.7	+0.7	+1.6	-1.1	34.6		+1.3	+3.3	-0.3	59.9	+0.7	+3.4	-2.0	65.8		+3.3	+4.6	+2.5	68.0	+2.0	+4.0	+0.6	64.3	
1970	...	...	...	29.6	...	...	...	28.4		...	...	...	50.2	...	...	...	42.0		...	...	...	63.9	...	...	...	56.7	148*
1971	+0.8	+2.0	-2.3	29.0	+1.5	+2.4	-1.0*	27.7		+0.9	+3.0	-1.2	48.3	+1.6	+3.4*	-0.9	41.0		+2.0	+3.1	+1.2	63.7	+3.3	+6.0*	+1.2	55.6	244*
1972	+0.8	+2.1	-2.2	28.1	+1.6	+2.6	-1.0*	27.0		+0.7	+2.7	-1.4	47.4	+1.7	+3.4*	-0.7	40.0		+2.5	+3.8	+1.5	63.3	+3.8	+6.0*	+2.1	54.6	315*
1973	+0.8	+2.1	-2.5	27.2	+1.7	+2.5	-1.0*	26.3		+0.6	+2.5	-1.5	45.6	+1.7	+3.4*	-0.8	39.0		+2.5	+3.9	+1.8	63.3	+3.9	+6.0*	+2.2	53.7	434*
1974	+0.9	+2.1	-2.5	26.3	+1.6	+2.6	-1.0*	25.6		+0.7	+2.4	-1.3	45.4	+1.8	+3.4*	-1.0	38.0		+2.5	+4.0	+1.7	62.3	+4.0	+6.0*	+2.3	52.8	260*
1975	+0.9	+2.0	-2.6	25.4	+1.7	+2.5	-1.0*	25.0		+0.6	+2.4	-1.6	44.8	+1.7	+3.4*	-0.8	37.0		+2.3	+3.6	+1.5	61.8	+4.0	+6.0*	+1.6	51.9	117*
1976	+0.9	+2.1	-2.6	24.6	+1.5	+2.6	-1.0*	24.3		+0.6	+2.1	-1.3	44.4	+1.9	+3.4*	-1.1	36.0		+2.4	+3.1	+1.9	61.1	+4.0	+6.0*	+2.0	50.9	240*
1977	+0.9	+1.6	-2.2	24.1	+1.2	+2.3	-1.3	23.7		+0.6	+1.9	-1.1	43.6	+1.7	+3.1*	-1.0	35.0		+2.1	+2.7	+1.7	60.8	+3.7	+5.6	+1.8*	49.9	266*
1978					+0.9	+2.0*	-2.3	23.0						+1.4	+2.8*	-1.0	34.1						+3.5	+5.3	+1.6*	49.0	
1979					+0.6[b]	+1.8*	-2.5*	22.4						+1.1[b]	+2.3*	-1.6	33.2						+3.3	+5.1	+1.4*	48.1	
1980					+0.3[b]	+1.6	-2.5*	21.7	71					+0.9[b]	+1.9*	-1.8	32.3	71*					+3.2	+4.2	+1.2*	47.2	
1981					0.0	+1.3*	-2.5*	21.1	139					+0.6	+1.5*	-2.0	31.5	139*					+2.7	+4.0*	+1.0*	46.3	
1982					-0.2	+1.0*	-2.5*	20.5	157					+0.4	+1.1*	-2.5	30.8	157*					+2.6	+4.0*	+0.8	45.5	
1983					-0.3	+1.0*	-2.5*	20.0	157					+0.3	+1.0*	-2.5	30.1	311*					+2.5	+3.8*	-1.1	44.7	
1984					-0.4	+1.0*	-2.5*	19.4	392					+0.2	+1.0*	-2.5*	29.3	244					+2.7[b]	+3.6*	-1.8	43.5	
1985					-0.4	+1.0*	-2.5*	18.9	432					+0.2	+1.0*	-2.5*	28.6	188					+2.4	+2.8*	-2.5	42.2	
1986					-0.5	+1.0*	-2.5*	18.4	469					+0.1	+1.0*	-2.5*	27.9	154					+2.3	+2.0*	-2.5	40.9	
1987					-0.2	+1.0*	-2.5*	17.8	514					+0.2	+1.0*	-2.5*	27.2	80					+2.5	+2.0*	-0.1	39.7	
1988					-0.2	+1.0*	-2.5*	17.3	349					+0.4	+1.0*	-2.5*	26.6	89					+2.5	+2.0*	+0.4	39.2	
1989					-0.2	+1.0*	-2.5*	16.9	409					+0.3	+1.0*	-2.5*	25.9	292					+2.5	+2.0*	+0.2	39.0	
1990					-0.2	+1.0*	-2.5*	16.4	374					+0.2	+1.0*	-2.5*	25.2	134					+2.5	+2.0*	-1.5	38.8	
1991					-0.1	+1.0*	-2.5*	15.9	357					+0.1	+1.0*	-2.5*	24.5	91					+2.5	+2.0*		38.4	
1992					-0.1	+1.0*	0.0*	15.5	359					+0.1	+1.0*	-2.5*	23.9	- 27					+2.6	+2.0*	-5.6	37.6	386*
1993					-0.1	+1.0*	0.0*	15.4	597					+0.1	+1.0*	-2.5*	23.3	- 74					+2.6	+2.0*	-6.7	35.8	671*
1994					-0.1	+1.0*	0.0*	15.1	632					+0.1	+1.0*	-2.5*	22.7	-104					+2.7	+2.0*	-5.2	33.9	736*
1995					-0.1	+1.0*	0.0*	15.0	577					+0.5	+1.0*	-2.5*	22.1	- 90					+2.7	+2.0*	-0.3	32.4	667*
1996					0.0	+1.0*	0.0*	14.8	622					+0.6	+1.0*	-2.5*	21.5	236					+2.8	+2.0*	0.0*	31.9	386*
1997					+0.2	+1.0*	0.0*	14.7	582					+0.9	+1.0*	-2.5*	20.9	276					+2.9	+2.0*	0.0*	31.3	306*+87
1998					+0.2	+1.0*	0.0*	14.6	525					+1.1	+1.0*	-2.5*	20.4	460					+3.1	+2.0*	0.0*	30.3	65+382
1999					+0.2	+1.0*	0.0*	14.5	457					+1.2	+1.0*	-2.5*	20.1	457					+3.1	+2.0*	0.0*	29.1	0+406
2000					+0.2	+1.0*	0.0*								+1.0*	-2.5*								+2.0*			

Source: From absolute data in appendix C.

Notes: * Assumed rates. Other rates are either given or derived by arithmetic.
a In thousands. b After deficits and surpluses appear, total rates refer to changes before implied population transfers, and all other rates and measures after.

*low and medium LSP can be expected to decline absolutely, but not by
more than -2.5 percent per year.* To decrease by less over most of the
period would mean that labor could not be supplied other than out of the
region of high LSP at a sufficiently high rate to meet the deficit of the
region of low LSP. To decrease by more over any length of time would
require unreasonable assumptions about the growth of productivity in
agriculture.

Condition No. 3. *The percentage of the working-age population
rural areas can be expected to decline, but not to below about 15 percent in
the region of low LSP and 20 percent in the region of medium LSP by the
turn of the century.* Together with the limit of a + 1.0 percent rate of
increase in the urban component and a -2.5 percent decrease in the rural, the
gradual decline of the percentage rural to 15-20 percent (outside of the
region of high LSP), it is felt, would be broadly consistent with the
achievement of developmental goals based on substantial but not
impossible increases in labor productivity in both urban and rural areas.

The actual calculation of the projections for each region were carried
out by hand, adjusting by "trial and error" to stay within the limits of the
conditions set forth above. The projections are reproduced in Table 3 in
terms of the annual percentage rates of change and the percentage of the
population in rural areas.

The end result of the projections is the emergence of measures of a
labor "deficit" in the region of low LSP, and the "balancing" of the
deficit with "surpluses" from the other two regions--measuring the
"deficit" from a "zero" base in the 1970's, that is, over and above any
"shortages" of labor in this region that may already exist.

It is shown that the deficit in this sense can be initially met, from 1980
to 1983, by the surplus from the region of medium LSP alone. From 1984
to 1988, the region of high LSP must also contribute from its surplus,
reaching the point (in 1988) where about half of the cumulative deficit in
the region of low LSP has been covered by each of the other two regions.
From 1991 to 1995, the region of medium LSP itself becomes a "deficit"
area, but from 1996 to the end of the century, under the respective rates of
growth in urban and rural areas assumed here, the surplus expands in both
the medium and high LSP regions--more than enough to cover the
projection deficit in the other.

These figures thus open the possibility that about half of the labor
deficit of the region of low LSP for the next ten years or so could be met
from the potential surplus of the region of medium LSP, entailing less
ambitious assumptions about the policies and practices of labor mobility
than if the region of high LSP solely were involved, as is implied by the data
of Table 1, above. Subject to the limiting conditions listed above, in other
words, the region of medium LSP appears capable of meeting its own needs
for labor as well as of supplying labor to the region of low LSP, well into
the 1980's. Whether Soviet authorities would be able to take advantage of
this approach to a labor "balance," of course, is debatable, but the
possibilities of moving labor from the medium to the low region of LSP

would seem to entail fewer institutional and cultural difficulties than from the region of high LSP alone.

The possibility of labor surpluses in the region of medium LSP also provides *time* in which to develop and introduce methods for drawing labor from the region of high LSP, recognizing the fact that by the early 1990's in all events the latter will have to be the sole source of additional labor.

As shown in Table 3, the needs of the region of low LSP for labor from outside sources continue into the next century--at about 500,000 persons per year, based on the assumption of a 1.0 percent increase in the urban working-age population and no change in the rural after 1991. Beginning about 1995, however, trends in the growth of the working-age population everywhere reverse themselves; the prospect for a "surplus" in the region of medium LSP reappears, and that in the region of high LSP sharply increases (shown in Table 3 as an "extra" surplus after 1996 beyond that needed to "balance" the deficit in the region of low LSP). Figures this far into the future, it must be pointed out, are illustrative, but they cannot be taken too seriously, because they are based on the arbitrary use of one of four fertility variants for the late 1970's on which the projections (from FDAD) are calculated.

It should also be stressed that all of the projections in Table 3 are not to be considered as "predictions" of what will happen or is even likely to happen. They are offered as one "plausible" scenario for regional labor supply relationships over the next two decades. Other scenarios are also possible. By developing a comprehensive regional framework, these other scenarios, based on alternative assumptions to those in Table 3, may be easily considered.

Finally, the framework of Table 3 (and the absolute data from which it is derived) will enable us to interpret the results of the 1979 census as they appear. Since the recent intercensal period, 1970-79, is very different from its predecessor, 1959-70, in terms of the dimensions of population growth, one immediate use of the hypothetical framework presented here will be the interpretation of even partial results from the 1979 census in a way that takes their wider implications into account.

Graph 3

Annual Percentage Change in Working-Age Population.

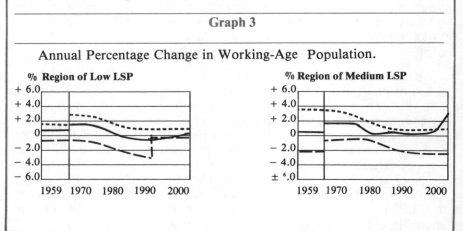

% Region of Low LSP

% Region of Medium LSP

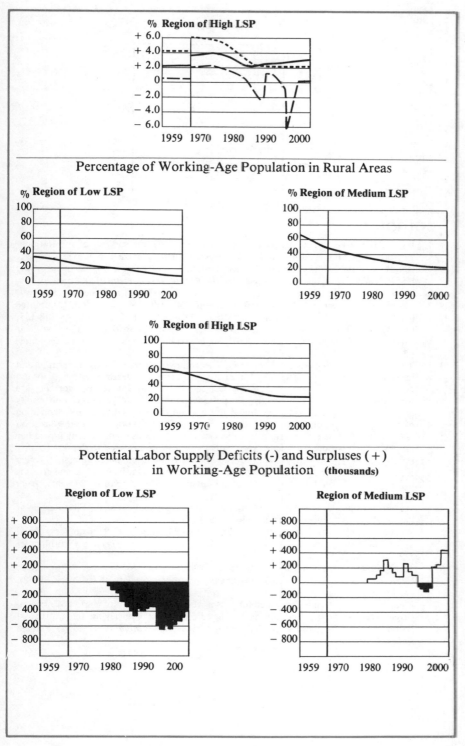

% Region of High LSP

Percentage of Working-Age Population in Rural Areas

% Region of Low LSP

% Region of Medium LSP

% Region of High LSP

Potential Labor Supply Deficits (-) and Surpluses (+)
in Working-Age Population (thousands)

Region of Low LSP

Region of Medium LSP

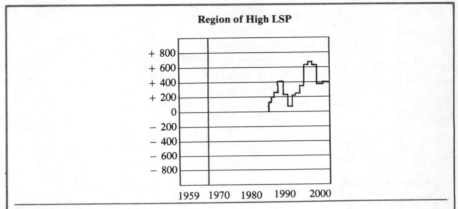

Region of High LSP

Footnotes

1.   Part of the research for this paper was carried out with the support of the National Institute of Child Health and Human Development, Contract No. NIH-70-2191.
2.   Recent published works include: Murray Feshbach, "Manpower Management in the USSR," W.A. Douglas Jackson, (ed.), *Soviet Resource Management and the Environment*, (Columbus, Ohio, 1978), pp. 26-44; Murray Feshbach and Stephen Rapawy, "Soviet Population and Manpower Trends and Policies", Joint Economic Committee (ed.), *Soviet Economy in a New Perspective* (Washington, D.C., 1976), pp. 113-153; and Murray Feshbach and Stephen Rapawy, "Labor Constraints in the Five-Year Plan", Joint Economic Committee (ed.), *Soviet Economic Prospects for the Seventies*, (Washington, D.C.) pp. 485-563.
3.   The information in Graph 1 is portrayed as follows: Secular trends in fertility and mortality are expressed in terms of annual crude birth and death rates per thousand population. Episodic events involving reduced fertility and increased mortality are identified by vertical bars bracketing the periods in time. Episodic events of low fertility and the most recent period of declining fertility can be expected to have a depressing effect 16 years later on the rate of growth of the working-age population; the direction and timing of these effects is indicated in Graph 1 by means of diagonally linked bar graphs. The episodic periods of low fertility can also be expected to depress fertility rates in the next generation, as the reduced number of potential parents passes through the reproductive ages. For purposes of illustration, this potential generational effect is indicated by Graph 1 by horizontal arrows each covering a span of 25 years, from birth to the mid-point of the prime reproductive years (20-29).
4.   Warren W. Eason, "The Soviet Population Today: An Analysis of the First Results of the 1959 Census", *Foreign Affairs*, (July 1959).
5.   Warren W. Eason, "Demographic Problems: Fertility," U.S. Congress, Joint Economic Committee, (ed.), *Soviet Economy in a New Perspective* (Washington, D.C., 1976), pp. 155-161.
6.   The general statement which follows is from Warren W. Eason, "Population Changes", Allen Kassof, (ed.), *Prospects for Soviet Society* (New York, 1968), pp. 236-237.
7.   This summary of trends for the country as a whole is drawn from Warren W. Eason, "Demographic Trends and Soviet Foreign Policy: The Underlying Imperatives of Labor Supply", in Seweryn Bialer, (ed.), *Internal Determinants of Soviet Foreign Policy*, (forthcoming).

Dr. Theodore Shabad

Current position:
Editor
Soviet Geography Magazine
145 East 84th Street
New York, NY 10028
USA

Main field of work:
Economic geography of the USSR

**Publications during
the last two years:**
(Co-author with Victor L. Mote)
Gateway to Siberian Resources,
New York, 1977.

(Co-author with Leslie Dienes)
The Soviet Energy System, New York
1979.

"The BAM: Project of the Century",
in Soviet Economy in a Time of
Change, U.S. Joint Economic
Committee (ed.), Washington, 1979.

"Some Aspects of Central Asian
Manpower and Urbanization",
Soviet Geography, February (1979),
113-124.

"Soviet Regional Policy and CMEA
Integration", Soviet Geography,
April (1979).

Author of regular News Notes' section
on Soviet economic geographic
developments in Soviet Geography
and Polar Geography (monthly
reports on Soviet development
projects, mainly in the energy and raw
materials sectors).

Labor Force and
Regional Raw Material Development

Siberia and the Soviet Far East Exploitation Policies in Energy and Raw Materials Sectors: A Commercial Assessment

Dr. Theodore Shabad

Soviet planners and policy-makers have historically been confronted with a basic geographical dichotomy: concentration of population and economic activity in the European part of the USSR and the presence of a large reservoir of resources in environmentally hostile and sparsely inhabited Siberia. If the Soviet Union is considered in terms of three macroregions--European USSR, Siberia and Central Asia--we find that the European USSR, with one-fourth of the national territory, contains three-fourths of the population and generates about 80 percent of industrial and agricultural output. Siberia with 57 percent of the territory and 10 percent of the population, accounts for 87 percent of the energy resources, 62 percent of timber resources and 70 percent of water resources.[1]

The significance of Siberia as a potential storehouse of resources has become enhanced in recent years by two basic factors: (a) the progressive depletion of the resource base in the European USSR and continuing economic growth have forced the Soviet planners to turn increasingly eastward to remote and inhospitable environments for sources of raw materials and, especially, energy resources; (b) the growing interaction of the Soviet Union with the world economy, which is generally regarded as a key ingredient of detente; the need for foreign exchange for the purchase of Western technology, and the upward trend in world prices for energy goods and raw materials seem to have stimulated the development of Siberian resources, traditionally distinguished by high costs, for export to the Western industrial economies.

The present paper, after a brief historical perspective on Siberian development during the Soviet period, will discuss the present rationale for Siberian development, the physical problems of such development, some of the major ongoing development projects, and the contribution that Siberia is now making to the Soviet economy.

141

I. Historical Perspective

Siberian resource development in the Soviet period has passed through several distinctive phases that varied in regional focus and in the character of development.[2]

Two generalized phases may be distinguished: the Stalin era and the post-Stalin era, beginning in the middle to late 1950's. In the Stalin era, when the regime had greater control over population movements, the avowed aim of Siberian development was permanent settlement and the building up of what the Russians call an integrated, or well-rounded economy. This development strategy, which began with the program of forced industrialization under the early five-year plans, was based on the ideologically motivated objective of achieving a more uniform distribution of productive forces through the development of new population centers and of industries near resource sites. It also evolved from strategic considerations calling for the construction of backup plants in key industries that would, to some extent, duplicate the output of establishments in the developed European part of the Soviet Union, but would be located in safer interior regions far from potential overland invasion corridors. This early eastward movement was facilitated to some degree by the availability of a large pool of forced labor that could be moved at will for use in construction projects in harsh environments that could not be staffed so readily with free labor.

A new phase in Siberian development began with the start of post-Stalin liberalization of Soviet society. With abolition of the massive use of forced labor, the Government encountered difficulties in attracting workers to Siberia for permanent settlement and integrated economic development. The labor shortage in the region became a serious constraint in continuing the previous development strategy. In addition, the increasing depletion of fuel and energy resources in the European regions focused attention on the need for moving fossil fuels and electrical energy from Siberia to the urban and industrial consuming centers of the European USSR. The problems of attracting population to Siberia and the growing appetite of the western regions for energy goods and raw materials gradually led to a geographical division of labor, in which manufacturing activities with large labor requirements were confined mainly to the well populated European part of the country while Siberian development became increasingly specialized in the extraction and, perhaps, some preliminary processing of resources as well as the development of power-intensive industries, such as aluminum, with large energy requirements. Instead of seeking to foster an eastward movement of population, as in the past, Soviet policy-makers adopted a conscious strategy of limiting labor inputs in the Siberian economy to the minimum required in staffing the various resource-oriented developments.

Within this overall pattern, Siberian development has been dominated over the years by a sequence of regional programs that focused investment on particular parts of Siberia.

1. The Urals-Kuznetsk Combine, the first such regional program, was associated with the integrated development phase of the Stalin era. It began in the early 1930's as an effort to build up a new iron and steel base in the eastern part of the USSR. It combined Urals iron ore and Kuznetsk Basin coking coal in a 1,400-mile-long shuttle operation aimed at creating new steel plants both in the Urals (at Magnitogorsk) and in Siberia (at Stalinsk, the present Novokuznetsk). This early effort, involving mainly primary industries, was supplemented in World War II by the evacuation of war-threatened manufacturing plants. This influx of industry during the wartime emergency led to the rapid development of cities in the population belt of southern Siberia served by the Trans-Siberian Railroad. Population and economic activity boomed in Omsk and Novosibirsk, in West Siberia, and in Krasnoyarsk, in East Siberia. The more distant reaches of Siberia to the east were less affected in this wartime boom because of the great overland distances separating them from the centers of economic activity in the west.

2. The second major regional program, beginning in the 1950's, was the development of the great hydroelectric potential of the Yenisey and Angara rivers, attracting power-intensive industries such as aluminum. This program, which is still continuing, was the first of a series of development projects that sought to take advantage of Siberia's resource potential, in this case hydro power, while minimizing labor inputs. It resulted in the construction of some of the world's largest hydroelectric stations in the capacity range of 4,000 to 6,000 MW (Bratsk, Ust'-Ilimsk and Krasnoyarsk). A fourth, the Sayan station on the upper Yenisy River, produced its first electricity in December 1978, and a fifth, the Boguchany station on the middle Angara River, is in early groundbreaking stage with completion scheduled for the middle 1980's. The Siberian stations account for more than 40 percent of the Soviet Union's hydro generating capacity as of the late 1970's, and their low-cost power has attracted roughly 50 to 60 percent of the nation's aluminum reduction capacity.

3. A third regional development program got under way in the mid-1960's in the Ob' River basin of West Siberia with the development of newly discovered oil and gas resources. The oil resources, in particular, soon turned out to be of crucial significance for the Soviet economy because of the peaking and reduction of oil production in older producing areas in the European USSR. The development of the West Siberian hydrocarbon resources has been extraordinarily rapid if one considers the difficulties of the long, cold winters, the swampy forest terrain and the lack of population centers and infrastructure. By 1978, 13 years after the first oil began to flow from the West Siberian fields, they accounted for 44 percent of Soviet petroleum production. The natural gas resources, situated in an even more northerly setting and more difficult of access, have been developed more slowly. The development of the northern gas resources posed less urgency than the oil because Central Asian gas sources temporarily filled the need as older gas fields in the European USSR became depleted. However, Central Asian gas resources were limited and, after a slow start, West Siberian gas development is now receiving high priority.

By 1978, the West Siberian gas fields furnished 25 percent of Soviet national production.

In addition to these three major ongoing programs, two more regional development efforts are now getting under way, with the impact likely to be evident only after the middle 1980's:

(a) The new Soviet energy policy of conserving oil and converting fossil-fuel power generation from fuel oil to coal is expected to focus in the 1980's on the development of the large low-grade lignite coal deposits in the Kansk-Achinsk basin of southern Siberia. Because the low-calorific lignite is not easily transportable (it crumbles and ignites on prolonged exposure to the air), present plans call for the "coal-by-wire" approach in which lignite would be burned in huge mineside power stations and the electricity would be transmitted to power-consuming areas over extra-high-voltage lines. Although plans have been announced for the construction of the first of a series of lignite-fired 6,400 MW stations and for the construction of a high-voltage test line operating at 1,150 KV, there still appears to be controversy over the economics and practicality of Kansk-Achinsk development. It may well be that the long-distance transmission of electricity will not be implemented and that a lignite-based power complex would instead attract energy-intensive industries to the area following the pattern set by the hydro development.

(b) The evident Soviet interest in greater interaction with the world economy has revived the old Baikal-Amur Mainline project of East Siberia and the Far East. The role of the BAM is to be discussed separately in this colloquium. Suffice it to say at this point that, aside from any strategic implications or its significance as an additional east-west transit route, the BAM may be expectaed to play an important role in resource exploitation. When completed in the middle 1980's, it will provide access to a new tier of potential energy and raw material sites north of the Trans-Siberian Railroad. Because of the huge overland distances separating these new resource areas from the economically developed western regions of the USSR, the exploitation of resources in the BAM zone is likely to be oriented eastward for export through the Soviet Union's Pacific ports.

Finally, mention should be made of a regional development that extends beyond mere resource exploitation and comes closer to the old Soviet concept of comprehensive development. This is the manufacturing complex emerging around the new Sayan hydro complex on the upper Yenisey River. This area, in southern Siberia, has relatively favorable living conditions (for Siberia) and, it is hoped, will attract population for permanent settlement to staff the projected manufacturing industries. Aside from the customary aluminum plant (under construction at Sayanogorsk), the Sayan manufacturing complex will include the production of transport equipment (freight cars, containers) in the Abakan area, and an integrated complex of diversified electrical equipment manufacture at Minusinsk.[3]

II. The Present Rationale for Siberian Development

The current development of Siberian resources can be attributed to two basic motives: (a) the exploitation of energy and raw materials required by the Soviet domestic economy, essentially the economy of the European USSR; (b) the development of resources that are likely to find a market abroad, generating foreign exchange for the acquisition of the advanced technology and industrial equipment sought by the Soviet Union in the West.

In view of the vast east-west spread of the Siberian landmass, it is useful in this context to divide the region into two parts, roughly by drawing a north-south line through Lake Baikal. The western half of Siberia may be said to orient its activities toward the west, both to the European USSR and to Eastern and Western Europe. The eastern part is, for most purposes, too remote to interact intensively with the western regions or with Europe, and is likely to be oriented increasingly toward the Pacific Basin.

The domestic factor in Siberian resource development is probably most evident in fossil fuels and energy as the depletion of energy resources in the European USSR has focused growing attention on the oil, natural gas and coal of the western half of Siberia. To the extent that the Soviet planners will be able to set aside West Siberian energy goods for export, for example, natural gas for Western Europe, the western part of Siberia will also perform important export-generating functions.

The foreign trade factor, about which the next speaker will have more to say, will probably be the predominant motive for development of the eastern regions of Siberia (east of Lake Baikal). These regions have long been only marginally involved in the Soviet domestic economy, mainly because of the vast distances separating them from the nation's economic centers in the west. The onset of detente, inviting greater economic interaction between the Soviet Union and the Western countries, and the upward trend in world raw material prices appear to have opened up new opportunities for the development of the Soviet Union's Far Eastern resources for export. In this context, the decision in 1974 to proceed with the construction of the Baikal-Amur Mainline can be viewed as a step toward the long-term implementation of a resource-export policy. The BAM will be providing access to known resources that could not be developed previously in the absence of transportation, for example, the Neryungri coking coal of southern Yakutia; the construction of the railroad is also likely to stimulate a renewed geological exploration effort to identify new resources within the BAM zone. A crucial aspect of the BAM is that, in addition to opening up new resource sites directly, it will also bring an even larger segment of eastern Siberia closer to the nearest railhead.[4]

Just as export functions will operate in the basically domestic-oriented development of the western half of Siberia, the eastern part will play a role in the domestic economy in addition to its projected basic export function. However, only high-value, low-bulk goods capable of overcoming the friction of distance across Siberia are likely to have a domestic orientation. In addition to gold, such specialized goods would include many of the mineral raw materials in which the eastern half of Siberia has a virtual monopoly, for example, boron, fluorspar, mica, tin and some other rare metals as well as diamonds.

The expanding electric-power complex of south-central Siberia, based so far mainly on the hydro potential of the Yenisey-Angara basin, but ultimately perhaps also on the lignite-fired power complex of Kansk-Achinsk, may be interacting both with the east and with the west. The locational attraction of low-cost power sources is so strong in the case of energy-intensive industries (aluminum in particular) that raw materials may be shipped over long distances to the power sources and the end-product may then be shipped back to market areas. The aluminum plant currently under construction at Sayanogorsk, for example, will be using alumina, the intermediate product, from a seaboard alumina plant on the Black Sea, at Nikolayev, which in turn will be importing bauxite from a Soviet-developed mine in Guinea. It is conceivable over the long term, world market conditions permitting, that the Soviet Union will be able to exploit its growing hydroelectric potential in the Angara-Yenisey region by importing raw materials needed by energy-intensive industries such as aluminum, and re-exporting the finished product. Despite its diversified mineral resource base, the Soviet Union is not well supplied with high-grade bauxite, and roughly 40 percent of its aluminum output is already being derived from imported materials, both bauxite and alumina.[5]

III. Physical Development Problems

The constraints in Siberian development, aside from the availability of investment resources, are well known, and focus essentially on the quality of the environment, the shortage of labor, and the absence of transportation. All these factors operate in the direction of enhancing the costs of development.

The environment operates mainly through climate, with its winters of six months or more and temperatures descending routinely to -40°C. These harsh conditions tend to raise the costs of construction by requiring better insulation of buildings, additional heating fuel and specially designed equipment for outdoor operation with Arctic specifications. Climate also affects transportation by reducing the usefulness of water routes to the brief ice-free shipping season, unless icebreakers are used, as on the Dudinka-Murmansk run of the western portion of the Northern Sea Route (see below). However, the long winters also have one positive impact on transportation by permitting the use of seasonal winter roads in regions like Yakutia, where the permanent road system is rudimentary. These seasonal roads are simply trails bulldozed across the country and used by heavy trucks to carry supplies to outlying settlements.

As in the case of transportation, climate also has conflicting impact on construction. Indirectly it poses engineering problems because of the presence of permafrost, with its thin, seasonally melting surface layer, which causes sagging of structures unless special precautions, such as the driving of deep piles, are taken. At the same time, the long winters are the prime construction season because the frozen ground makes possible the movement of heavy equipment over terrain that provides no support in the brief summer season, as in the West Siberian swamps and in parts of the Arctic tundra.[6]

Since the abolition of forced labor as a mass institution in the middle 1950's, Soviet planners have come to the conclusion that labor inputs in Siberia will have to be limited to a bare minimum. At first an effort was made to attract workers by expanding a variety of material incentives, such as regional wage differentials, Arctic supplements, longer vacations and other benefits. However, it turned out that these devices helped to attract labor only for fixed contract terms and did not induce permanent settlement. The planners appear to have come to the realization that the promotion of permanent settlement would require the provision of living conditions, services, housing and supplies of consumer goods that are not only equal to the developed and populated European regions of the USSR, but in fact superior to the western living levels. But the provision of such a high level of services, it has been recognized, is far costlier under Siberian conditions in view of the higher costs of goods, many of which must be hauled from the west; the difficulties of providing equivalent services over a vast territory with a scattered population; the need for warmer clothing, greater heat insulation, and so forth. For the time being at least, the goal of promoting further permanent settlement in resource development areas has therefore been shelved.

Programs to attract labor to Siberia are now limited largely to the work force actually needed to staff particular development projects; settlement for settlement's sake no longer seems to be an immediate goal. But even when it comes to these developmental requirements, the authorities appear to be having difficulties. Workers, for the most part, go to Siberia for temporary tours of duty, causing a high rate of labor turnover, with its inherent inefficiency, the increased cost of training programs, loss of experienced workers, etc. A two-year migration survey for 1968-69 that was included in the 1970 census showed migration intensity (a measure of population turnover equal to the sum of in-migration and out-migration) to be high through most northern areas of Siberia and the Far East. In Magadan Oblast, for example, in northeast Siberia, as much as one-fourth of the total population either arrived or departed during the two-year period, and in Kamchatka Oblast, one-fifth participated in migration. This migration pattern also included Tyumen' Oblast, the center of oil and gas development.[7]

In an effort to minimize labor requirements and reduce turnover, the Soviet Union has been experimenting with two techniques: the work-shift method and the expeditionary method. In the work-shift method, workers and their families are housed in larger, permanent base cities designed to provide more amenities, and workers are airlifted (by helicopter or fixed-wing aircraft) to dormitory settlements near remote work sites for work shifts of a few weeks, followed by time off in the base city. In the expeditionary technique, workers are flown to work sites, not from Siberian base cities, but from cities in the European USSR, for longer tours of duty. The expeditionary technique has been applied mainly in the oil fields of West Siberia, where the local work force has proved inadequate for the growing drilling program needed to maintain critical oil supplies. Beginning in 1977, drilling teams have been flown to Siberia from the older oil fields of the Volga-Urals, where depletion of reserves has been setting in and the need for a work force in the oil industry has been reduced.

Transportation, either overland transportation or waterways, is essential to provide access to resource sites that generate bulk movements of freight. High-value, low-bulk mineral resources such as gold and diamonds have been developed in remote areas through the extensive use of airlift capacity, but air transportation is obviously inadequate to serve coal mines, metal mines and logging areas that generate large volumes of outgoing material. Two basic approaches have been adopted to improve transport access to Siberian resource sites: feeder railroads running north from the Trans-Siberian mainline, and the development of Arctic navigation along the Northern Sea Route.

Feeder railroads running north from the Trans-Siberian have long been limited to logging areas. A number of such rail lines into new timber-felling regions were built in the 1960's, most of them 200 to 300 km long. The oil and gas development in West Siberia has stimulated the construction of a more ambitious south-north rail project, the 1,300-km line running from Tyumen' on the Trans-Siberian north through Tobol'sk and Surgut (an oil center) toward Urengoy (a gas center). The railroad reached the Surgut region only in 1975, 10 years after the start of oil production in the area, suggesting that oil development with its reliance on pipeline transmission is not totally dependent on railroad access. However, the further development of outlying oil fields in West Siberia and, especially, of the more northerly gas fields appears to have been a factor in the present northward extension of the railroad from Surgut toward Urengoy. This railroad, which will be the first to cross Siberia from south to north, reached the vicinity of Lat. 64° N in early 1979, and is proceeding along the Pyaki-Pur River, a tributary of the Pur, toward Tarko-Sale. Although this project is being given priority, the advance is being slowed by the swampy terrain, requiring long hauls of materials from the outside for roadbed construction.

This access route toward the Arctic gas fields from the south was decided on after a period of controversy over the restoration of another northern railroad that had been started in the early 1950's under Stalin. That line, running from Salekhard, on the lower Ob' River, toward Igarka, on the Yenisey River, had been designed as part of the earlier concept of comprehensive Siberian development and, at the time, actually had virtually no economic justification. Having been constructed by forced labor, the project was abandoned by the middle 1950's, when it had reached the area where vast gas resources were to be discovered a decade later. A prolonged debate on whether to rehabilitate the old railroad was finally resolved in favor of the southerly approach, which appeared to be more useful for purposes of oil-field and gas-field development along the way. The Salekhard railroad, moreover, would have required a costly bridge across the lower Ob' River if it were to be connected to the rest of the Soviet rail system. The Surgut-Urengoy railroad is ultimately expected to be extended to Igarka and Noril'sk, thus providing the first year-round overland outlet for the crucial Noril'sk metals mining complex, the Soviet Union's major producer of nickel, copper, cobalt and platinum-group metals.

Pending the availability of such an overland transport route, Noril'sk has been dependent on upgrading of the Northern Sea Route through enhancement of the Soviet Union's icebreaker capabilities. The shipping season on the route between Dudinka, the Yenisey River port for Noril'sk, and Murmansk used to be limited to about four months. The expansion of Noril'sk mining operations clearly called for more regular transport services, and the shipping season was gradually extended both through the use of powerful nuclear icebreakers, to keep the main sea lanes open, and through the operation of specially designed shallow-draught icebreakers suitable for river mouths. In addition to the older nuclear-powered Lenin, a 44,000-horsepower icebreaker in operation since 1960, the Soviet Union now has two larger nuclear icebreakers, the Arktika and the Sibir' (sister ships of 75,000 horsepower each), functioning in the Arctic. In 1977 and 1978, two powerful (20,000-horsepower) conventional icebreakers suitable for shallow waters in the mouth of the Yenisey River--the Kapitan Sorokin, in 1977, and the Kapitan Nikolayev, in 1978--also entered service. Like most modern conventional Soviet icebreakers, they had been built in Finnish yards. The stage was now set for an attempt to insure year-round navigation along the western segment of the Northern Sea Route, between the Noril'sk district and Murmansk, and shipping operations were in fact maintained throughout the winter 1978-79, for the first time.

A by-product of improved Arctic navigation, which was fostered mainly by the requirements of Noril'sk, has been the development of a great new gas field on the west coast of the Yamal Peninsula, at Cape Kharasavey. Starting in 1976, cargo vessels under icebreaker escort have approached the prospective gas site early in the year, using the fast ice offshore as a platform for the unloading of supplies (shallow water off Yamal prevents ships from coming close inshore). The Yamal gas development operation (production is not expected before the early 1980's) is the first example of a gas development from the seaward side on the Siberian coast; other Arctic gas fields have been developed from the landward side.[8]

In areas without railroad access, development continues to be hampered by transport problems, as can be illustrated by the case of Yakutia. This vast region, with a variety of mineral developments, ranging from gold to tin and diamonds, is dependent for 80 to 85 percent of its incoming supplies on the seasonal water route of the Lena River.[9] Equipment destined for Yakutian mining sites is often manufactured in the European USSR, and must be transported over the Trans-Siberian and the Tayshet—Ust'kut branch line to the upper Lena port of Osetrovo in time for the summer shipping season opening around mid-May. Until the freeze-up in early October, around 3 million tons of cargo must be moved through Osetrovo and down the Lena River. Despite an active dredging program, shipping is often hampered by shallow depths in the upper reaches, requiring the loading of ships below their capacity to reduce the draught and the transshipment and fuller loading of ships at downstream ports (Kirensk, Vitim, or Lensk). After the cargo finally reaches a river landing closest to its destination, it must wait until freeze-up before it can be hauled by seasonal winter road to its destination. It sometimes takes eight months or more to deliver supplies to remote Siberian development sites. Until the development of the Osetrovo navigation head in the 1960's, most of the supplies for Yakutia were brought in by the Northern Sea Route, whose share is now down to about 3 percent of all incoming freight. In view of the bottleneck that has been developing at Osetrovo and the navigation difficulties in the upper reaches of the Lena River, there have been demands for a revival of the Northern Sea Route's eastern segment, especially in light of the enhanced icebreaker capabilities of the last few years.

The Yakutian situation may also be improved by the construction of the Little BAM, the transverse north-south line crossing the Baikal-Amur Mainline at Tynda. The Little BAM was built in the 1970's to provide an outlet for the coking coal from Neryungri in southern Yakutia for export to Japan; the first coal moved out of the Neryungri strip mine in 1978[10] for local steam-electric stations; coking coal movements to Japan will begin only in the early 1980's. While serving mainly the needs of the coal project, the Little BAM has also improved the transport situation of the nearby gold and mica producing district around Aldan in southern Yakutia. There are likely to be increasing demands for early extension of the Little BAM northward toward Yakutsk, the Yakutian capital, to replace the present motor road running northward from the Trans-Siberian Railroad.

While the Little BAM thus emerges as a crucial element in improving the transport situation in southern Yakutia, the Baikal-Amur Mainline itself will be a significant new element in the development of a broad zone between the upper Lena River and the lower Amur to the north of the Trans-Siberian. Although the outlines of future raw-material development are still vague and may have to await the drafting of the next five-year plan (1981-85), it is evident that in addition to Neryungri coking coal, the future exploitation program will involve the asbestos of Molodezhnyy in the northern Buryat ASSR, the copper of Udokan in Chita Oblast and tin in the Badzhal area west of Komsomol'sk. (More detailed discussion will be left to the session on transportation.)

IV. Overview of Major Resource Projects

Because of limitations of space, the following review of major Siberian resource development projects will be limited to the most recent events, current status and future outlook.*

By far the most significant projects in the westward oriented part of Siberia are those concerned with fossil fuels and energy, with the focus on the oil and gas resources of Tyumen' Oblast. This region is on the way to becoming the principal supplier of hydrocarbons to the Soviet domestic economy as well as a source of exports of natural gas and, to the extent that domestic oil needs can be curbed, of crude oil. The development effort is evident alone from the magnitude of investment going into Tyumen' Oblast, which in 1975 (the last year for which regional investment data were published) exceeded that of any major civil division of the USSR outside of the city of Moscow.[11] Until recently the oil development program was concentrated around relatively accessible and large fields near the base towns of Surgut and Nizhnevartovsk, notably the giant Samotlor field. But these fields are now leveling off in production, and continued expansion of production requires a costlier strategy of developing many smaller, medium-size fields. The current effort is proceeding in two directions. The more significant expansion of oil development is taking place to the north of Nizhnevartovsk and, to a lesser extent, north of Surgut toward the more northerly gas fields. This northward movement is being assisted to some extent by the concurrent construction of the Surgut-Urengoy railroad; however it also requires maximum use of tributaries of the Ob' River during the brief summer shipping season and of winter roads during the longer coldweather season. A less significant thrust is under way in the southeast portion of West Siberia, into the Vasyugan Swamp of Tomsk Oblast. So far, however, Tomsk Oblast has been contributing only a negligible share of West Siberian crude oil production; in 1978, Tomsk Oblast produced 8 million tons of crude oil compared with 246 million tons in Tyumen' Oblast. The combined West Siberian output represented 44.4 percent of total Soviet oil production in 1978.[12]

The development of the West Siberian oil fields has resulted in increasingly large movements of crude oil from Siberia to refineries in the European USSR. This westward movement rose from 15 million tons in 1970 to 113 million tons in 1975 (23 percent of all Soviet oil). The original plan for 1980 was 240 million tons of westward transmission (or 37 percent of planned output), with about 70-80 million tons being refined in the Asian USSR, mainly at the Siberian refineries of Omsk and Angarsk, the Far Eastern refineries of Khabarovsk and Komsomol'sk, and the new refinery at Pavlodar, in northeast Kazakhstan, which went on stream in 1978.[13] The increasing demands of westward transmission have now required the construction of yet another pipeline, from Surgut

---

*For more detailed information and a historical perspective, the reader is referred to Theodore Shabad, "Siberian Resource Development in the Soviet Period," in: Shabad and Mote, Gateway to Siberian Resources (The BAM), New York, 1977, pp. 1-61, and to the News Notes section in Soviet Geography.

westward through Perm', Gor'kiy and Yaroslavl' to the Belorussian refinery at Novopolotsk. Great priority is being given to this project to insure that the growing production of West Siberia will not be constrained by inadequate pipeline capacity, both to refineries in the European USSR and to export terminals. West Siberian oil began to be exported in 1972, and now contributes a substantial part of net Soviet exports, running at the rate of 140 to 150 million tons, or one-fourth of production. The outlook for Siberian oil is that of an increasingly large share in national production as production is declining in older oil producing areas, especially the Volga-Urals. In 1978, West Siberia achieved an output increment of 36 million tons, but this was eroded by a decline of 10 million elsewhere in the USSR, so that the national gain in production was 26 million, from 546 million in 1977 to 572 million tons in 1978. The trend is likely to continue. The projected 1979 increment for Siberia is 31 million tons, and the expected decline in other fields 10 million, making for a projected national gain of 21 million tons in the 1979 plan. The continuing erosion of West Siberian increments would seem to suggest that Soviet oil production may indeed peak sometime in the early to middle 1980's, although it is difficult to say how long the peaking can be held.

Natural gas production in Siberia has been slower to develop because of the more northerly and remote location of the Arctic fields, but the reserves are not the constraining factor that they appear to be in the case of oil. The first giant field, Medvezh'ye, was put into operation in 1972, and reached an output level of 71 billion cubic meters in 1978, actually somewhat above its original designed capacity of 65 billion.[14] The second giant field is Urengoy, which yielded its first commercial gas in April 1978 and is expected to reach its first-stage capacity of 100 billion in the early 1980's. Urengoy was once envisaged as the source of gas for the North Star project, involving United States cooperation in gas-field development and the tanker shipment of liquefied natural gas to the East Coast of the United States. The joint venture did not materialize because of financing problems and the Russians have now gone ahead with the development of Urengoy on their own. Gas from this field, reputed to be the world's largest in reserves, is initially being transmitted through the gas pipeline system serving Medvezh'ye, to the west. However, most of the Urengoy gas flow will be moving through a new southerly tansmission system, both for consumption in the European USSR and for export to Eastern and Western Europe. The first pipeline of this southern transmission system reached the field at Urengoy this year. In 1978, West Siberian gas production was 92 billion cubic meters, or 25 percent of the national total; its share is expected to increace to about 35 percent by 1980. Unlike the situation in oil, West Siberian increments in gas have not been seriously undercut so far by declines elsewhere as some of the older fields are holding steady. But their reserves are limited and production appears to be approaching a peak, especially in Central Asia, so that West Siberian gas is expected to assume a dominant position in the 1980's. The basic problem in the case of gas is that pipeline transmission of gas is inherently less efficient than pipeline transmission of oil, and ways are under study to make more effective use of the Siberian supplies. One plan that appears to have gained favor is to burn more gas in a power generating complex under development at Surgut and transmitting the electricity over long-distance lines at least to the Urals.[15]

In solid fuels, the Kuznetsk Basin of the southern Siberia continues as the Soviet Union's second largest coal producer (after the Donets Basin in the Ukraine). Its significance will increase as production in the Donbas begins to level off, if not decline. The high-grade bituminous coal of the Kuzbas, now being produced at a rate of 150 million tons a year, represents one-fifth of all Soviet coal output, and the coking-coal component represents as much as one-third of Soviet supplies. Because of its high heating value and the need for coking coal in the expanding iron and steel industry of the European USSR, much of the Kuznetsk coal is being hauled over long distances to the Urals and beyond at prices that are competitive with Donets Basin coal. In 1975, about 30 million tons of coal moved by rail from Siberia beyond the Urals, mostly from the Kuzbas; the 1980 plan was about 45 million tons.[16]

The Kuznetsk Basin is also the locale of most of the Siberian iron and steel industry, with two plants at Novokuznetsk: the older Kuznetsk mill and the newer West Siberia mill. Together they are now producing about the rate of 11-12 million tons of steel, or 7 to 8 percent of the national total. In general, the steel industry does not appear to have much of a future in Siberia because, in contrast to many other minerals, the region is poor in iron ore. Most of the iron and steel capacity in recent years has been added in the European USSR, closer to the two great iron-ore basins, the Krivoy Rog district and the Kursk Magnetic Anomaly.

As mentioned earlier, the full-scale development of the lignite resources of the Kansk-Achinsk basin remains a matter for the 1980's. Although the start of development has been announced on both the first giant strip mine and its first associated mineside power station, progress appears sluggish and the development, for the time being at least, does not appear to receive high priority. The original plans called for the first strip mine and power complex, known as Berezovskiy No. 1, to go into operation around 1982, near the projected city of Sharypovo, but judging from present indications such a schedule will not be maintained.

In the hydroelectric power program, of the Yenisey-Angara River system, the principal current project is the Sayan hydro station at Sayanogorsk, with a designed capacity of 6,400 MW. The first of ten 640 MW generating units started up in late 1978, and two more were to be added in 1979. However, the main power consumer, the Sayanogorsk aluminum plant, is behind schedule, as has often been the case in Siberian power and aluminum projects.

Aside from aluminum, a major industry associated with the Siberian hydro projects has been woodpulp manufacture, requiring both water and power inputs. One of the largest Soviet pulp mills, with a capacity of one million tons a year, is operating at Bratsk, and a second major mill, with a designed capacity of 500,000 tons, is under construction at the Ust'-Ilimsk hydro station as a joint venture of Comecon. The manufacture of pulp is part of a new development strategy to process a greater share of Siberian roundwood to reduce the costs of long hauls of roundwood to the European USSR. Siberia is now felling around 34 percent of the Soviet Union's timber, but accounts for only 29 percent of the sawnwood. The Siberian share of processed wood products is even smaller.

One of the most important development projects, being expanded under particularly harsh conditions, is the Noril'sk metals complex, yielding nickel, copper, cobalt and platinum-group metals. Dating originally from World War II, the Noril'sk operation was greatly enhanced by the discovery, in the 1950's, of additional large and high-grade ore bodies deep underground at nearby Talnakh. Some of the largest and deepest mines in the Soviet Union are under development, with the so-called Taymyr mine being driven to a depth of 5,000 feet; a second nickel smelter is approaching completion to handle the increasing flow of ore. However, smelting facilities even then would not match the area's mining capacity, and a large portion of the concentrates will continue to be shipped over the Northern Sea Route to Murmansk for processing in smelters of the Kola Peninsula.

Both the Sayan hydro and manufacturing complex and the Noril'sk operation are part of Krasnoyarsk Kray, which was long the leading Siberian investment area until oil and gas development moved Tyumen' Oblast into first place in 1973. The third largest investment region is Irkutsk Oblast (2 billion rubles in 1975), where, in addition to the pulp-mill project at Ust'-Ilimsk, a major chemical complex is under development in the Zima area, at the new town of Sayansk; it will use local salt deposits and ethylene from the Angarsk petrochemical plant to produce caustic soda, chlorine and polyvinyl chloride. The Sayansk chemical project is only one of several chemical ventures that are expected to develop in Siberia during the 1980's; the two principal sites are the petrochemical projects of Tobol'sk and Tomsk, which are both expected to use hydrocarbon feedstocks from the West Siberian fields.

In considering the resource development projects of the eastward, export-oriented portion of Siberia, we have already dealt with the prospects associated with the BAM in the southeast quadrant of Siberia. Farther to the north is the potential gas producing region of Yakutia, in which both Japan and the United States are expressing interest. Without impinging on the report to be given by Mr. James Lister, I would just say that this project had been predicated on the proving of adequate reserves to support the delivery of natural gas, in LNG form, to both Japan and the United States over at least a 25-year period. Of the minimum requirements of one trillion cubic meters, about 800 billion had been proven by the end of 1977. The reserves are in two widely separated areas--460 billion in the Middle Vilyuy field of central Yakutia, and 340 billion in the Middle Botuobuya field, 350 miles to the southwest. The Soviet side expected to meet the one trillion cubic meter goal by the end of 1979.

V. Siberia's Contribution to the Soviet Economy

Siberia's contribution can be measured on a percentage basis and related to its share in the total population of the USSR. Although Siberia has a somewhat higher rate of natural increase than the nation as a whole, net out-migration has kept the Siberian population at a stable level, of about 10.5 percent of the Soviet population. This population share may be used as a yardstick against which Siberia's production in various commodity groups can be assessed.

Table 1 presents the Siberian percentage contribution in selected commodity groups for which official statistics were published until 1973. Since then, the Siberian share of USSR production is no longer being systematically published. For some goods, notably energy resources, iron and steel, wood products, cement, consumer goods and food, it has been possible to gather data from scattered sources. The table does not contain mineral commodities for which no official statistics are published. Minerals and metals in which Siberia is estimated to contribute at least around one-half of Soviet production are:

Aluminum	Indium	Selenium
Beryllium	Liithium	Tellerium
Boron	Mica	Tin
Cobalt	Nickel	Tungsten
Diamonds	Niobium	Tantalum
Fluorspar	Platinum group	
Gold		

Among the officially reported commodity groups, energy resources and wood products stand out as percentages far in excess of Siberia's population share. Coal and timber have been traditional Siberian products since the early years of development, as shown by the 1940 share (23 percent of USSR production for each).

In the energy field, coal has been joined since the late 1960's by oil and since the early 1970's by natural gas; the Siberian share of these two commodities is likely to increase rapidly through the 1980's. The coal share may also be enhanced, depending on the rate of development of the controversial Kansk-Achinsk lignite basin.

The electric power share is roughly double the population share and, in the case of hydro power, quadruple the population share. This reflects the availability of a power surplus for local power-intensive industries and, if the long-distance transmission problem can be resolved, for transfer to other regions. The predominance of electric power generation is likely to be further enhanced through the 1980's as the development of hydro sites in the Angara-Yenisey region continues and if a vast power-generating complex is realized on the basis of Kansk-Achinsk lignite.

In the wood products group, the characteristic aspect has been the emphasis on roundwood removals and sawmilling, with relatively less development of deeper wood processing. This lag is slowly being rectified, in particular through the development of woodpulp capacity as well as the manufacture of paperboard, mainly containerboard. The Siberian share of paper production, which is a highly market-oriented activity concentrated in the European USSR, remains small (at 7 percent of the USSR total). There may be prospects for newsprint production for export to the Pacific Basin if technology and product quality can be improved.

Table 1
Siberian Share of USSR Production Selected Commodities (percent)

	1940	1950	1960	1970	1973	1975	1978
Energy resources							
Coal	23.0	27.0	28.0	32.0	33.0	34.0	35.0
Coking coal	17.0	29.0	26.0	29.0	30.0	31.0	32.0
Oil	1.6	1.6	1.1	0.6	21.0	31.0	45.0
Natural gas	--	1.5	0.7	5.0	8.5	14.0	26.0
Electric power	6.6	11.0	15.0	18.0	18.0	18.0	
Hydro power	4.4	3.6	10.0	36.0		40.0	
Iron and steel							
Iron ore	1.6	5.5	5.7	6.5	6.9	6.4	6.1
Pig iron	10.0	10.0	7.1	8.5	9.5	9.0	
Crude steel	10.0	13.0	8.4	8.1	8.3	10.0	
Chemicals							
Caustic soda	--	8.9	9.1	10.0	12.0		
Man-made fibers	--	--	16.0	13.0	11.0		
Soda ash	2.5	8.2	3.1	1.2	7.2		
Sulfuric acid	1.1	1.7	3.8	5.9	5.2		
Fertilizers	6.8	6.7	4.4	5.0	4.0		
Machinery							
Machine tools	1.4	5.2	4.3	2.3	2.6		
Tractors	--	9.5	8.8	7.3	7.4		
Grain harvesters	--	5.0	15.0	18.0	27.0		
Wood products							
Roundwood	23.0	23.0	26.0	33.0	34.0	34.0	
Sawnwood	23.0	19.0	23.0	26.0	27.0	28.0	
Woodpulp	--	4.3	9.3	20.0	22.0		
Cement	8.8	13.0	13.0	12.0	12.0	12.0	
Consumer goods							
Cotton fabrics	0.8	2.0	2.9	3.6	3.2	3.3	
Radio sets	--	13.0	19.0	24.0	20.0		
Meat	13.0	12.0	11.0	9.1	10.1	9.0	
Population	8.9		10.8	10.5	10.5	10.5	

Source: Shabad and Mote, p. 54.

Siberia presents no unusual advantages for iron and steel production, largely because iron-ore resources of adequate quality appear limited. Table 1 shows that the output share of iron ore is less than the pig iron share (6.4 percent and 9 percent in 1975), suggesting that roughly 25 to 30 percent of ore requirements must be shipped *into* Siberia, mainly from the Rudnyy mine in Kazakhstan.

No outstanding contribution is evident in reported inorganic chemicals, except perhaps for caustic soda (favored by abundant salt deposits and electric power for electrolysis). However, the chemicals contribution may undergo significant change in the 1980's as the great petrochemical complexes of Tobol'sk and Tomsk go on stream. Tobol'sk is designed as a major producer of monomers (isoprene, butadiene) and ultimately synthetic rubber; Tomsk is slated to become the largest Soviet producer of polyethylene and polypropylene.

The relatively low share of machinery manufacture is illustrated by machine tools, a basic machinery group, although the Siberian contribution is greater in some specialized types of machinery such as farm equipment for the West Siberian grain regions. Cement production, a rough index of construction activity, is only slightly higher than the population share, demonstrating that the greater share of industrial construction remains in the developed western parts of the USSR.

The existence of a high cost-of-living index in Siberia is suggested by the low output share of soft consumer goods, such as textiles. An exception is found in consumer durables, with new radio and other appliance manufacturers being located in Siberia in an apparent effort to provide female employment opportunities in the largely male-oriented Siberian economy.

Footnotes

1. A.A. Mints, "A Predictive Hypothesis of Economic Development in the European Part of the USSR," *Soviet Geography,* (January 1976), pp. 8-9.

2. For a detailed account of the history of development, see: Theodore Shabad, "Siberian Resource Development in the Soviet Period," in: Theodore Shabad and Victor L. Mote, *Gateway to Siberian Resources (The BAM)* (New York, 1977), pp. 1-61

3. V.V. Soklikova. *Sayanskiy narodnokhozyaystvennyi kompleks.* Moscow, 1974, for recent progress reports, see *Sotsialisticheskaya industriya,* August 7, 1976; *Ekonomicheskaya Gazeta,* 4 (1979), p. 10.

4. See V.I. Poponin, "Changes in Transport Accessibility of East Siberia and the Soviet Far East Through Construction of the BAM," *Soviet Geography,* (September 1978), pp. 470-474, for maps showing the increase in accessibility resulting from the BAM construction.

5. Theodore Shabad, "Raw Material Problems of the Soviet Aluminum industry," *Resources Policy,* (December 1976), pp. 222-234.

6. For detailed discussion of these environmental problems, see: Victor L. Mote, "Environmental Constraints to the Economic Development of Siberia", 2 vols., December 197 (Discussion Paper No. 6, Project on Soviet Natural Resources in the World Economy), Geography Department, Syracuse University, Syracuse, N.Y. 1310.

7. Theodore Shabad, "Soviet Migration Patterns Based on 1970 Census Data," in: Leszek Kosinski (ed.), *Demographic Developments in Eastern Europe.* (New York), pp. 173-196, particularly pp. 191-192.

8. For regular reports on Arctic shipping operations and their impact on Soviet resource development in Siberia, see the periodic notes on the Northern Sea Route by Terence

Armstrong in *Polar Record* and by Theodore Shabad in *Polar Geography.*

9. *Pravda,* Nov. 29, 1977; *Vodnyi Transport,* March 31, 1978.
10. *Soviet Geography,* 10 (1978), p. 742.
11. *Narodnoye Khozyaystvo RSFSR v 1975 g.* (Moscow, 1976), p. 329. Tyumen' Oblast accounted for 3.26 billion rubles of investment in 1975, or one-sixth of the Siberian total of 19.3 billion.
12. *Soviet Geography,* (April 1979); Leslie Dienes and Theodore Shabad, *The Soviet Energy System.* New York, 1979.
13. *Soviet Geography,* (October 1978), pp. 583-584.
14. *Soviet Geography,* (March 1979).
15. *Soviet Geography,* (April 1978), pp. 281-285.

James P. Lister

Current position:
Vice President, New Projects
Development
El Paso LNG Co.,
2919 Allen Parkway,
Box 1440,
Houston, Tx., 77001

Main field of work:
Plant operations, venture analysis and
project development for both
domestic and foreign liquid natural
gas projects. He has had a direct
role in the development of El Paso's
Algeria I project which is now in
operation delivering Algerian LNG to
the United States.

Labor Force and
Regional Raw Material Development
Siberia and
the Soviet Far East:
Exploitation Policies
in Energy and
Raw Materials Sectors:
An Economic Assessment
James Lister

I. Introduction

Adiscussion of development policies in the Soviet Far East requires consideration of a great many interrelated factors that are almost as overwhelming as the immense area and mineral resources of Siberia. Historical, political, economic and technical factors continuously interplay to determine Soviet policy and plans concerning development of the vast Siberian resources.

I recognize that any analysis of Soviet development policy is affected by the availability and validity of pertinent statistics and information. In my case, it must also be remembered that such an analysis is the result of Western-oriented thinking, contemplating a culture, socio-economic system and a political philosophy markedly different from its own. We are keenly aware of such limitations and try to keep them always in mind as we continue to work with the USSR to jointly develop our project. In this regard, I am fortunate in that my involvement with the USSR has been on a front line basis in a major project which would develop natural gas resources in Eastern Siberia. Our project is immense and has many ramifications beyond the strictly commercial aspects.

The joint development of the Yakutia Gas Project to discover, develop, transport and export large quantities of natural gas involves a great many ministries, agencies and governmental offices, and provides a unique look at the functioning of the Soviet system. It is apparent that such a project could have a significant impact on the USSR and on the rest of the world's energy balance. Ultimately, Soviet as well as US governmental policy will determine whether this project goes forward.

II. Evolution of Siberian Development Policies

The victory of Japan in its war with Russia in 1904-05 amply demonstrated that for Russia to hold Siberia against foes in the East, it had to develop and colonize Siberia. Considerable effort was made by the Tsarst government to downplay the infamous penal aspect of the region in order to attract quality settlers from the Western areas of the Empire. Even so, internal economic and political necessities brought about by the disastrous 1914 War, plus the Revolution and Allied intervention prevented large scale development programs in Siberia: there were simply higher priority needs elsewhere. During the 1930's, the collectivization policies, together with the purges also deflected planners' attention to other areas. During World War Two, however, the importance of the region east of the Urals to the survival of Russia became much more acute for the country. Siberia now began to serve as a vast reserve arsenal for supplies, manufacturing and a safe area far from enemy bombers. As a result, in the post-war years, Siberia and the Far East as a geographical, economic, and political frontier, somewhat similar to the Western portion of the USA in the eyes of the relatively well developed Eastern United States in the late 19th century, began to emerge. This 'frontier' aspect of the Soviet regions east of the Ural mountains pervades current Soviet thinking toward the region: it is viewed as an area of both visible riches and of undefined promise. There seem to be three main driving forces behind present Siberian development policy:

1. *Strategic*--The Soviet preoccupation with the threat of invasion has been vividly etched in the current leadership's mind by World War II, not to mention the invasion of the 'Motherland' by the Allies in 1918-19, Japan in 1904-05, Poland, Turkey, France and a host of other countries in the last 150 years. In this respect Siberia is viewed as reservoir of raw materials as well as a gigantic buffer zone against a real or perceived invasion.

2. *Resource Supply*-The vast natural resources of Siberia represent in their view an almost unlimited source of raw materials for development of the Soviet economy—both military and non-military segments. As demands increase and traditional raw material sources in the Western USSR are depleted, Siberia, by necessity, will assume ever increasing importance.

3. *Financial*—The USSR will soon become the world's largest exporter of natural gas. The resources of Siberia represent a tremendous pass-key to future hard currency income for the USSR. Major timber and coal projects are already functioning with Japan. The hard currency income from such commercial transactions is an integral part of the USSR's future plans to import Western technology and equipment to improve all aspects of its sagging domestic economy and boost its very low productivity.

To meet these three important needs, the USSR presently attaches a high priority to increasing the population of Siberia; to the development of major infrastructure systems (the BAM Railway being one significant example); and to an expansion of industrialization in much of the region. Whole cities and industries are created where none existed before. The con-

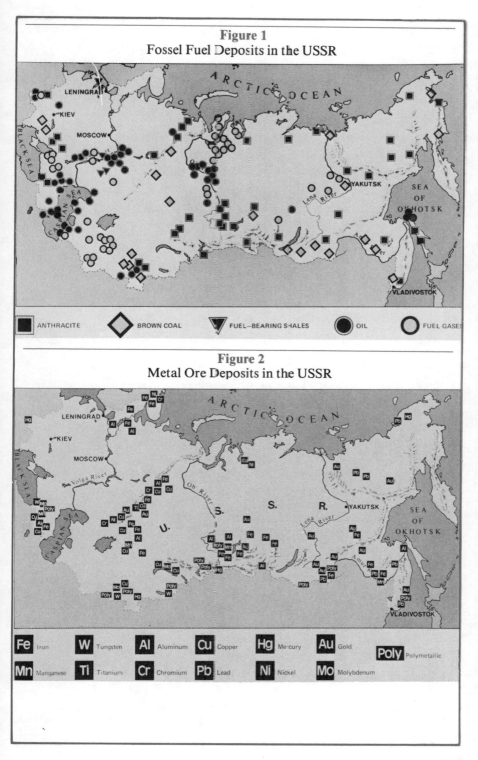

Figure 1
Fossel Fuel Deposits in the USSR

■ ANTHRACITE	◇ BROWN COAL	▼ FUEL–BEARING SHALES	● OIL	○ FUEL GASES

Figure 2
Metal Ore Deposits in the USSR

Fe Iron	**W** Tungsten	**Al** Aluminum	**Cu** Copper	**Hg** Mercury	**Au** Gold	**Poly** Polymetallic
Mn Manganese	**Ti** Titanium	**Cr** Chromium	**Pb** Lead	**Ni** Nickel	**Mo** Molybdenum	

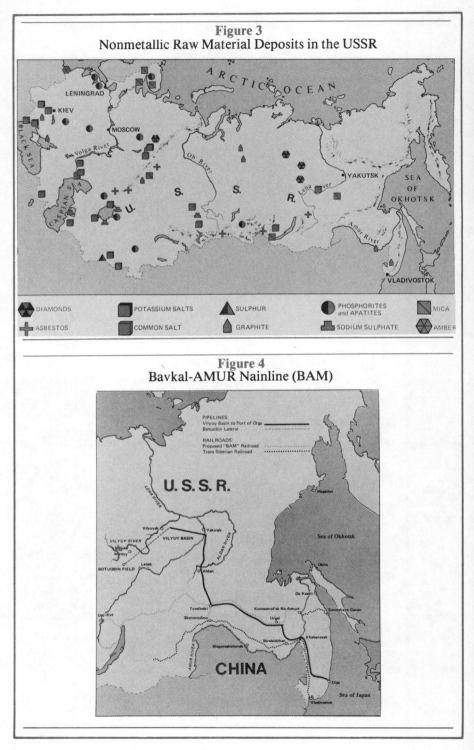

Figure 3
Nonmetallic Raw Material Deposits in the USSR

DIAMONDS   POTASSIUM SALTS   SULPHUR   PHOSPHORITES and APATITES   MICA

ASBESTOS   COMMON SALT   GRAPHITE   SODIUM SULPHATE   AMBER

Figure 4
Bavkal-AMUR Nainline (BAM)

ditions are hostile, the problems are immense, long delays in implementation are the rule, and the availability of labor is limited. But, in spite of these obstacles, there can be little doubt as to the long-term commitment and importance of Siberian development in Soviet plans.

III. The Riches of Siberia Opportunity and Obstacles

Figures 1, 2 and 3 show the concentration of basic raw materials in Siberia and the Soviet Far East.[1] Figure 1 shows the location of deposits of fossil fuel substances, including anthracite, brown coal, fuel-bearing shales, oil, and fuel gases. Figure 2 shows the location of major deposits of metal ores, including iron, manganese, chromium, titanium, nickel, tungsten, molibdenum, aluminum, copper, etc. Figure 3 shows asbestos, graphite, mica, phosphorites and apatites, sulphur, potassium salts, common salt, sodium sulphate, amber, diamonds. The minerals shown on these figures are only the major discoveries which have been made to date—the ultimate potential discoveries could be considerably greater.

Having these important resources and developing them are, of course, two different things. Besides the incredible distances involved, Siberia faces climatic and natural obstacles of the highest magnitude. However, the Soviet plan is to capitalize on the riches of this unique region and, in certain instances, it has been done remarkably well. The huge rivers of Siberia are being harnessed to provide hydroelectric power. The creation of complete industrial cities like Bratsk in the Siberian wilderness are worthy achievements. The Baikal-Amur Mainline (BAM) Railway in eastern Siberia, currently under construction, is an enormous undertaking that will greatly augment future Eastern Siberian development (Figure 4).[2]

One of the ways the Soviet Union has chosen to expedite development is through the introduction of Western know-how and technology. The Soviet attitude toward the use of Western help to develop Siberia was recently expressed by the Director of the Moscow-based Institute of the USA and Canada, Georgi Arbatov, in a recent interview. He was asked, "The economic development of Siberia is the next big step for the Soviet Union on the economic front. Is this going to make it more important to have intensive economic and political cooperation with the West?" Mr. Arbatov replied, "You know we will develop Siberia anyway. At the same time, of course, cooperation with the West as well as cooperation with our allies and friends from Socialist countries can speed up this development and can really make it easier.[3]

Since the days of the early Soviet international trade projects, the USSR has initiated and successfully conducted projects with many countries of both the West and East.[4] The Occidental fertilizer exchange, the Orenburg gas pipeline and the Japanese timber and coal projects are more recent examples of the concept of successfully using trade to gain access to Western technology (and in some cases Eastern European labor) to further the development of Siberia.

The Yakutia Gas Project, involving the US, Japan and the USSR, is another undertaking that fits this pattern. It is a project that matches—in size and degree of difficulty—the expansiveness and harshness of Siberia.

IV. Soviet Energy and the Yakutia Gas Project

There is no area that is more representative of both the problems and opportunities facing the USSR's Siberian development plans than that of hydrocarbon fuels, particularly oil and natural gas.

The extent of the Soviet Union's position as a major producer and marketer of oil and natural gas is often unrecognized, even by many actively involved in the energy business. In 1978, the USSR produced crude oil at a rate of 11.4 million barrels per day.[5] Extending its lead as the world's largest producer of crude oil, the USSR produced almost 19% of the entire world's oil production and 32% more oil than its nearest rival, the United States.

The Soviet Union is no small factor in the natural gas business either, although it now produces natural gas at only about half the rate of the USA. However, a very high priority has been assigned to natural gas in future Soviet plans and this industry is developing rapidly at about 8% a year. The Soviet Union's theoretical potential to produce natural gas exceeds by far any other nation's. Proven reserves total about 30% of the total world reserves, dwarfing its nearest competitors, the USA and Iran (Figure 5). Soviet plans call for gas production in 1980 to reach 415 to 420 billion cubic meters.[6]

Figure 5
World Wide Natural Gas Reserves

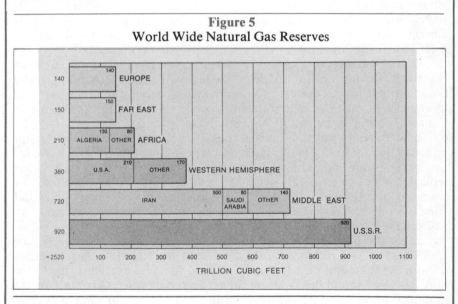

The Soviet Union is currently a major exporter of gas, and it may well become the world's largest gas exporter in the not too distant future. Both Eastern and Western Europe are to become major purchasers. In 1976, the USSR exported about 25.8 billion cubic meters—split about equally between Eastern Europe and Western Europe.[7] By 1980 the USSR will be exporting 30 to 33 billion cubic meters per year to Eastern Europe—providing about one-third of Eastern Europe's supply—and at least 25 billion cubic meters to Western Europe or approximately 10% of Western European consumption. This percentage may well increase to about 25% by 1985. Recipients in Western Europe include West Germany, France, Italy, Austria and Finland.

Figure 6
Soviet Geological Basins and Gas Pipeline Systems

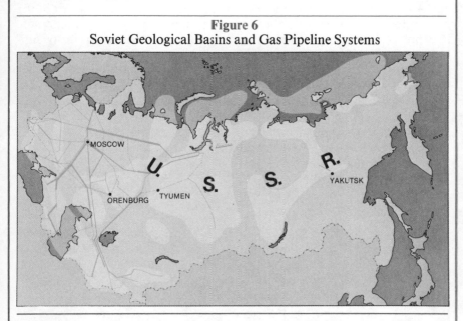

The light shaded areas on this map of the Soviet Union (Figure 6) represent those geological areas, both onshore and offshore, that potentially contain hydrocarbons. Although these geological areas are spread fairly evenly throughout the Soviet Union, more than 90% of the presently known gas reserves are in the western half of the country. Exploration originally started in the south and west but production from these older areas has been declining for several years. Today, and in the foreseeable future, the most active and promising area is the West Siberian Basin, north of Tyumen up to the Yamal Peninsula on the Kara Sea. As much as 20% of all the gas in the world may be located here. New, large fields in this area are being brought into production and tied into gas pipeline systems, shown here, which serve both the western Soviet Union and Europe.

El Paso's interest is in the Vilyuy Basin in the Yakutia region of Eastern Siberia. Exploration efforts in this eastern region have been relatively minor when compared with the western region, but enough work has been done to establish the prospects of substantial amounts of natural gas. This area is separated from the western distribution system by thousands of miles of frozen, largely uninhabited countryside. Because of the vast distances to their western market and because of the abundance of gas reserves in the basins to the west, the USSR plans to move the gas from the Yakutia region eastward, consuming some of it in Eastern Siberian cities and exporting the rest in lieuqefied form to the USA and Japan.

I do not intend to deal extensively with the question of the need and desire for LNG imports to the USA, but it might be helpful to briefly describe some important aspects of LNG projects. Many in the gas industry and American government recognize the desirability of LNG as a part of the answer to our growing natural gas supply problem, although I should note that present energy policymakers view LNG as a rather low priority supplement for the USA. This may very well change as OPEC oil prices continue to rise. On the other hand, Europe and Japan have placed a higher priority on LNG and continue to actively develop LNG projects.

Figure 7

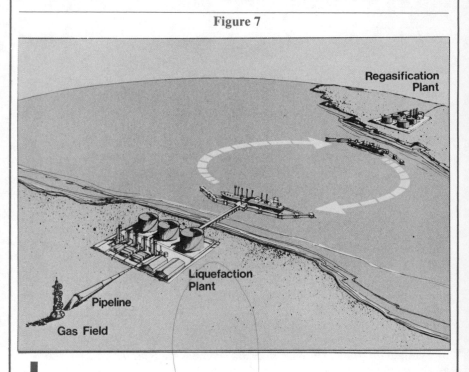

Regasification Plant

Liquefaction Plant

Pipeline

Gas Field

Liquefied natural gas projects have several elements in common (Figure 7). First, gas is produced from fields and, after preliminary treatment, is pipelined by basically conventional methods to a coastal location. The natural gas is then liquefied in a series of refrigeration steps whereby the gas is reduced to a temperature of -260°F. At this temperature the gas becomes liquefied at atmospheric pressure.[8]

The reason for going to all of this trouble is to put the gas in a form where it can be economically transported over long distances. Six hundred cubic feet of gas occupy only one cubic foot as a liquid. Thus, the liquefied natural gas can be loaded on specially built carriers and transported to receiving terminals where LNG is returned to a gaseous form and transported to markets in conventional pipelines.

El Paso began talking with representatives of the USSR Ministry for Foreign Trade about gas exports from the Yakutia region in 1972. In June 1973, a Protocol of Intent was signed with the Ministry of Foreign Trade. This Protocol in essence states that when adequate gas is found in the Yakutia region, El Paso would buy it in liquefied form for shipment to the United States, and that the equipment for the necessary facilities in the Soviet Union would be purchased by the Soviets using western credits, with the credits to be repaid from LNG sales revenues.

Shortly after signing this Protocol a consortium of Japanese companies headed by Tokyo Gas agreed to enter the project, purchase half of the LNG for export to Japan, and supply half of the necessary equipment and financing to the Soviet Union. El Paso believes the participation of the Japanese will add a significant element of political stability to the project in addtion to the obvious financial advantages.

The next major development occurred in December of 1974 when a General Agreement on Exploration was executed that defined the roles of the three countries during the exploration phase of the project. This General Agreement provides for the purchase of $50 million of exploration equipment, half from Japan and half from the USA. Financing for this equipment was provided on a 50/50 basis by the Japanese Eximbank and the Bank of America.

The General Agreement states that the Soviets will confirm and dedicate adequate reserves to support exports to the USA and Japan of the liquefied equivalent of 2 billion cubic feet of gas per day, for a twenty-five year period. The Soviet side has been quite successful in its exploration efforts, and has indicated that it has about 30 trillion cubic feet of gas in place.

This map (Figure 8) shows the approximate location of the proposed pipeline route, the LNG plant at the port of Olga and the trade routes for the LNG carriers. The project will require total production from the gas fields of about 3 billion cubic feet per day: 2 billion for ultimate export and another 1 billion to power the pipeline and LNG plant and for deliveries to a number of local Soviet communities along the pipeline route.

The main pipeline will be larger in diameter and almost three times as long as the Alaskan oil pipeline. Like the Alaskan line, the Yakutia gas pipeline will cross permafrost for well over half of its distance. At Olga the gas will be liquefied, and half of the LNG will be transported 4,700 miles to the American west coast. The other half will be shipped to receiving terminals in Japan.

The USSR will purchase, outside the Soviet Union, essentially all of the machinery and equipment needed to complete the project, including drill rigs, well completion equipment, gas treating facilities, pipe and compressor stations, a liquefaction plant, tankage, port facilities and construction equipment. Preliminary studies show that the total cost of foreign procurement for the Soviet Union will be $4 to $5 billion (in 1978 dollars). Half of the equipment will be supplied and financed by Japan. The other half will be provided, if possible, by the United States, or if necessary, by other countries, depending on export credit and trade policies at the time.

Figure 8
Yakutia Project Trade Route

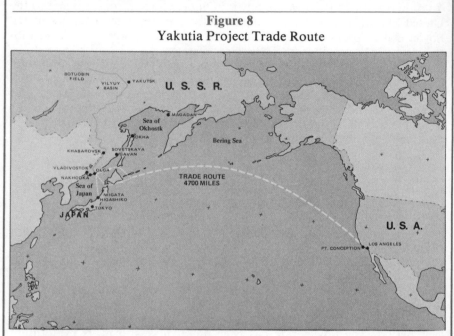

Investment by American entrepreneurs for this project will be in excess of $2 billion for LNG carriers and a receiving terminal on the west coast. The Japanese investment would be much smaller (about $400 million), since the shipping distances are much smaller and because LNG receiving terminals already exist in Japan.

The immense size of this project has forced all three participants to find solutions to some rather basic and difficult problems.

One of the first and most fundamental questions is the need to obtain detailed data on natural gas reserves. In general, Soviet reserves data are very closely held. However, since the existence of adequate reserves is the cornerstone for billions of dollars of financing and investment, the General Agreement on Exploration provides that the Soviets will supply both the U.S. and the Japanese with detailed data on gas reserves. American and Japanese geologists and reservoir engineers have visited the fields near Yakutsk on two occasions to review the exploration progress and to study, on a preliminary basis, some of the reserves data thus far gathered.

The three countries are also working to define a method of jointly conducting future feasibility and engineering studies. The nature of an LNG project requires that all facilities, from the gas wells to the receiving terminals, be designed and built as a single, optimized, integrated system. The USSR wants to design and build the facilities in the USSR, but it is impossible to design and finance the necessary facilities outside of the USSR (the LNG carriers and receiving terminal) without a thorough understanding of the nature and reliability of the Soviet facilities. We know that it has been difficult in the past for American engineers to visit sites in the USSR and to participate in the detailed Soviet engineering work, but it is absolutely essential if a project of this type is to be financed and is to receive government approval. The Soviets seem to appreciate this fact and are working closely with us to find ways to meet the needs of the project.

Perhaps the biggest challenges do not lie in the Soviet Union at all, but rather in the United States. The Yakutia Project combines two subjects, both of which cause strong emotional reactions in the latter: first, technological transfer to the Soviet Union, and the on-going fear that Soviet military power may be enhanced by *any* purchase of advanced Western technology, and second, imports to the Americans of liquefied natural gas. Both of these subjects are hot items in Washington. Regrettably, these discussions are not based entirely on reason, but are sometimes involved with emotion and politics.

The timing of the development of our project is such that policy decisions and commitments from Washington will not be needed for several years, and we are hopeful that during this period policies will develop in both these areas to permit us to go forward.

This project brings together three very different systems of government. It is significant enough to ultimately require major policy decisions at high levels in each of the countries. In both the Soviet Union and Japan the major governmental policy commitments are made at an early stage in the project development, while in the United States the government remains relatively uninvolved until major commercial contracts have been signed, reserves are proven and preliminary engineering, economic and financing studies are completed. In view of what has transpired with attempts of American companies to buy Mexican gas, this may change. Both the Soviets and the Japanese are concerned about the lengthy American review and approval process for LNG projects, a process which historically takes two to three years. They also recognize there is a chance that, at the last minute, the Yakutia Project could be cancelled by a small group of policy-makers in Washington. However, the potential benefits to each of the three parties are great enough to keep everyone committed to crossing hurdles as they come.

The benefits to the USA and Japan are fairly obvious. First, a secure source of needed energy imports from another geographical and political source besides OPEC. The Soviet Union will be making a substantial financial commitment to this project and is committed to providing a long-term, reliable source of LNG. On the consumption side, natural gas provides more than 26% to 28% of the total energy consumed in the nation and is the source of about one-half of its non-transportation energy. There are now in the United States approximately 42 million homes that use natural gas.[9] Many industrial plants and commercial establishments also depend on natural gas for heating and processing purposes. Many different supplemental sources of natural gas, including this project, are needed to meet only the most essential future American requirements.

A second major benefit is the opportunity for jobs and export trade. If conditions in the USA allow for the sale and financing of petroleum technology to the Soviet Union, this project could generate in excess of $2 billion in American export trade. Further, American investors will be investing an additional $2 billion for the construction of necessary ships and the terminal. Because of these opportunities the project could have significantly positive employment and balance of payments benefits, particularly when compared with imported OPEC oil.

The benefits to the USSR are also very great. The project will generate a large and stable long-term source of hard currency, which will help finance additonal purchases from the western world. Hard currency earnings from oil and natural gas exports are of great importance; exports of oil and oil products earned 9.4 billion rubles for 1977, with more than half of this amount in the form of hard currency from the West. Sales of solid fuels and natural gas added another one billion rubles each to the Soviet export account.[10]

Of equal significance is the opportunity for a self-financing project to develop the infrastructure of Eastern Siberia and to provide natural gas for industrial development in the area. The pipeline will pass through several cities where electric power plants are already located; and thus the gas could ultimately be used to provide electricity to most of the Soviet Far East.

With these very strong driving forces on all three sides, we see the project as a logical and natural development with a good probability of eventual success.

V. Concluding Remarks

There is no question that Siberia represents a vast wealth of resources, not only for the USSR, but the entire world. Its potential is such that the adequacy of future worldwide supplies of many important materials may well depend on the extent of Soviet success in developing this potential. Nowhere is this more true or obvious than in oil and gas. Will the USSR be an energy importer in the 1980's, thereby worsening an already strained worldwide supply picture? Or, will be USSR continue to be a major energy exporter, thereby helping to alleviate potential shortages and the frictions that are created by such shortages? We must not lose sight of these worldwide benefits in the debate over how and whether the West should "participate" in one way or another in the development of Siberia.

Debate, particularly in the USA, often centers on whether the export of modern equipment and technology to the USSR is in the national interest.

To my knowledge, no one advocates the transferral of know-how that has obvious direct strategic and military application in the USSR. Such a course would be folly. Indeed, NATO countries have an effective, albeit somewhat lengthy, mechanism for ensuring that sensitive export products are withheld from Communist countries. This is proper and should continue. However, appropriate equipment and technology sales from NATO countries could play an important part in the development of Siberia.

There are few aspects of international life that are not directly or indirectly influenced by American-Soviet relations. It is certainly in everyone's interest to welcome and encourage improvement in this relationship. It is unrealistic to expect that the competitive aspects of these relations will ever entirely be transformed into cooperative efforts. Of course, our hope is that the shift will be toward cooperation, but both elements are an integral part of the relationship and there is nothing inconsistent in dealing with both the competitive and cooperative aspects at the same time. As Marshall Shulman, a former advisor to the Secretary of State, has said in testimony before Congress, "Common sense dictates that we should, while advancing our own interests and purposes energetically, seek to regulate the competitive aspects of the relationship to reduce the danger of war and at the same time to enlarge the areas of cooperation where our interests are not in conflict." Further explaining his ideas, Shulman noted, "....Substantial progress over the long run will be better served by specific actions on concrete problems based upon mutual self-interest than by symbolic gestures or abstract declarations about detente."[11] I believe the Yakutia Gas Project is one example of such a long-term, mutually beneficial opportunity.

Those of us involved in the Yakutia Gas Project attach some degree of importance to the dialogue and mutual understanding that are necessary and logical in such a long term venture resting on a foundation of mutual interest. Discussion and contact are certainly not a cure-all nor a guarantee of anything. But, in our minds, learning how to deal constructively with both the routine and complex issues raised in such a project unquestionably lessens the chance of misunderstanding in other areas.

Last, but not least, no observations on the Siberian development plans would be complete without mention of China. The Sino-Soviet relationship obviously deeply influences Soviet thinking and plans on many fronts. The recent dramatic moves to resume normalization of political and economic relations between the USA and China as well as Chinese purchases of Western military equipment may well speed up or alter Soviet Siberian development plans, although the general thrust and the planned end results will probably not change very much. The long term effect of the "China card," and all that the phrase implies, is certainly beyond my capability to predict. It is probably an understatement to say that the development of this triangular relationship will be a crucial and intriguing subject for all of us to watch during the coming decade.

Footnotes

1. *Deposits of Useful Minerals* (map). Edited by V.N. Prohorova. Prepared by Scientific-editorial map preparation division of GUGK in 1971 and corredted in 1977. Moscow: GUGK 1974, with changes in 1977.

2. T. Shabad and V.L. Mote, *Gateway to Siberian Resources (The BAM)*. New York, 1977.

3. J. Power, "Moscow's No. 1 American-Watcher Keeps Wary Eye on U.S. - China Ties", *International Herald Tribune*. November 11-12, 1978.

4. On the early Soviet trade treaty efforts, see B. Considine, *The Remarkable Life of Dr. Armand Hammer,* New York, 1975.

5. National Foreign Assessment Center, CIA. *International Energy Statistical Review.* ER IESR 78-015. Washington, D.C., November 29, 1978.

6. National Foreign Assessment Center, CIA *USSR: Development of the Gas Industry.* ER 78-10393. Washington, D.C., July, 1978.

7. *Ibid.*

8. El Paso LNG Company, *The LNG Carrier*. Houston, Texas, 1978.

9. American Gas Association, *Gas Facts 1977*. Arlington, Virginia, 1978.

10. P. Kuhl, "Soviet Foreign Trade", *Soviet Business and Trade*. Vol. VII, 12 (November 8, 1978).

11. M.D. Shulman, "Overview of U.S. — Soviet Relations", *The Department of State,* Bureau of Public Affairs, Office of Media Services. Washington, D.C., October 26, 1977.

Comment

Dr. Terence Armstrong

Dr. Shabad is an acknowledged authority on these matters, and I find much to applaud and little to criticize in his paper. But I will comment on a few points, and then elaborate a little on the shipping question, which interests me particularly.

I am not quite sure that I go along with his contention that Soviet planners have a "conscious strategy" for limiting labor for Siberia, or have "shelved further permanent settlement." Have they not been forced into this situation by lack of volunteers, and would they not take more labor if they could get it? The shift and expedition systems are by no means universally accepted, and the latest book on them (P. I. Zimin and V. G. Lazareva, *Vakhtennyye zhilyye kompleksy dlya severa,* Leningrad, 1978) concludes by listing their disadvantages as well as their advantages. But whatever the planners' intentions, the result, I agree, is the same--too few hands.

Long-distance power transmission is so obviously a key factor in the utilization of Siberian energy potential that it is slightly odd no solution seems to have been found yet. The west does not have the same incentive to find one, and perhaps this is an area where Soviet technology is deficient.

The likely delays in the Kansk-Achinsk complex were further confirmed by two *Pravda* articles on 22 and 23 March (after Dr. Shabad's paper was written), one on the mine and one on the town. But I daresay he would agree that lateness, even in a planned economy, is an inconvenience rather than a disaster. Things mostly get done in the end.

Now I should like to elaborate on his interesting and accurate remarks on shipping off the Soviet north coast. There has been a steady increase in activity here over the past several decades, so that besides ships, the USSR now has an invaluable (and unique, because no other country has it) pool of manpower trained in Arctic seafaring. How will these be deployed?

The claim is made that navigation in these waters is now year-round. First of all, that claim can refer only to the south-west part of the Kara Sea, and not to the other four-fifths of the route between Novaya Zemlya and Bering Strait, where the season remains about four months maximum. Secondly, even in the south-west Kara Sea the claim is barely substantiated, judging by press reports. Two separate operations take place at the start of each season in this area. One is to supply oil and gas exploration teams in Yamal. This has to be done when the ice is still present and frozen to the shore (fast ice); shallow water will not permit ships close inshore, so the fast ice is used as a quay stretching into deeper water. In the 1978 season voyages to Yamal started on 15 February and were completed by early

April. The second operation is the most important one on the whole northern sea route, servicing the mineral and timber industry on the lower Yenisey river. Traffic to the Yenisey started on 29 March--the earliest ever-- but the first ship arrived at its destination, Dudinka, only on 1 May. Another came a week later, but then there was a gap until late June. There- after traffic flowed more or less continuously until November, when the intention was expressed to keep the route open round the year. Press reports of continuing activity appeared at about fortnightly intervals until mid- February 1979 (thus completing the year?). After that there was one report (25 February) describing, without giving a date, how some very difficult conditions were surmounted, and then silence until 19 April, when a convoy was reported to be trying to reach the Yenisey through very heavy ice. It looks as if the spring months are still too difficult--but there is reason to believe that the present spring, and perhaps that of 1978 too, were anomalously bad for ice (the summer of 1978 certainly was). However, big advances were unquestionably made, and year-round operation may be achieved soon. The new ships are impressive in performance and may be able to continue to offset the longer-term deterioration of ice conditions which has now been fairly firmly demonstrated.

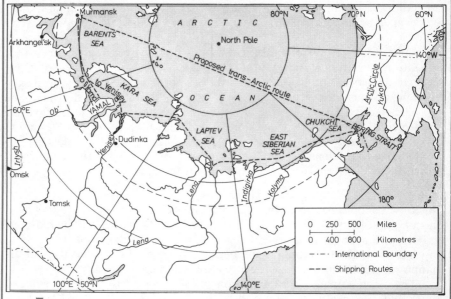

also want to draw attention to the new idea (dating from 1977) of pioneering a direct trans-Arctic sea route, as distinct from the now existing coastal route. The coastal route is the one giving access to northern Siberia, and we know it is increasingly needed for this purpose. Let us note in passing that it will be used this summer to transport major components of a French petro-chemical plant to Omsk and a British methanol plant to Tomsk. But the astonishing voyage of the icebreaker *Arktika* to the Pole in August 1977 (a 3,850-mile round trip completed in 14 days at an average speed of 11.5 knots) was stated by the Minister of the Merchant Fleet immediately after the voyage to be motivated by the desire to explore the possibility of a trans-Arctic route across the middle of the Arctic Ocean. Such a route would be 1,300 km shorter than the coastal route. There was a follow-up in 1978 when *Sibir,* the other large nuclear icebreaker, took a freighter across, in a more southerly latitude but at a more difficult time of year (May-June). The USSR could probably pioneer a route of this kind and use it for some months of the year--though freighters adequate in both strength and capacity would have to be built for the purpose. But it is hard to see why they need such a route. The northern sea route as a whole (as distinct from its parts) is very little used, and there seems to be no Soviet freight crying out for direct passage from Murmansk to Bering Strait and beyond. Nor is it clear that the gain in distance would not be nullified by the delays caused by heavier ice. But the deeper water should allow use of larger ships. Maybe the USSR prefers to pioneer and manage such a route, even if most users are non-Soviet, rather than see others do it. Long-term intentions here are still not clear.

Comment

Tony Scanlan

Before commenting on the interesting paper presented by James Lister on the Yakutia gas project, I feel it would be appropriate if I commented on the oil situation under the general heading given to this session on energy in Siberia and the Soviet Far East. I should like to draw some parallels between the Soviet position and that in the rest of the world. By approaching Mr. Lister's paper in this way I hope to provide three points:

1. There is a strong parallel between the problems caused by pressures on oil supplies in Comecon and the same pressures elsewhere.
2. The acceptability of "long-haul" gas is closely dependent upon the pressure on oil supplies.
3. The regional significance of Yakutia gas is quite different from that of oil in Asiatic USSR.

1. ■ Soviet oil reserves remain a state secret but for those in non-Communist areas we have a reasonable perspective of the amount of proven reserves that are technically recoverable and also of the annual rate at which we are adding new oil reserves. The BP annual Statistical Review (1978) currently lists these as about 555 billion (thousand million) barrels. Consumption is nearly 20 billion barrels each year. In simple terms it looks as though there are 28 years supply remaining, plus whatever is added from new discoveries or higher recovery.

Closer examination is not so reassuring. New discoveries are not keeping pace with consumption, indeed the last unique field of giant proportions (i.e. 5 billion recoverable barrels in one reservoir), was discovered ten years ago, on the North Slope of Alaska. I decline to use the older definition of "giant" meaning 100 million (repeat million) barrels which dates from an earlier age in the USA: now such an amount is used in less than a week in that country alone. Other oil provinces are, like the North Sea, precious additions to the world's "stocktank" of oil, but the trend to smaller fields and regional accumulations is inevitably meaning greater effort and above all longer *time* on the supply side of the oil equation, while on the other side, demand continues to rise. It may be that Mexico will arrest this disparity for a time, but a close reading of what Pemex are actually describing as the necessary logistics and *timescale* for some of their new finds will add to, rather than detract from, these comments.

In order to maintain flow rate, it has been observed that a comfortable relationship between rate of extraction and remaining recoverable reserves is that the latter should amount to the equivalent of 15 years extraction rate.

This is known as the "R/P Ratio" and although not a scientific term, the reserves/production ratio is a useful perspective. This means that remaining reserves are not equivalent to 28 years at current flow rates but only 13 years may elapse before daily flow rates become difficult to maintain. New discovery rates, if they continue to fall below annual consumption, will only defer the problem, and additional oil recovery from existing reservoirs is a slow process which may add a few percentage points to the amount of oil in place that is recovered, but over *time* rather than adding to the daily rate of flow. In a perfect world, you may observe, the problem is not immediate because we are constantly adding to reserves and still have at least a decade in hand before flow rates are jeopardised: but this once more is where the existence and location of the supergiant fields is critical. Two or three countries contain some 30 percent of recoverable world oil reserves and they by chance contain less than 0.5 percent of the population. Clearly, the position would be very different if this oil had happened to be located among the leading consuming nations.

If we consider the Soviet position, again by consulting the BP Statistical Review which quotes as far as possible official or authoritative sources, we can use the same criteria and it is immediately apparent that the USSR and its European associates in Comecon are already close to the 15 years R/P ratio. Oil reserves, if about 70 billion barrels, will have to support production at or above 600 million tons for CMEA countries in 1979 and 600-650 million tons next year. This will deplete existing reserves at between 4.4 and 4.8 billion barrels annually, so that whatever is added to either reserves or production will be starting from a 15:1 relationship.

This, in turn, focuses the burden on Siberian oil production. Looking back at my paper here in 1974, I am struck by the fact that so much was predictable, five or even ten years ago, about the prospects for oil in Western Siberia, especially the Tyumen region. What, in contrast, do we now see as the next "Tyumen" for the middle and late part of the next decade? What region contains the next Samotlor?

The total significance of Western Siberia can perhaps best be summed up in numbers. In 1980 it represented less than 10 percent of USSR production. Production in all other regions of the USSR last year combined was lower than in 1970, whereas Western Siberia was 5 million barrels per day above 1970 levels. Unless there is an unexpected shift in the pattern of development of useful but relatively tiny oil discoveries in areas such as the Baltic littoral, Sakhalin, and in the degree of success in attempts to arrest decline in the Caspian and Ural-Volga area, dependence upon Western Siberia will further increase. This is not to say that further major new areas may one day be added to the main producing regions of the USSR, but if these lie significantly further East or North, time would appear to prevent them from being capable of major development in the next decade.

2. It is in this context that there is increasing interest in the USSR gas potential. I would have little to disagree with in Mr. Lister's chart of world recoverable natural gas reserves by region except perhaps to suggest that there was even more in some Middle Eastern areas: but the award of first place to the USSR is widely accepted and the existence of a pipeline network from the Ob delta to Trieste and from the Iranian border to Western Europe is there for all to see. Both the USA and the European Community have taken a positive line against over-rapid substitution of gas for oil, for example in power generation, and it remains to be seen how the USSR will treat its use of gas: but if it is the case that current moves towards the accelerated use of nuclear power imply a selective use of the very considerable gas reserves, then the use of gas in export potential, both into the rest of CMEA and also as an earner of hard currency, partly in place of oil, is a major feature of the future Soviet energy scene.

3. ■ The Yakutia gas project is in a special place in this regard, because unlike any other major oil or gas producing region it is totally dependent on export viability. Mr. Lister has told us that only one-third of the production can be absorbed in the USSR If one had any doubt as to why this is so, his clear use of maps demonstrates that Yakutsk gas is far further to the East than Tyumen oil or Urengoi gas. It suffers from the same geographical disadvantage to the highly developed areas of the USSR as the brown coal deposits and hydropower schemes of the Lake Baikal area: it is further from Moscow than we are today. But as a currency earner the Japanese market it is competitively located in comparison with any other major source of Japanese gas imports.

It leaves may questions unanswered, however. If, as James Lister has described, it combines a pipeline over twice as long as Alyeska with a 5,000 mile LNG tanker voyage across the Pacific, what is the cost? Estimates of Eastern Hemisphere LNG delivered to the main continental USA start from $4 MMBTU or in the more familiar oil equivalent, $20 per barrel. This Yakutia project will surely exceed this cost. The $5 bn. capital estimate must be sensitive to delay and indeed I wonder whether one can really ascribe completion to the 1980's. Will not one of the major hurdles here, on all recent form, be in the USA and its lengthy procedures for approval? If the total volume for export could be absorbed in Japan, several of these problems would be removed. But I understand there is no question of a bilateral project so we are left with a 10,000 mile LNG round voyage with the hassle of entry into the US west coast at the end of it.

On the other hand, the rising pressure on oil supplies all over the world is bound to make "long-haul" gas more competitive and Mr. Lister has made it clear that the technical aspects of the project, including compatibility of equipment, and the financial implications have received careful study. It is an attractive diversification of hydrocarbon resources for Japan and the development is logistically attractive to the USSR in bringing to the Soviet Far East a major energy asset at acceptable cost, together with a valuable new source of hard currency earning, neither of which would be viable solely within the criteria of the internal economy of the USSR. The currency earning will have to allow for the effect of any compensating deliveries to pay for pipeline and other material imports used in the project: but by the time the Yakutia scheme may be developed it will be accelerating the net earning effect of the total Soviet gas export drive.

First we observe that the only statistically significant value is the correlation coefficient for the 1976-80 period: its level and sign indicate a strong inverse relationship between real income and welfate levels (as measured by our urbanization ratio proxy) and growth, suggesting a strong income distribution objective. But this is best approached within the entire context so let us look first at the others.

We note first that ranks are assigned in such a way that a positive correlation coefficient r_s implies that relatively faster growth is associated with lower urbanization ratios and negative values of r_s with higher growth rates for republics with higher urbanization ratios. Thus, a positive correlation coefficient implies a positive association between the rate of industrial growth and poverty, as indicated by the urbanization proxy.

We must, of course, avoid mechanical interpretation of the results, an effort aided, to be sure, by the fact that very little emerges which is statistically significant at conventional levels (5 percent or less). The 1971-75 attained rate suggests that, on the whole, inter-republic welfare differentials were reduced. The really interesting thing, though, is that this r_s was observed.

What happened? The rank correlation for planned growth was seriously affected by the change in the rank of a few key republics: Moldavia (planned rank 11, attained rank 2); Turkmen SSR (planned rank 15, attained rank 3)); and Armenia (planned rank 1, attained rank 8). The much higher attained than planned growth for the first two may have reflected the increasingly tense relations between the Soviet Union and the adjacent foreign countries, Moldavia adjacent to Rumania and Turkmenia next to Iran and Afghanistan, but growth in the latter also reflected the rapid development of the Turkmen oil based industries. Thus, while the much greater attained than planned rate for these two republics may well have been prompted by foreign policy and growth maximization concerns, it also worked in the direction of more equitable income distribution.

When we come to the 10th FYP, however, we observe a striking pattern of planned republic growth rates and urbanization levels. The high correlation coefficient—and the correspondingly high value of t—would occur purely by chance only with very low probability, less than once out of every five hundred times that such an experiment was conducted. While, as we have seen, it is possible for some republics to be both strategically situated and have low urbanization ratios, it is also possible for some to be strategically located and not (Armenia, for example). Thus, while a policy of satisfying strategic concerns might also have salubrious effects on income distribution, as it appears to have had in the previous quinquennium, as noted, a correlation coefficient as high as the one observed for the 10th FYP would seem to be more directly related to a conscious pattern of developing the poorer regions. But satisfying strategic concerns may also work against welfare equalization, as indeed seems to be the case in the pattern of planned growth rates for 1976-80, with a high rate of industrial growth being planned for Armenia, a republic with the fourth highest urbanization ratio. Incidentally, a greater concern with human side in the 10th FYP also shows up in the planned growth rate for group B—1.5 percentage points higher than that of group A.

Regarding the attained growth rates, however, the picture is rather different, the rank correlation coefficients for the first three years of the 10th FYP being, respectively .35, .5, and .2. While the last two coeficients (those for 1977 and 1978) are at least positive, they are so low as not to be inconsistent with a pattern of industrial growth which is random in relation to the urbanization ration, while in the first (that for 1976) the pattern of republic growth rates actually runs counter to urbanization patterns and, hence, works against the equalization of welfare levels.

It is interesting to examine the individual republic records of attained growth and urbanization which caused the rank correlation coefficients for attained growth to differ so sharply form that for planned growth in the 10th FYP and to explore the hypothesils that strategic considerations may have intervened to cause a pattern of growth rates which was inconsistent with promotion of welfare equalization. The most dramatic difference is observed in the shift from the significant and positive coefficient of the plan to the negative coefficient for 1975-76. Armenia did have a high attained rate, as in the plan although not actually equal to the planned rate, but the rates for a number of other republics changed drastically. Moldavia, so favored earlier in the plan and in the previous quinquennium, slipped to 11th place; this would seem to conflict with the hypothesis of strategic necessity until it is noted that its 10th FYP projected rate of growth of agriculture, the highest in the country, is 6.5% per year, over 50% higher than the republic next on the list, Armenia. Agriculture is probably capable of producing faster short term effects on living standards. On the other hand, a number of other strategically situated republics with high industrial growth plans— most notably all five Central Asian Republics — slipped sharply between their planned and attained growth rates. it is not that their planned rates were overly ambitious—except perhaps that the Kazakh Republic; the others were close to or less than their attained rates for 1971-75. It may simply be that, while in principle the government still would like to bolster these republics to levels projected in the plans, the enormous expenditure of resources further east is simply too much to support and still achieve.

Conclusions and Prospects

In this paper we have attempted to detect the main forces behind the pattern of attained and planned industrilal growth rates since 1965. No single broad social or economic policy emerges, and indeed, we scarcely expected that one would. Indeed, I am surprised that there was much coherence as has been observed—an apparent concern with reducing inequalities in real welfare levels being observed during the 10th FYP. to say this, of course is not to suggest that the regime in 1975 was inherently socially conscious; we must allow for the possibility of recognition on the leaders' part that the best way to minimize the threat of subversion and ensure that far-flung republics adhere to the national structure may be by putting bread on their tables. Nor does recognition of this basic tendency require that income distribution explicitly or implicitly be the only concern of national policy-making or that some investment may take place which undoes some of the equality which might otherwise be attained.

What does this general pattern as well as the specific developments of recent years presage for the future? As noted earlier, the rates of industrial growth are falling in almost all republics, suggesting that there may be real problems at hand. Part of it may be due to overcommitment and grandiose ambitions in the east and we must await the completion of some before there is a resurgence elsewhere (recall the tremendous share of investment in the Ural Kuznetsk Kombinat—25-40% of the total investment in industry and transportation).

Comment

Ann Helgeson

By now it is inexcuseable not to know about Soviet demographic problems, the resultant impending labor shortages and their regional outlines. One of the reasons for the recent increased interest in Soviet regional problems and perhaps the reason for the choice of the topic for this colloquium is a recognition of the problems created by regional differentials in population growth and labor supply.

I congratulate Professor Eason on a very interesting and informative paper and especially for his efforts in collecting and processing oblast-level data. He says that the purpose of his paper is "to examine the changes in the population variables that underlie the changes in labor supply, and in particular to examine their regional manifestations." He has accomplished this laudably--certainly at least with respect to the natural increase of population and its regional diversity.

In Eason's discussion of the dimensions of the demographic problem he lists declining fertility and its localization in the Slavic regions of the country, the resultant labor imbalances and the pressures which these cause for labor planners. But it should be pointed out that there are two components of population change in a system of regions: natural increase (or decrease) and migration.

Most regions of the USSR have experienced a demographic transition from high levels to low levels of fertility and mortality, with the commonly observed intermediate stage of rapid population growth. Populations also experience a mobility transition at the end of which high levels of migration and complex patterns of circulation occur. Most of the USSR has experienced this--with the exception of Central Asia. Once migration has been established as a common phenomenon it can yield much quicker results for the regional redistribution of labor. (You don't have to wait for a newborn child in a labor deficit region to reach the age of 16.)

The projections done by the Foreign Demographic Analysis Division, extremely useful as they are as Prof. Eason has shown in his paper, are based on the assumption of no internal migration. Yet migration increases annually in the USSR and today about 12 million persons change their place of residence every year.

n principle labor supply problems in Soviet industry might be alleviated by a redistribution of the working-age population into line with the territorial distribution of economic activity. The net results of internal migration in recent years, however, indicate that, far from effecting a rational redistribution of population, internal migration has exacerbated the

Table 1
Age-Specific Net Migration 1959-70 (in thousands)

Eastern USSR:[1]

10-19	+ 28	2.3%
20-29	+ 554	45.7%
30-39	+ 111	9.2%
40-49	− 271	22.4%
50-59	− 97	8.0%
60-69	− 52	4.3%
70-79	− 98	8.1%
10-79	+ 174	

Siberia & Far East:

10-19	− 355	23.0%
20-29	+ 270	17.5%
30-39	− 227	14.7%
40-49	− 308	20.0%
50-59	− 185	12.0%
60-69	− 149	9.7%
70-79	− 48	3.1%
10-79	− 1,003	

Southern USSR:[2]

10-19	+ 985	31.4%
20-29	+ 124	4.0%
30-39	+ 823	26.3%
40-49	+ 475	15.2%
50-59	+ 363	11.6%
60-69	+ 316	10.1%
70-79	+ 47	1.5%
10-79	+ 3,133	

Regions containing Republic capitals + Leningrad Oblast:

10-19	+ 919	28.4%
20-29	+ 1,054	32.6%
30-39	+ 602	18.6%
40-49	+ 288	8.9%
50-59	+ 183	5.7%
60-69	+ 129	4.0%
70-79	+ 59	1.8%
10-79	+ 3,234	

RSFSR:

10-19	− 700	32.6%
20-29	− 29	1.4%
30-39	− 569	26.5%
40-49	− 272	12.7%
50-59	− 298	13.9%
60-69	− 254	11.8%
70-79	− 25	1.3%
10-79	− 2,147	

Moscow, Leningrad, Kiev, & Minsk Obs.:

10-19	+ 525	25.6%
20-29	+ 815	39.7%
30-39	+ 345	16.8%
40-49	+ 191	9.3%
50-59	+ 77	3.7%
60-69	+ 56	2.7%
70-79	+ 43	2.1%
10-79	+ 2,051	

Central Asia & Kazakhstan:

10-19	+ 383	30.0%
20-29	+ 284	22.2%
30-39	+ 338	26.4%
40-49	+ 37	2.9%
50-59	+ 89	7.0%
60-69	+ 97	7.6%
70-79	− 50	3.9%
10-79	+ 1,178	

[1]Eastern USSR includes Central Asia, Kazakhstan, Siberia and the Far East.
[2]Southern USSR includes the Ukraine, Moldavia, the Caucasian Republics, Central Asia and Kazakhstan, the North Caucasus Economic Region and Volgograd, Astrakhan and Kalmyk regions.
Source: Ann Helgeson, *Soviet Internal Migration and its Regulation Since Stalin: The Controlled and the Uncontrollable,* (Unpublished PhD thesis, University of California, Berkeley, 1978), p. 85.

maldistribution problem. Chronic labor deficit regions like Siberia and the Far East lost net migrants to other Soviet regions and Central Asia gained migrants. (See Table 1)

Eason implicitly considers the role of internal migration in defining labor supply potential as roughly equivalent to the rural population reservoir. He has held up the possibility of, although he has certainly not prophecied, compensating migration from his medium LSP region to the low LSP regions. But based on the experience of net migration in recent years, I find this highly improbable. The rural surpluses or potential surpluses are only potential migrants. (See Map : rural-urban migration during the last intercensal period, 1959-1970.)

Although net rural losses are ubiquitous on the map, the rates of rural out-migration show an important regional variation. Above average rates of rural out-migration are nearly all in the north. With the exception of oblasts around Kiev, Belorussia, a couple of places in the Caucasus, Tashkent Oblast and three oblasts in northeastern Kazakhstan, all of the above average rates of rural out-migration are in the RSFSR. Below average rates, again with few exceptions, notably the Far North and the Far East, are concentrated in the non-Russian republics. All of the exceptionally low rates are in Kazakhstan and Central Asia.

In the RSFSR almost all regions lost over 20 percent of their rural populations; many lost over a third. Nearly two-thirds of rural losses were under the age of 30. Among persons aged 20-29 in 1970, those who had moved from rural areas to the towns outnumbered those who remained. These are the parents of the entrants to the workforce in the 1990's, and the number of their offspring will be less than if they had remained in rural areas. Those remaining in the countryside will not reproduce even the deficit numbers of agricultural workers present today in European Russia. To give some idea of the composition of the agricultural labor force in European Russia we might repeat that in 1967 in the Central Economic Region 55 percent of all men and 80 percent of all women employed in agriculture were under the age of 20 or over the age of 60.

So, the numbers of rural-urban migrants in European Russia and the demographic effects of the departure of those in the childbearing ages on future natural growth in the countryside suggests that the rural reservoir of urban labor is drying up.

On the other hand, rates of rural out-migration are below average in the non-Russian republics and in the southernmost region of the RSFSR, the North Caucasus. This lesser inclination to make the move to the towns is not entirely explained by ethnic factors. Certainly in Central Asia the language and cultural barrier to movement into the urban 'Soviet' culture is operating. Yet in the Ukraine and the North Caucasus this cannot explain the lesser propensities to move. We might suggest that life is better in the villages of the south, positively luxurious in some of the large rural settlements in, for example, Krasnodar Kray in the North Caucasus where agricultural success not only provides high quality food, but kolkhoz profits which enable the construction of modern housing and even resort sanatoria. And urban migrants are attracted into the cities of these labor surplus regions. So, left to their collective inclinations, the rural population of the south cannot be expected to move to cities in their own regions to say nothing of northern regions of labor shortage.

Eason's high LSP regions are characterized by, in general, the lowest rates of rural out-migration. On the other hand the low LSP regions, those facing impending labor shortages, in European Russia and West Siberia, are characterized by the highest rates of out-migration. A comparison of this map with Map 1 in Eason's paper suggests that rural-urban migration will not solve the problem.

Rural Out-Migration Rates 1959-1970
(Cohorts aged 10-79 in 1970)

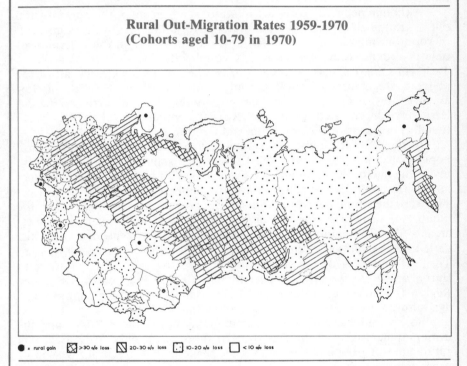

● = rural gain   ⊠ >30 o/o loss   ⧄ 20-30 o/o loss   ⬚ 10-20 o/o loss   ☐ < 10 o/o loss

Finally, it is important to realize that, unlike the situation in earlier periods, Soviet labor cannot be moved around at the will of the planners. We must expunge from our minds the image of platoons and divisions of Orgnabor recruits dutifully lined up at the railroad station. At a time when a finely-tuned and efficiently distributed labor force is essential to the success of Soviet industrial goals, control over the behavior of workers has been eroded. Workers, and the population in general, are more free to move about the country according to their individual inclinations than ever before in Soviet history. Stalinist programs geared to labor mobilization and the prevention of unplanned mobility have been either repealed (the 1940 decree making unauthorized job-leaving a criminal offense was repealed in 1956), reduced in scope (Orgnabor in the 1960's placed only a fourth of the recruits placed in the 1950's), or reorganized in principle (under the 1974 passport regulations collective farmers will receive passports as everyone else, ending special mobility restrictions on this class; the residence permit system for the entire population has been streamlined, although not abolished). These and other institutional changes have made migration destinations a matter of personal choice. The result has been a demonstrable conflict between the residence preferences of individuals and those of industrial planners. We can no longer speak of the Soviets *moving* labor, as Eason does in his paper, but only of *attracting* labor.

All this is not to detract from Professor Eason's excellent paper, but rather to supplement his remarks with another dimension of population change.

Dr. J. N. Westwood

Current Position:
Reader,
Center for Russian Studies,
University of Birmingham,
Birmingham, England

Other remarks:
Lectured in the Universities of Florida
State, McGill and Sydney, economic
consultant to Canadian National
Railways, (1957-59).

Transportation and the Military Significance of Regionalization

Variations in the Transport System at the Regional Level: the Role of BAM (I)

Dr. J.N. Westwood

Full details are lacking about the Soviet railway crisis in January, 1979. Apparently the Southern Urals and Western Siberian lines were the worst affected by the exceptionally harsh winter, and for a few days all efforts were concentrated on passing coal and oil trains. Since parts of the east-west main line between Novosibirsk and Cheliabinsk are said to work on a normal day at over 95 percent of their theoretical capacity,[1] it is hardly surprising that technical failures occasioned by remarkably low temperatures should cause massive breakdowns in traffic flows. Press comment was expectedly sparse and superficial,[2] but it can hardly be doubted that this alarming, if temporary, crisis will affect the attitude of the Soviet leadership towards transport policy. Over the last decade or so there has been a greater awareness of transport costs than in the more distant past, when the overriding criterion was the sheer ability to deliver goods at any price. The January 1979 difficulties must surely have put this new attitude in question or, as some would express it, have emphasized that a transport system which offers the lowest cost per ton/kilometre is not necessarily the cheapest.

A railway operating at over 95 percent of its theoretical capacity is, in practical terms, perilously overloaded, and it is this overload that is the fundamental explanation of Soviet transport difficulties. A policy of integrated regional development offers an alleviation of the problem because to some extent it enables shorter-haul intra-regional traffic to replace the longer inter-regional hauls.

Regionalization means different things to different people. For the Soviet leadership it means a distribution of new economic activity that requires the minimum investment in new transport facilities. For transport managers, those actually responsible for freight movement, it seems to have little significance except as a slogan with which to buttress proposals for new or improved facilities. It is among the academics and the planners that the concept has best flourished, primarily as a new way to look at old problems. However, expository difficulties arise because transport is, from the economic point of view, both the subject and object of regionalization. Regionalization depends absolutely and unavoidably on transport, and the transport system is intended at the same time to be a main beneficiary of regionalization. Once this is established, further theoretical discussion gravitates towards statements of the obvious, a difficulty which Soviet scholars manfully tackle, either by pretending that old topics (like the choice of new routes or the coordination of different forms of transport) are essentially regionalization topics, or by using turgid language to disguise platitudes like 'The particular significance of transport resides in the circumstance that with its assistance connections are accomplished between separate components of an economic region...'[3]

Another academic wrote a more useful declaration in 1952 about the role of transport in regionalization, '...transport of production must satisfy the requirement of the least possible expenditure...for the maximum economic result'. When this was published (twenty years later),[4] it became perhaps the most rational of the standards against which Soviet transport researchers evaluate regionalization projects. Moreover, it required the proper costing of operations, and the intellectual discipline that such costing demands. In the more distant past there was a much vaguer approach to regionalization, usually limited to ascribing to regional policy decisions that would have been made in any case. Thus the early regionalization scheme associated with GOELRO in the 1920's, which proposed 'super-mainline' electrified railway links, was quoted as theoretical justification for the policy of restoring to reasonable standards just the most crucial routes, a policy which was in reality imposed by the

Table 1[5]

	Kilometres of railway per 100 square km of territory	Kilometres of road per 100 square km of territory	Kilometres of railway per 1000 inhabitants	Kilometres of road per 1000 inhabitants
USSR	0.6	6.0	0.5	5.4
RSFSR	0.4	4.4	0.5	5.7
Ukraine	3.6	34.7	0.5	4.3
Byelorussia	2.6	31.7	0.6	7.1
Lithuania	3.0	51.0	0.6	10.3
Latvia	3.8	38.0	1.0	9.0
Estonia	2.2	57.0	0.7	18.2
Moldavia	3.3	30.3	0.3	2.7
Georgia	2.0	30.3	0.3	4.5
Azerbaijan	2.1	24.7	0.3	3.9
Armenia	1.9	30.0	0.2	3.1
Kazakhstan	0.5	4.0	1.0	8.0
Uzbekistan	0.7	6.5	0.2	2.3
Kirgizia	0.2	10.2	0.1	6.4
Tadjikstan	0.2	9.2	0.1	4.1
Turkmenia	0.5	1.9	0.9	3.7

combination of war-torn railways and scarce resources.

A statistical approach to regional transport became possible through the concept of 'proportional development' as an objective of Soviet regionalization. Progress towards this goal could be measured by comparing the densities of regional transport networks. The resultant tables were commonly used to illustrate textbooks; they were less helpful than they might have been because they compared republics rather than regions and because the Russian Republic, with its broad expanse of virgin territory, is both dominant and untypical. Here is one recent such table, more useful than most because it treats two forms of transport.

Tables like this do at least suggest the wide variation in transport facilities to be found in the USSR. The exceptional situation of the Baltic republics--Lithuania, Latvia, and Estonia--is evident. These three regions represent one extreme of the Soviet transport patterns, resembling Eastern Europe more than the other parts of the USSR. They have arrived at a stage when transport facilities may be redundant rather than insufficient; in fact over the last decade their railway mileage has declined in the face of highway 'competition'. The opposite extreme is not well represented in the table; while the smaller Central Asian republics certainly present low indices (as opposed to Kazakhstan, which has benefitted greatly from Soviet transport policy), they are nevertheless well-off in comparison not with other republics, but with certain other regions. Perhaps a good example of very elementary regional facilities is the area of the Upper Kolyma and Indigirka rivers in the Far East. This is one of those areas where the definition of an economic region is simple because there is a single transport artery (in this case the Kolyma Highway from the coast into the interior) which forms the axis, and defines the limits, of economic development.

The great difference between transport facilities in this eastern region and the Baltic republics may be ascribed to their different stages of economic development. Categorization by development stage is a useful technique, but there are others. Notably, regional transport patterns may be affected by geography. In the Caucasian republics there is a discernible difference between Georgia and Armenia on the one hand, and Azerbaizhan on the other. Most of the economic activity of the latter takes place in the extensive lowlands, and railways and highways tend to follow the same routes, whereas in Georgia and Armenia, mainly mountainous, much of the highway mileage is in areas devoid of railways. (Nevertheless, say the Georgians, more roads are needed because of the depopulation of roadless mountain districts).

Even without the six exceptional situations presented by the three Baltic and three Caucasian republics, the Soviet regions are too numerous to permit a grand tour within the limitations of this paper. Instead, just a handful will be examined, including the region of the new Baikul Amur Railway. These variations reflect their history as much as their geographies or stages of economic maturity, for there is a time in the life of every economic region when a permanent transport pattern may be established by one key decision. Such key decisions are affected by the technical, political and social possibilities of their time, which means that the period in which they are made can determine the present-day situation. For the region of the Baikal Amur Railway that decisive period is evidently right now, but in European Russia there are regions whose shape derives from the first years of the railway age, if not earlier. Over a century ago, Tsar Nicholas I's St. Petersburg to Moscow Railway set the pattern for the region through which it passed. Even though many roads and railways have been built since, that pattern still dominates; Novgorod now has good links with the two capitals, but it has never recovered from the reverse it suffered when the Tsar's railway passed it by. Some Soviet geographers now see this Railway as the axis of a new territorial production complex, given the expansion towards each other of the electrified Moscow and Leningrad rail commuter services.[6] Such an axial conurbation, 400 miles long, is not an inviting prospect, although it would enable those who now are not permitted to live in the two capitals to at least settle in a place that they could imagine to be Moscow or Leningrad. There is, of course, among Soviet geographers an unflagging zeal for the uncovering of new territorial production complexes, and this may be one result of such assiduity. All the same, the suggestion of a *randstad* along the October Railway does emphasize how long-past decisions affect today's transport patterns.

The economic development of the North Caucasus by means of the Vladikavkaz Railway in the 19th century seems likely to remain a classic example of a long-term, stage-by-stage, establishment of a regional transport system and of successful colonization without the intervention of planners in the modern sense of the word. Barely a decade after that region had been cleared of hostile tribesmen a private company began to create a new economic unit for the tsarist empire. This company, the Vladikavkaz Railway, finished its 698 km (434 mile) main line from Rostov-on-Don to Vladikavkaz (now Ordzhonikidze) in 1872. It would be an exaggeration to ascribe the economic blossoming of the region, which the railway brought, simply to the benefits of free enterprise, for in many important respects state organizations and dignitaries assisted the company. Both for reasons of state and for private gain there were many powerful figures who had an interest. The Vice-Regent of the North Caucasus was all in favor of economic development, and regarded the Railway as the best possible catalyst. The War Ministry welcomed the Railway because it aided troop movements in a border region. The Ministry of Finance shared the vision that first inspired the Company's promoters, of North Caucasus wheatfields bringing in foreign currency through the Black Sea ports.

After 1884, when the recently virgin territory served by the Railway at last began to produce profitable traffic, a succession of extensions and branches were built to enlarge the grain-growing hinterland and to connect with ice-free Novorossiisk on the Black Sea. At this location the Company created a new port with modern elevators and loaders, and at the same time erected other elevators at inland stations; the Company's management, which consisted largely of engineers, may not have used the word *kompleksnost'*, but this did not prevent it from evolving an integrated grain operation. Nowhere else in Russia was grain traffic handled so efficiently. Meanwhile the Railway extended itself to Petrovsk (Makhach Kala), where it provided an icebreaker and erected oil storage tanks. A long branch to Tsaritsyn (Volgograd) enabled timber brought down the Volga to be sent on by train into the North Caucasus. The Kislovodsk branch and its associated developments created a tourist industry.[7]

The North Caucasus still produces one tenth of Soviet grain, and that other creation of the Railway, the Grozny oil industry, has since become the basis of a flourishing chemical industry. The Railway's port of Novorossiisk is now the biggest port of the USSR. In Soviet times further railways have been built, notably to the Black Sea resorts, and tourist possibilities have also brought a better-than-average provision of highways and of air services. But in general the transport pattern is still recognizably that created by the Vladikavkaz Railway. In brief, the Railway fulfilled the requirement of 'the least possible expenditure...for the maximum economic result'. It may be noted that the initial stimulus had been provided by the potential of just one kine of traffic, grain, and other traffics were picked up on the way, as extras. This seems to be a frequent pattern in Russian transport development, and is paralleled by colonizing railways elsewhere in the world.

In the early 20th century there were two other large railway-based colonizing ventures, the Trans Siberian of the tsarist regime and the Murmansk project of the early Soviet years. The Trans Siberian scheme is too well-known to warrant description in detail, but it is worthwhile to recall a few fundamentals. It was certainly a case of deliberate regional development, but its initial motivation was the exploitation of a single valuable resource, in this case farmland. Rather like the present-day Baikal Amur Railway, where another resource, oil, is the prime motivation, the opportunity was taken to achieve other desirable economic objects at the same time. In other words, a 'complex' approach was adopted, and in the end more money was spent on the secondary objects than on the primary. However, the exploitation of farmland was carried out successfully, and in Western Siberia the beginnings of what might nowadays be called agricultural production complexes can be discerned in the processing and marketing facilities that were provided for the farming communities. To regard the Siberian butter trains, carrying animal oils to Britain, as precursors of the unit trains that will carry Siberian mineral oils to Japan, may be fanciful in terms of scale but is consistent from the technical point of view. That there was little integrated industrial development along the line was simply because the time was not right, not because the imagination was lacking. In any case, the exploitation of on-line coal deposits for the benefit of the Railway's locomotives can be taken as an elementary manifestation of integrated development. Noteworthy, too, was the carefully considered coordination of river and rail, with the provision of boats and transhipment facilities to enable the north-south rivers to act as feeders to the east-west Railway. In the Soviet period much more was done, and the line can be regarded as the spine of a widely spread economic belt.

Why then was the Trans Siberian Railway not an unqualified success? One reason was that it was built in a hurry. Among other things, this meant that during its construction not enough money was available to provide a well-built line. The American expedient was adopted of building to low standards and relying on future traffic to pay for infrastructural improvements. But what worked in the USA did not necessarily work in Russia. Another difficulty was that the economic motivation and justification of the line, the agricultural development of Western and Central Siberia, was soon submerged by other considerations, especially military, naval, and political considerations. These led to the spending of large sums on building the Railway through Manchuria and later along the Amur, sums which could hardly be justified in terms of economic return and whose military and political objects can be seen, in retrospect, to have been negative and directly or indirectly giving rise to enormous military as well as constructional costs. At the same time as resources were found for building unprofitable line, thanks to military demands, the section of the Railway which did have good prospects was starved of capital. Lastly, however carefully the planners might plan, cardinal assumptions had to be made and it is unsurprising that some should have been falsified by events. As with the Baikal Amur Railway, much depended on assumptions about what the Chinese and Japanese might do, and the reactions of these two nations were not accurately foreseen. Providing a common-carrier transport facility is very much a wager, and one factor which makes it so is the inability to forecast accurately the traffic that will present itself.

The Karelo-Murmansk development scheme, based on the Murmansk Railway and determining the future transport pattern of that region, stands outside the mainstream of Russian and Soviet regional development. Its exceptional feature was that the role of transport (in this case the Murmansk Railway) was not the exploitation of a particular resource. It was rather the resources which were to exploit the Railway. The Murmansk Railway had been hurriedly completed in 1916 as a means of connecting the Russian war economy with a warm-water port open to Allied shipping. As the Civil War drew to a close the line was in a threadbare condition and there were proposals for its closure. After all, it served an undeveloped and largely unpopulated region and, with the end of hostilities, it seemed to lack any worthwhile traffic. The Railway's management had other ideas, and with little difficulty persuaded the Transportation Commissariat to take up its proposal. This proposal was for the 'Canadization' of the line; that is, to save the Railway by the Canadian or American land-grant device. This was a period when Russian state bodies were open to all kinds of novel suggestions, and the North Western Economic Council and the State Colonization Research Institute accepted the idea, which envisaged the transformation of the Railway into a colonizing agency, with the grant to the Railway of a 40-verst belt of territory along the 1,045 km (650 mile) Petrozavodsk-Murmansk line. Exploitation of this land would provide the money to rehabilitate the Railway, and parcels of land could be offered to incoming settlers. The scheme was bitterly opposed by the Northern Timber Trust, which asked how the management of a 'second-rate railway...rich only in deficits'[8] could find the experience and the means to indulge in territorial development. Moreover, claimed the Timber Trust, giving over vast areas of forest to the Railway would undermine its own rights and lead to harmful competition. In the end, the scheme was approved by the government, but thanks to the opposition, the Railway received less territory than had been hoped, and some of its activities could only be undertaken in cooperation with the baleful Timber Trust, or under the supervision of the Commissariat of Lands. In general, then, the scheme was integrated, but at the same time did not represent a coordinated approach by a group of involved departments. It was rather a plan worked out, and intended to be carried out, by one state agency against others. Or, as it was expressed at the time, the plan was a 'dialectical synthesis'.[9]

The new combine divided itself into five departments (railway, forestry, fisheries, colonization and Murmansk port) and began to build a miniature planned economy in the region. Integration of the five departments was very close, with the railway providing boilers for the forestry department's steamers, and the latter providing timber to make the fisheries' boats and barrels. There was a satisfying growth in all departments, albeit from a very low level. But despite its success, the combine was dissolved in 1927, its constituent parts going to the appropriate ministries. Evidently it did not fit the changing face of the USSR, and it may be surmised that those who had opposed its establishment had been working actively for its downfall. But short-lived though it was, the combine had succeeded in its main aim, the preservation of the Murmansk Railway. In time, enough mineral traffic was generated to make worthwhile the electrification of the Railway's northern section, and the line is still the main artery of the region, new rail and road facilities being very restricted and built in connection with, or in reference to, the original main line.

The general relationship in the interwar period between transport and regional development is well known.[10] The stated aim of evening out development levels between the regions was a very long-term ambition, and in those years carried out only partially. When transport facilities were built in formerly neglected areas they were for the purpose of obtaining a particular raw material; regional objectives were very much secondary, even though some regions, like Kazakhstan, did benefit disproportionately from new access railways. Transport objectives were evaluated in terms of physical means and possibilities, with little reference to costs apart from the fixing of cost-unrelated freight rates to make the economics of a project look more attractive. The first of the great undertakings, the Urals-Kuzbas Combine, was preceded by a rate concession for Kuzbas coal which the railway authorities believed was intended to help the then-depressed Kuzbas coal enterprises to find a market in European Russia.[11] Two decades later the burdens imposed on the railways by this combine were realized;[12] the location of processing industries closer to their raw material source then received more attention and irritable references to excessive length of freight hauls grew in frequency. But it has to be remembered that the pre-war desire to shift the center of industrial gravity more towards the east would have been difficult to achieve without an increase in the average length of haul.

The transport development of Northern Kazakhstan in connection with the Virgin Lands project of the 1950's may be taken as an intermediate stage in regional transport policy. Again it was the physical possibilities that determined the choice of facilities, but there was serious discussion in which both comparative costs and the integrated approach received more attention. Unfortunately, most of the discussion seems to have occurred only after the initial decisions had been taken.

The Virgin Lands lie south of the Trans Siberian Railway between Cheliabinsk and Omsk, and north of the South Siberian Railway between Kartaly and Pavlodar. These two lines are roughly parallel and about 400 km (250 miles) apart. In September 1954 a third east-west line was authorized, to run midway between these two for some 830 km (515 miles); passing through the heart of the Virgin Lands, this Central Siberian Railway was intended to open up a belt of territory too far distant to be well-served by the existing lines. This belt could be regarded as some 100 km (62 miles) wide on each side of the line, which in a grain area implies a high level of traffic. Perhaps the most interesting feature was that this line was to be of narrow gauge.

The start of the Virgin Lands campaign was accompanied by narrow gauge railway projects elsewhere in the region, often involving lines of more than 100 km (62 miles) in length, designed as feeders to the main broad gauge lines but at the same time expected to constitute an interconnected narrow gauge system with its own organizational structure. Of the 2,132 km (1,324 miles) of new line scheduled for construction in 1955-57 by the Party directives, 1,950 km (1,211 miles) were to be of narrow gauge. Only 3,500 km (2,173 miles) of new road were scheduled for the same period.[13] This programme soon ran into difficulties, and was only partially realized. Not all the lines were finished. Some remained projects only, others were finally built to broad gauge or, quite often, converted to broad gauge after completion. Others still remain as isolated narrow gauge lines. In 1961-65, 800 km (496 miles) of narrow gauge lines were laid in the Virgin Lands, and several hundred had already been laid in the preceding six years. But this burst of narrow gauge activity was short lived. As for the Central Siberian Railway, this was built less as a mainline narrow gauge railway than as a succession of short lines, some broad and some narrow, which happened to make end-on connections with each other. Usually the earliest sections were narrow gauge, and the later sections broad gauge, while some lines were begun as narrow gauge but completed as broad gauge. Evidently it had become clear at some point that narrow gauge trackage was not, after all, the best option. The present situation of this line is that it is now entirely broad gauge, some of the most hastily built sections are being upgraded to the mainline standards of the other sections, and its last line (Kustanoi-Uritskoye) is listed for completion in the present Five Year Plan, more than a quarter century behind schedule.

The odd reversion to narrow gauge, usually considered to be an outmoded form of transport, was a manifestation of the spirit of that time. The Virgin Lands scheme was carried out by men in a hurry, and the narrow gauge option may well have seemed to be that which was most likely to provide the needed carrying capacity in the shortest possible time. It was cheaper and quicker to build than broad gauge, and in the circumstances of Northern Kazakhstan, where roadstone had to be obtained from afar, it was also quicker and perhaps cheaper to build than light hard-top roads, for it could be laid directly on the surface of the land without any need for special infrastructure. In the case of the Central Siberian Railway, it is hard to repress the suspicion that the Ministry of Transport had its own reasons for keeping to itself any doubts about the choice of narrow gauge; in the end the Ministry got what it had long wanted, a new east-west main line paralleling a busy section of the Trans Siberian. The needs of the Virgin Lands and the apparent cheapness of narrow gauge construction perhaps made palatable to the Soviet leadership a new railway alignment which in other circumstances it would have rejected. Once the decision was made to lay a line, plans could be made to upgrade it to the standard required by the Ministry. This, of course, is what happened; the intra-regional narrow gauge railway has become a broad gauge route of considerable inter-regional importance.

Professor Osorgin, in his 1957 assessment of Northern Kazakhstan transport,[14] wrote some polite comments about the narrow gauge, but the cost data that he presented implied quite plainly that these lines could not be justified on strict economic grounds. At best, the narrow gauge railway could be the most suitable form of transport for routes of from 100 to 300 km carrying a moderate traffic (100,000 ton/km per km total of both directions). The highway was cheaper for all tonnages up to 100 km and for small tonnages up to 300 km, while the broad gauge railway was best over 100 km where the traffic exceeded 100,000 ton/km per km. The basic conclusion of Osorgin's study was that thousands of kilometers of new hard-surfaced roads were needed (highway truck costs on average double over unsurfaced roads). Some of his proposed main roads, like the Cheliabinsk-Akmolinsk-Karaganda route, were to run alongside railways, a mature recommendation for that period. Perhaps to mollify those critics who asserted that Northern Kazakhstan was not a true economic region because it lacked industry, the study suggested how new roads might help the development of local industry; the latter would be orientated towards agricultural needs, but there was also suggested a more intensive exploitation of Ekibastuz coal, which would be moved to Omsk by a new direct railway. A few of these recommendations have since been put into effect, so although research was too late to deter the initial false steps, it may perhaps have assisted in determining subsequent choices.

Current emphasis on the integrated development of economic regions seems to have been stimulated, or at least reinforced, by the problem of exploiting the Western Siberian oil reserves revealed in the 1960's. The aim of 'complex' development, a minimization of long-distance freight traffic by the establishment of inter-related industries close to sources of energy, is complemented by new methods of transporting energy, notably by pipeline and high-tension electric cable. In the case of Western Siberia it has been the pipeline rather than territorial production complexes which, so far, has been the most significant resort.

Investment in Western Siberian transport is very different from that required by a previous re-orientation of the Soviet oil industry. When the Volga oilfields were developed a good railway network already existed, because this was a region of long-standing development. Only one major new railway needed to be built, from Ufa to Ishimbaevo. Elsewhere, new short roads were sufficient. But Western Siberia was a territory at that primitive stage of development when the helicopter and the snow-train become the essential mechanical links with the outside world, and where the main trunk route is a river open for only half a year. Rationally enough, oil and gas pipelines were chosen as the transport media most suitable for moving the output to the consuming centers; it was this task which has dominated discussion of the exploitation of these resources, although there is talk now of establishing more local industries, based largely on timber resources. However, pipeline is only a single-purpose medium, and the problem remained of supplying the oilfield with all the materials needed for development and all the goods required to make life less unattractive. As waterway transport was already established, there was a strong current of opinion that held that other forms of long-distance transport, like a railway, were not really needed.[15] The case for the waterway was particularly strong because construction costs of both railway and highway were very high because of the swampy terrain.

Nevertheless a rail link was chosen. Of the several alternative routes, that proceeding north-eastwards from Tyumen' through Tobol'sk to Surgut (the presumed center of the new oilfield) was selected. An immediate benefit, on the line reaching Tobol'sk, was that the existing river shipments could henceforth use the latter as a transhipment port, thereby shortening the river segment of the haul. Despite the swamps and despite above-estimate expenditure, the line was pushed forward. Beyond Surgut there were two possibilities. One was an extension northwards into the oil and gas areas of the region, with an eventual terminus in the Far North at Noril'sk; this ambitious scheme is already underway. Secondly, to embrace oil areas north of the Ob' and east of Surgut, an extension eastwards was advocated in some quarters (and opposed in others).[16] This easterly extension in due course was to become a segment of the proposed east-west route known as the North Siberian Railway. However, since the River Ob' and the proposed railway are parallel, the arguments for developing the waterway instead of building a railway were quite strong, and could be demonstrated in comparative costings which showed that for most tonnage/distance permutations waterway transport would be cheaper.[17]

Nevertheless, the eastward extension as well as the northern are proceeding. Although the waterway is still used east of Surgut, it is uncertain how long it will survive as a major carrier. Throughout the Soviet period neither official exhortations nor favorable cost comparisons have done much to direct to the waterways traffic normally carried by the railways. This is a problem about which volumes could be written; here a few observations must suffice. Firstly, in terms of regional development and with some notable exceptions like raw timber and sand traffic a general rule may be propounded that waterway transport can be of first significance only where railway transport is lacking. Secondly, that shippers defy economic advice (in the form of cost comparisons) probably does not signify that shippers are dull and obstinate; more likely those adjectives fit transport economists who turn a blind eye to factors which cannot be quantified. Thirdly, tariff manipulations to encourage combined river/rail shipments may do more harm than good. For example, they encourage some shippers to use a combined routing in situations where an all-rail route has lower costs; probably, though, few shippers swallow this tariff bait because it is the buyer who pays for transport but the shipper who is blamed for late deliveries. Having said all this, it is only fair to add that the use made of Western Siberian waterway transport in the initial stages of oil and gas development (and its continued use there in outlying areas, especially in aid of the timber industry) seems a good example of the rational exploitation of this form of transport.

The Baikal Amur Mainline (BAM) railway was also inspired by the needs of the Western Siberian oilfield. But whereas in Western Siberia the pipeline preceded the railway, with BAM the sequence is reversed (that is, if a pipeline along the BAM route is ever built). At the period when the idea of exporting oil to Japan was first discussed it was assumed that a pipeline would be built across Siberia to the Far East, with Japanese and American assistance. This did not preclude a railway later, BAM being a pre-war concept and already in existence at its eastern and western ends. As negotiations with Japan dragged on there were second thoughts, and in 1974 it was announced that BAM would have priority over a pipeline. The main reason given for this decision seems quite plausible; a railway offered many more possibilities for the region through which it passed, and in this case there was great potential for the creation of new production centers based on proven but untouched resources of energy and metals. No doubt there were other reasons and circumstances. It can hardly be imagined that during the course of the Soviet-Japanese negotiations the thought did not occur that a large-diameter pipeline, once built, would be a hostage whose future would be dependent on relations with Japan. Secondly, there is the technical consideration that it is generally possible, though not always desirable, to lay a pipeline within a railway's infrastructure, but the reverse is impossible. Thirdly, there is the unspoken but presumably quite powerful consideration that a duplicate main line to the Pacific, a hundred miles or so further from the Chinese frontier, would be a strategic asset. To sum up, the winding course towards a Soviet-Japanese agreement provided an ingredient hitherto lacking in Soviet projects, an involuntary pause-for-thought.

The alignment and purpose of BAM have been exhaustively discussed elsewhere.[18] Briefly, it will be a heavy-duty, singletrack railway of an advanced, but not futuristic, technical standard. It starts at Taishet (west of Lake Baikal on the Trans Siberian Railway) and runs eastwards, north of Lake Baikal, to the Pacific at Sovietskaya Gavan'; in fact its eastern and western ends (Taishet-Bratsk-Ust Kut and Komsomlsk-Sovietskays Gavan') have been in operation for many years. It is the 3,162 km (1,965 miles) central section, passing through seismic and unstable terrain, whose effect on reliability and maintenance costs can only be estimated, which is the line on which work is now feverishly proceeding. Target date for completion is 1983. Meanwhile the so-called 'Little BAM' whose construction started in 1971, is virtually complete. This runs north from the Trans Siberian, cuts the BAM at Tynda, and then continues northwards into Southern Yakutia where, among other resources, lie the substantial coal reserves of Neryungri and the iron ores of Aldan. Eventually, the distribution of mineral, timber and energy resources along BAM and 'Little BAM' is expected to give rise to territorial economic complexes in which raw materials will be reduced to more transportable products. The sequence and delineation of these complexes is still imprecise, but the older-established developments around Bratsk, where hydro-electricity has become the basis of aluminium and timber processing industries, suggests the shape of things to come. But the intra-regional significance of BAM will, at least initially, be overshadowed by its inter-regional and transit function. That is, by its oil traffic. It is true that some timber, coal and ores are also expected to be carried for shipment from Pacific ports, but Western Siberian oil will at first be the main traffic, being loaded from pipelines into railway cars at Taishet and transhipped to another pipeline at Urgal' in the Far East for distribution to refineries and to ocean tankers.

At this point, four years before its scheduled completion and decades before the region takes shape, evaluation of the project is necessarily speculative. Nevertheless, it is not too early to foresee some of the likely problems, and the remainder of this paper will survey the BAM project in relation to certain general difficulties facing the Soviet freight system and, firstly, against the background of those earlier regional transport projects already described.

There is little in common between BAM and the Vladikavkaz Railway. The latter might be regarded, with a century's hindsight, as a superbly successful venture in railway-based regional development. It is possible to suggest the basis of this success: the enterprise was above all allowed to mature over several decades. Once the decision to build the first main line was taken, further construction was undertaken only as tempting opportunities occurred. There was no grand plan, only willingness to let the project spread its roots in a natural sequence. This was perhaps the last major development in Russia where such a leisurely progression was permitted. The Trans Siberian project was hurried, and so were later projects. With BAM, however, it is just possible that a viable substitute for leisurely organic development has been found in the form of well-considered planning, faithfully executed. As for the Trans Siberian project, in some ways the closest equivalent of BAM, a main weakness was its excessive multiplicity of aims. Parallels with BAM are perhaps hard to draw here, but may well appear as time passes. The lesson of the Murmansk Railway is less fundamental but no less contemporary, for it is an example of a well-conceived project bedevilled by inter-ministerial squabbles, a phenomenon nowadays known as a 'narrow departmental approach'. Already, with BAM, there are well-known cases of lack of cooperation between ministries. The timber industry is felling trees close to the railway despite protests that they help to prevent landslides. A certain lack of coordination was also demonstrated in the case of those hundred-odd miles of track near Bratsk which had to be re-sited when it was discovered that they passed through territory scheduled to become the bottom of a reservoir. This kind of problem threatens to get worse rather than better as more territorial complexes are developed; the greater the *kompleksnost'* the more numerous will be opportunities for misunderstanding and friction.

The Virgin Lands transport policy as adopted in the 1950's is not only an example of haste, but raises at its starkest the whole question of Soviet highway facilities, a problem also encountered in the intra-regional implication of the BAM project.

Possibly intra-regional is the wrong term here, because it is usually used to describe the large-scale movement over BAM of traffic between integrated components of the region's industry. This intra-regional freight will probably be well-handled by the Railway. But there is also what can best be described as local traffic, and it is here that poor road services will be felt; small-volume movement to or from lesser centers is unlikely to flourish on the presently-planned highways associated with the BAM project. A really useful road network, as distinct from a succession of unconnected feeder roads, would include a road built along the BAM route. 1,200 km (745 miles) of such a road have already been created, according to a recent report.[19] Yet instead of upgrading this service road it is intended to abandon it once the line is finished. A Soviet critic[20] observes that in many places this road is already breaking up, and regrets the intention to abandon it.

Without such an all-weather highway, traffic between the smaller stations will have to be handled by stopping trains handling small consignments, the kind of train for which there is little place on a tightly scheduled heavy-duty main line. To this criticism the Soviet reply would be that it is not intended to have a massive population shift into the BAM region, so railway stations are not expected to form the nuclei of expanding settlements. There is indeed some justification for avoiding an interpretation of BAM in terms of western experience. The concept of a railway as some kind of fairy-tale prince whose coming awakens a sleeping princess dies hard. It is a concept that is well founded in US experience, but in other countries, Canada and Australia for example, the princess has been revealed as not only dormant, but sterile too. There is little likelihood that every station on BAM will or should become anything but a railway facility. On the other hand there is every likelihood that some stations will have the prerequisites for expansion, and such expansion will certainly be retarded if the present scale of road-building is not enlarged.

Neglect of road transport is not unique to the BAM project. It is a characteristic of most parts of the USSR, and is probably the greatest weakness of the transport system. In the last two decades there have been serious efforts to overcome this, first by exhortation (ineffective) and recently by an expansion of road-building (effective but insufficient). In the Soviet period as a whole roads have been neglected partly because building materials are short, partly because highway transport seemed to have very high costs, and partly because railways offered the mass long-distance transport which the economy most demanded. One of the great contributions of transport economists in the post-war period has been the progressive clarification of highway costs. Like their colleagues abroad, they have still a long way to go, but they did at least, and at last, emphasize that loading/unloading costs had to be included in any road-versus-rail comparisons. This approach revealed that many more hauls were better suited to road movement than had hitherto been thought.

Some of the indices for the post-1950's period seem impressive. Hard-surfaced roads increased from about 177,000 km (110,000 miles) in 1950 to about 660,000 km (410,000 miles) by 1975.[21] In the same period common-carrier motor trucks increased their traffic from less than one billion ton/km to about 100 billion.[22] And yet in 1975 common-carrier trucks moved only 1.7 percent of Soviet freight ton/km.[23] This implies that the railways are still handling small and short-distance traffic for which they are not at all suited; even collective farms sending their cabbages 25 km into the neighboring cities still choose to use the railway. And yet on the railways a 25 km haul costs twelve times more per ton/km than the average. Moreover, that cabbage-laden railway car spends ten hours at the unloading station, whereas a truck might be turned round in less than an hour.

Soviet highway transport is simply not capable of carrying the traffic for which, theoretically, it is most suitable. There are only a few bright spots in this gloomy picture. One is the Baltic republics. Another is the North Caucasus Railway which, serving a region relatively well provided with roads, has succeeded in transferring all local short-distance traffic to road vehicles. Elsewhere in the USSR small freight stations have been closed, with the aim of using road vehicles for pick-up and delivery over longer distances. However, in some cases this seems to have presented clients with serious problems when their shipments were terminated at stations with which they had no road access. Another measure of doubtful utility was that undertaken by the Northern Railway, which cooperated with local common-carrier truck enterprises by transferring rail freight to the highways where otherwise trucks would return empty to their base. This was very successful in its aim of reducing the empty mileage of motor trucks, but it increased the empty mileage of railway cars by a corresponding factor.[24]

This seems to be one of those problems which are a product of many factors, no one of which can usefully be tackled in isolation. It is an immense problem, too, which seems likely to persist for decades simply because there is no easy way around it. Progress made between 1950 and 1975 is recorded in the figures quoted above, but these have to be measured against the inauspicious statistics which follow. Firstly, of the 660,000 km of hard roads existing in 1975 only about 16 percent had a surface (asphalt/concrete) suitable for heavy traffic.[25] Most of the road classified as hard is in reality rather soft, being of gravel laid with or without a thin coating of tar. One indication of the difference between the best and the average is that fuel consumption over concrete is said to be 15 percent less than the average over hard roads.[26] It is reckoned that an asphalt/concrete road costs 150,000 rubles more than a singletrack railway.[27] Thus the Soviet mileage of good heavy-duty roads is less than the railway mileage, and it is cheaper to build railways. This situation appears differently when less substantial roads are included in the discussion, but these are not really suitable for heavy axleloads; they are easily damaged by heavy traffic and by the weather and therefore expensive to maintain. Turning to highway truck operations, on average one third of trucks are off the road under repair (or, more likely, awaiting spare parts).[28] About 45 percent of truck mileage is empty mileage.[29] Labor productivity in highway operations is nine times lower than on the railways. Average cost (insofar as this can be determined) of common-carrier truck movement is 52 kopeks per ton/km against the railways' 2.50 kopeks.

These comparative costs can be misleading, and not only because it is difficult to apportion highway construction and repair costs. The railways' average represents a favorable permutation (a haul of 866 km in a 2,600 gross-ton train, with 28 percent empty mileage factor) whereas the highway average is far from being the optimum operation (15.9 km haul, a proportion of dirt road mileage, and trucks of 3 to 4 ton capacity). If the trucks' 'working conditions' could be improved they would seem a much better proposition from the cost point of view. But it is precisely these working conditions, that is, the state of the roads, which is such a daunting problem.

It would be wrong to presume that the share of highways in total traffic should increase to the American level. The latter is probably not the optimum for that territory and US conditions are very different from those of the USSR. Nevertheless it is clear that the Soviet situation implies that full advantage cannot be taken of the technical virtues of the motor truck. In a sense, a repetition is being enacted on the highways of the Soviet railways' dilemma of the 1920's. Then, the railways' capacity was limited because the rails could not support the axle loads of locomotives big enough to do the job. Now, Soviet highways cannot support the axle loads of heavy trucks. Most highway freight is carried in trucks of up to 4 tons capacity, an uneconomic unit of transport which goes some way to explain the current abysmal labor productivity. Moreover, the large proportion of roads which are poorly surfaced, unsurfaced, or badly maintained, further raises costs by enforcing low speeds, higher fuel consumption, and frequent break-downs. A denser network of better-surfaced roads is technically desirable, but seems out of reach simply because of the vast resources that would be required. So great is the gap between the desirable and the feasible that it seems questionable whether in this century the rubber-tired vehicle will ever play in the USSR the role of which it is theoretically capable. This being so, the relative neglect of roads in the BAM project becomes more understandable.

Judging from experience elsewhere in the USSR, a potential weakness of BAM will be the railway's attitude to the smaller shipments. Railway managements, concerned above all with passing heavy bulk traffic, habitually adopt a take-it-or-leave-it approach to lesser consignments. Fundamentally, this attitude arises because the managements are custodians of scarce resources, and it is likely to persist so long as transportation facilities are limited to what the government considers to be the bare minimum. This bare minimum is probably a very uneconomic minimum, but because its consequences are hard to quantify they are usually ignored; when a spare part has been sent to the most convenient station for the railway and the least convenient for the receiver (a typical history), it is not easy to determine how many rubles this arbitrary decision may have cost the economy, but the cost is nevertheless there. In the BAM region, as elsewhere, small shipments may well have a crucial, if underrated, importance. There are few industrial processes, for example, which do not require in addition to their bulk imputs the occasional but punctual carload of additives or less-than-carload of spare parts.

It is possible that this circumstance is one of the reasons why recent Soviet textbook writers stress that, ideally, the boundaries of railway administration should coincide with the boundaries of economic regions. To take a recent example,[30] a textbook on transportation geography has an introductory chapter on this theme, and then the author goes on to describe the economic regions as though they coincided (which they do not) with the boundaries of the USSR's railways. In any case, the advantages of such a coincidence seem exaggerated, for it does not automatically follow that a railway which exactly fits an economic region will give the latter a better service than otherwise. The recent move to eliminate the fourth tier of railway management (essentially station managements), making the railway division the smallest administrative unit, emphasizes that the shape of railway administrative areas is still determined not by regionalization, but by operating convenience.[31] Nevertheless, because regionalization is now a

206

widely publicized aim, there are those who advocate a restructuring. Presumably the latest such restructuring in Central Asia, resulting in the formation of the Virgin Lands Railway, is one manifestation of this trend. No longer, as in the 1930's, is the slogan 'one railway for one region' condemned as a manifestation of the 'opportunistic' concept of 'intra-regional socialism'.[32]

It will be interesting to see whether a separate administration will be formed to manage BAM, or whether it will be split between the Far Eastern and Eastern Siberian railways. As it happens, operational convenience may coincide with regional circumstances in this case. BAM will almost certainly use non-standard rolling stock, and this will tend to isolate it from the rest of the network. The oil tank cars that will carry the bulk of the initial traffic will be in captive service between the two pipeline terminals, never needing to leave the BAM tracks. At the same time, passing loops on the line are not as long as desirable from the point of view of future operation. The standard length of 1,100 meters is said to have been a compromise between operating ideals and the difficulty of building long loops in the inhospitable terrain. The offer of such an unconvincing explanation surely suggests that there is a less creditable reason lurking in the background, and this is probably that somebody decided that 1,100 meter loops should be installed because that was the existing standard elsewhere in the USSR. With this length of loop, maximization of carrying capacity would be best obtained by using cars of higher capacity but of the same length. This implies increased height or width, and in fact BAM is not being built to the All-Union general clearance limits, but to a new, enlarged standard. This permits tank cars with an internal diameter of 3,400 mm instead of 3,000 mm, giving a significant increase of capacity. Moreover, whatever the clearances, it is intended that traffic will be carried in 8-axle cars, and there are good safety reasons why conventional 4-axle cars should not be included in trains of these vehicles. Both these circumstances mean that the terminal stations of BAM will also be technical boundaries, making a separate administration almost inevitable and thereby demonstrating the 'one railway for one region' concept.

B AM's function as an inter-regional carrier is peculiar in that its main transit traffic, oil, will operationally be intra-regional, since it will be both loaded and unloaded in the Railway's own territory. When other traffic flows develop, the technical level of the Railway promises effective handling, although how BAM traffic will fare over adjoining and often overloaded railways is less certain. BAM will probably do little to relieve the hard-pressed east-west connections. Except insofar as the regional development made possible by the Railway will hold the growth of traffic to a level below what it might have been if all materials had been hauled out of the region for processing, its relieving effect will be small. But this conclusion does leave military traffic out of account. For commercial traffic, BAM is not a relief line for the older Trans Siberian because that sector of the latter which it parallels is not overloaded (and for that reason will be the last section to be electrified). The critically overloaded part of the Trans

Siberian runs westwards from Novosibirsk, which is far to the west of BAM's western terminus. However, the role of the Trans Siberian as provider of military transport, especially along the Amur, is important, and it may well be that even in peacetime the burden of troop deployments along the Chinese frontier will be enough to make BAM worthwhile as a diversionary route for non-military traffic.

The last transport facility to be accorded, like BAM, the title of Great Project of All-Union Significance was the Volga-Don Canal in the 1950's. At that time this expensive undertaking was commended for its revolutionary effect on inland waterway transport. Two decades after its opening, this revolution has yet to be glimpsed; even in a planned economy there is a strong gambling element in the choice of new routes. BAM is a gamble too, but it is being constructed against a background of considerable investigation, research and discussion which, together, have improved the odds on a successful outcome. All the same, it is worth remembering that its cost is not accurately known, that its reliability will be established only by trial and error, and that its traffic levels are uncertain.

Whether the resources invested in BAM might have been better invested elsewhere is an intriguing but virtually unanswerable question. It has been roughly estimated that the BAM project annually demands one percent of total Soviet investment,[33] or a final total of around $15 billion. For a single undertaking, this is an enormous sum, but nevertheless it is tiny in comparison with, say, the needs of Soviet highways.

The Soviet government still relies on high and often unreasonable utilization rates of existing facilities in preference to additional investment. Perhaps it is right to do so, but a consequence is that transport will remain at best, a wasteful process, and at worst a bottleneck. Excessive hopes have long been placed on two assumptions. One of these is that as output increases, demand for transportation increases at a slower rate. However, the published statistics which demonstrate this effect have been questioned.[34]

The second comforting assumption is that better coordination of transport will result in the overloaded railways transferring traffic to other media, even to the waterways which, despite disappointments, are still regarded as ready-made traffic arteries requiring negligible investment. This has been a theme of Soviet planning since the 1920's, and no textbook on transportation economics is complete without the following kind of table.

Table 2[35]
Percentage Share of Freight Traffic

	1940	1960	1975
Railways	85.2	79.8	61.9
Ocean Shipping	4.9	7.0	14.9
Waterways	7.3	5.3	4.2
Pipeline	0.8	2.7	12.5
Highway (total)	1.8	5.2	6.4
Air			0.1

At first sight this table does suggest that the railways' share has declined from four fifths to three fifths (although not to the benefit of the waterways). But if ocean traffic (mainly foreign trade now) is excluded, and if some caution is attached to the figures for highway traffic, it will be seen that the railways still carry more than two thirds of the freight. Almost all the genuine shift is accounted for by pipelines, which have expanded greatly and thereby relieved the railways of much traffic associated with high empty car-miles. With the exception of oil (and, of course, passengers), the share of the railways has scarcely decreased. The BAM project, which gives rail transport pride of place not only over waterways and highways but also over pipelines, represents an imposed retreat from the earlier priorities of Soviet transport coordination policies. Even though the BAM circumstances are special, in general the future still seems to lie with the railways; this must be a comforting thought for those who respect the historic role of the Soviet Union as conserver of 19th century virtues.

Footnotes

1. *Zheleznodorozhnyi transport,* 12 (1978), p. 16.
2. The railway newspaper *Gudok* took the opportunity during January 1979 to berate railway managements for the crisis in a series of I-told-you-so articles.
3. I.I. Belousov, *Osnovy ucheniia ob ekonomicheskom raionirovanii,* (Moscow, 1976), p. 185.
4. N.N. Kolosovskii, in *Voprosy geografii, 90* (1972), pp. 45-54.
5. A.I. Kerenchkhiladze, *Geograficheskiye problemy transporta Gruzii,* Tbilisi 1976, p. 50. The table, slightly abridged, relates to 1973.
6. *Soviet Geography,* No. 5, 1973, pp. 308-9.
7. Recent literature on the Vladikavkaz Railway appears in *Istoricheskiye zapiski,* Vol. 78, 1963, p. 297; *Slavic Review,* Dec. 1966, pp. 669-675.
8. G.F. Chirkin, *Transportno-promyshlenno-kolonizatsionnyi kombinat Murmanskoi zheleznoi dorogi,* (M-L, 1928), p. 12.
9. *Ibid.,* p. 19.
10. See, for example, H. Hunter, *Soviet Transportation Policy,* (Cambridge, Mass.,), 1957, pp. 21-40.
11. A forthcoming book by T. Kirsten will examine the odd circumstances surrounding the acceptance of this project.
12. Costs and tariffs for the metallurgical industry are discussed in M. Clark, *The Economics of Soviet Steel,* (Cambridge, Mass.,), 1956.
13. *Zheleznodorozhnyi transport,* 12 (1954), pp. 25-34.
14. A.V. Osorgin et al, *Voprosy kompleksnogo razvitiya osvoeniia tselinykh i zalezhnykh zemel' severnogo Kazakhstana,* Alma Ata, 1957, pp. 45-50.
15. *Soviet Geography,* No. 6, 1969, pp. 312-325.
16. *Soviet Geography,* No. 8, 1970 pp. 655-59.
17. *Ibid.,* p. 659.
18. T. Shabad and V. Mote, *Gateway to Siberian Resources (The BAM),* (New York, 1977), pp. 63-160.
19. *Zheleznodorozhnyi transport,* 12 (1978), p. 70.
20. *Ekonomika i organizatisiia promyshlennogo proizvodstva,* 4 (1978), p. 32.
21. L.A. Bronshtein and A.S. Shul'man, *Ekonomika avtomobil'nogo transporta,* (Moscow, 1976), p. 82.
22. *Ibid.,* p. 57.
23. B.G. Nikitenko and E.G. Gutsev, *Transport v narodnokhoziaistvannom komplskse BSSA,* (Minsk, 1978), p. 9. If non-common-carrier trucks were included, the share of highways would be 6.2 percent.
24. Yu. Tikhonchuk, (ed.), *Ratsional'noye raspredeleniye gruzovykh perevozok mezhdu*

          zheleznodorozhnyi i avtomobil'nym transportom, (Moscow, 1972), pp. 109-10.

25.   Bronshtein, p. 83.
26.   Kverenchkhiladze, p. 88.
27.   Bronshtein, p. 34-5. This rough figure is the cost per kilometer.
28.   In Kazakhstan, for example, in 1976 an average of 37 percent of all trucks were under repair. *Narodnoye Khoziaistvo Kazakhstana,* (Alma Ata, 1977), p. 123.
29.   *Ibid.,* p. 123; in Kazakhstan 52 percent of the mileage was loaded mileage in 1976. In Murmansk in 1975 the Oblast's trucks somehow contrived to register only 44 percent for loaded mileage; *Narodnoye khoziaistvo Murmanskoi oblasti v deviatoi piatiletke,* (Murmansk, 1976), p. 69.
30.   N.N. Kazanskii et al, *Geografiia putei soobshcheniya,* (Moscow, 1969).
31.   Nikitenko, p. 73.
32.   *Sotsialisticheskii transport,* 8 (1934), p. 109.
33.   Shabad and Mote, p. 67.
34.   *Trudy TsNII MPS,* No. 406 1970, p. 10. This article points out that the belief in a declining transportation/output ratio is based on a misleading comparison of the tonnage of freight with the value of output.
35.   Bronshtein, p. 24 (abridged).

Professor Dr. Johannes F. Tismer

Current position:
Chairman of the Osteuropa-Institut
Freie Universitat Berlin
Garystrasse 55
1000 Berlin 33
Germany

Main field of work:
Transportation economics
Regional economics
Comparative economics (economic systems)

Publications during the last two years:
"Verkehrspolitik der Staatshandelslander (Transportation policy of countries with government controlled economies)", Internationales Berkehrswesen, 3 (1977), 139-154.

Transportation and the Military
Significance of Regionalization
Variations
in the Transport System
at Regional Level:
the Role of BAM (II)
Professor Johannes F. Tismer

I. Preliminary Remarks

Variations in transport systems at the regional level are often directly related to develpments of regional economy, on which the transport system has an important influence. Transport development in a region is one precondition for activating its economic resources and the extent to which services are provided in an economic region rests on the basis of the transport infrastructure which has been created.

Intra-regional transport systems are supplemented by inter-regional ones. The function of the latter is to connect the economic activities being performed in various economic regions. The effectiveness of economic interrelations between various spatially separated producing centers which are far apart depends to a large extent on the efficiency of interregional transport systems. When we examine the regional aspects of the Soviet Union's transport system, our study will be based on the current Soviet practice of dividing the USSR into 19 economic regions. Fourteen of them comprise the so-called Macro-Region-West (MRW), covering the European part of the Soviet Union, and five comprise the Macro-Region-East (MRE), which covers the Asian part of the Soviet Union. Because it is a traditional industrial center, the Ural Region, which was of some economic significance even before the Revolution, is considered part of the MRW even though it is geographically part of the MRE.[1]

There are two alternative principles of regionalization. The first applies to nodal regions. They have a single main nucleus, an urban metropolis sometimes with subordinate centers, all surrounded by rural territory. The internal exhange of goods and services dominates in this kind of region. Examples are the highly industrialized regions in the European part of the USSR. The other principle of regionalization applies to homogeneous regions which are defined on the basis of internal uniformity, for instance the exploitation of mineral resources. The whole region renders a surplus supply of this kind of output that is to be exported in large quantities. Internal exchange, therefore, is of minor importance. Examples are the economically underdeveloped regions of Soviet Asia, where extractive and basic industries substantially dominate over high-order manufacturing compared with the industrialized regions of the MRW.

To simplify matters we will distinguish between developed and underdeveloped regions and between industrial and raw material producing regions, respectively. In addition, three aspects of variations in the transport system at the regional level will be given special attention in this context:

1. Transport services in the economically developed regions;
2. Communications between economic regions, particularly between the economically developed and underdeveloped regions;
3. Transport development in the underdeveloped regions as part of their overall economic development, giving special consideration to the territory traversed by BAM.

In this analysis it will only be possible to present a broad outline of the variations in transport systems at the regional level which are of importance at present and will be so in the future. It is not possible to provide detailed analyses of how specific transport situations have changed regionally.

When choosing the time period for our analysis, it should be taken into account that variations in transport systems at the regional level usually take place during the course of long-term development programs. Changes which are taking effect now may have been introduced over ten years ago. On the other hand, regional transport development projects such as BAM will hardly produce results until the 1980's. For this reason it will sometimes be necessary to examine transport developments which occurred in the 1960's in order to arrive at a meaningful analysis of current regional transport situations and of how they are likely to develop in the future.

II. Some Aspects of Transport Services in the Economically Developed Regions

It is characteristic of the Soviet Union's regional economic development that long-term economic growth has been concentrated in the European part of the country (MRW), with an orientation toward the traditional industrial clusters in the Donets-Dnepr Region, the Center, the Northwest, and the Ural Region.

A generally observable phenomenon in the industrialization process is a tendency toward the locational persistence of existing production centers or consolidation of locational patterns.[2] In the Soviet Union this tendency was favored by a policy of forced industrialization which occasioned still more regional concentration of economic activities in already existing manufacturing centers. On the other hand, economic development in areas with insufficient transport facilities, scattered settlement patterns, labor shortage, and unfavorable climatic conditions in many parts of Soviet Asia has been slowed down. Thus, in the European part of the Soviet Union, the formation of industrial agglomerations was encouraged. The advantages of localization economies taken by the management of an industrial branch, and also of urbanization economies to improve cooperative economic relations between its own enterprises and those of various other manufacturing branches, greatly accelerated the agglomeration process. In economic regions with relatively rich distributional, transport and infrastructural facilities, well-populated with skilled labor, clustered industry, etc., ministers found it more convenient to deal with their economc tasks. In virgin areas they are confronted with higher investment and operational costs for plants. Though urban activity is subject to substantial agglomeration economies (internal, external or both), expansion cannot proceed indefinitely because of capacity limitations. When they will be reached is difficult to determine and depends on the developmental possibilities of each industrial agglomeration center. The socially and economically optimal size of a city may range between 50,000 and 300,000 inhabitants.

The growth of cities necessarily must be accompanied by structural improvements of the transport system. As a rule, larger cities represent important traffic centers. To the extent to which their transportation facilities become increasingly burdened, additional capacities have to be installed. Such installments may be very comprehensive in cases when space for expanding circulation downtown is narrowing in the cities and/or when their access and/or exit roads threaten to run out of capacity. Capacity extension then will turn out to be very expensive or not even economically feasible. Burdens like this have already arisen at different places or are expected to arise in the foreseeable future in the industrial regions of the Soviet Union. Therefore, it is considered useful to foster decentralization of industrial locations instead of further concentrating them in narrowing metropolitan areas. Economic activities are then to be dispersed to suburban or rural areas around industrial clusters or outside industrial regions into areas that are still to be economically developed. The latter alternative of regional economic decentralization aims at locating industries within regions of Soviet Asia and will be discussed below with reference to transport development.

It is said that traffic in many manufacturing centers exceeds the capacity of motor roads, the consequence of which is slow and expensive trucking.[3] In past economic planning, road construction has been greatly neglected and therefore did not keep pace with traffic development in industrial centers and elsewhere. For example, traffic requirements of large cities for communication with their suburban and surrounding rural areas cannot at present be met satisfactorily. While auto freight traffic increased 15.5 times from 1950 to 1975, hard-surface road mileage in the Soviet Union rose only 3.4 times during the same period, and the annual production rate of motor vehicles increased 5 times (imports excluded).[4] This helps to explain why traffic density on roads in and around industrial centers has increased considerably, especially in the course of the past decade, even though there are currently only about 50 vehicles per 1,000 residents.[5]

In many cases the capacity of railroad junctions and industrial tracks connecting with mainlines is also heavily loaded. This is one important reason why railway cars are not being moved for four-fifths of their average turn-around time. Many shipments over short distances cannot be shifted to trucks, because the road network is poorly developed.[6] This in turn hampers coordination of truck and railway transportation at junctions.[7]

At the CPSU's XXV Party Congress, L. Brezhnev made the following statement:

> "During the forthcoming period we will have to make more resources available to accelerate transport development, for what is generally called infrastructure. In the past it simply was not possible to devote sufficient attention to many of these activities...especially to road construction. Now it is necessary to deal with them, and to do so seriously."[8]

In these remarks one can sense the leadership's concern that the failure to develop the road system sufficiently, especially where there are not enough hard-surface roads between central sites of metropolitan areas and their surroundings, could impede the process of economic development. The industrial cities of Astrakhan, Orenburg, Perm, Izhevsk, and Kirov are given as examples of places which badly need more road construction.[9] Indeed, any traveller to these or other Soviet cities will readily discern the poor quality and lack of a sufficient road network.

The necessity of dispersing industrial locations is underscored by the fact that, since 1959, when a census was taken, 88 percent of total population growth in the country as a whole, and an even larger percentage of the increase of working people, took place in the fairly limited space of cities with over 100,000 inhabitants.[10] The further concentration of population and industrial establishments, therefore, becomes more and more subject to spatial limits at different places. Insufficient local traffic, including public transit services, prevents the location of manufacturing activities in peripheral areas and hampers regular commuting between them and the center. In those areas where buses regularly provide transport services between cities and rural settlements up to 15 times daily the number of village residents increased by 23 percent from 1960 to 1970. By contrast, in rural areas where bus connections to cities are lacking, the population declined by 13 percent from 1950 to 1970.[11]

There are many indications that the success of decentralizing economic activities depends strongly on what kind of communication prevails between central and peripheral areas. It must be well established in order to cause larger segments of the population to move to peripheral areas and to slow down the heavy influx of rural population into the urban metropolis.

216

It should be possible to cover an 80 to 160 kilometer distance between the center and the periphery in two to three hours.[12]

There are proposals to include the construction and organization of efficient local transport systems in regional development programs to ensure that industrial output growth rates will be achieved mainly in suburban areas in the near future. An adequate work force also has to be attracted to locations outside of any major population center.[13] A locational pattern is visualized according to which industrial enterprises should be assigned to certain rural or suburban areas and be located along routes which radiate from the urban centers. Decentralization of industries into suburban and rural areas, which entails variations of the transport system, will be bound up with a rural resettlement program within a period of 15 to 20 years. In 1970, 292,000 of 469,300 rural settlements had 100 inhabitants or fewer. Approximately 40 percent of the rural population lives in villages with 200 inhabitants or fewer.[14] There is talk of reducing the total number of rural settlements fivefold. Amalgamation of communities is now in progress in the Non-Black-Earth-Zone (roughly north of the line Briansk-Saransk-Izhevsk-Sverdlovsk). These intentions are closely related to the constantly propagated plan to eliminate the socio-economic differentials between town and country, a claim that could not be met with much consistency because the development of transport facilities in rural areas has been neglected for decades. Roads are either poor or non-existent. The extent of road construction considered necessary to make these areas accessible is considerable. Minimum needs are set at 1.5 to 1.8 kilometers of road per 1,000 hectares. This would require a volume of new construction amounting to 850,000 to 900,000 kilometers of roadway.[15] Such construction measures could make it possible to locate more food processing industries in rural areas on the basis of raw agricultural products in order to promote 'industrialization' of the countryside. Even for heavy industries, it is useful to ship substantial portions of their output on roads. It is well known that road transport widens the choice of locations significantly, since the road network is more finely branched than the rail network and has more stopping places to choose.

During the tenth Five Year Plan (1976-1980), measures for expanding and improving the road network will concentrate primarily on rural areas. Over 50,000 km of road construction is to be added to the rural road network. Regional emphasis is to be placed on areas of the Non-Black-Earth-Zone. According to a decision taken by the CPSU's Central Committee and Council of Ministers, 25,000 km of hard surface roads shall be constructed in this area. This measure is seen as prerequisite to improving conditions for economic and social development in this zone and is intended to promote industries processing agricultural products, but above all to combat migration of rural residents to the cities. It is said that many of them would stay if their villages were to get a dependable daily transportation connection with a city.[16] On the other hand, there are strong restrictions on industrial expansion into rural areas which absorbs fertile land. Yet, it remains to be seen whether these ambitious plans are to be realized. The fact thet Brexhnev has made repeated statements about transportation deficiencies in the last two years may indicate that the Plan target will not be met.

The formation of a regional economic system with the inter-related territorial functions historic nucleus, green belt (recreation area), and the surrounding rural territory as the economic development zone, in as organizational problem. It is considered insoluble as long as municipal administrative and industrial management make decisions not in accordance with plans for functional intergration.[17] Transportation infrastructure in particular is involved, since industrial management is engaged in the construction of feeder lines and sidings. They not only link large enterprises with railway main lines, but also with processing and consuming centers. In 1976, 133,000 km of feeder lines were in operation. However, their services are limited to the requirements of the enterprises of authorities operating them and do not meet the transport needs of the general public.[18] Effective local traffic is one element of a functional system that must be organized between the center and the peripheral areas.

The BAM railway advances through the Siberian Taiga towards Amur on the Pacific coast. The 3,200 km-long railway is due for completion in 1982.

II. Communications Between the Economic Regions, Especially Between the Economically Developed and Underdeveloped Regions

The pronounced spatial concentration of economic growth which resulted in very high levels of industrial agglomeration in the European part of the Soviet Union (the European area MRW) accounts for about eighty percent of gross industrial and agricultural output,[19] whereas Siberia represents only about nine percent has led to an enormous increase in energy requirements that by no means can be satisfied here. This need to import energy placed an extremely heavy burden on the long-distance transport systems[20] which connect the economic regions, especially on those transport routes carrying vital raw materials to the western part of the country.

The railroad continues to exhibit high growth rates of freight traffic. Most of this growth is occurring on trunk lines which run west from the Kuznetsk Basin, as well as on the eastern connections to the Ural area and the lines running from here to the Center. Exceptional growth is also taking place on the freight lines which lead west from the Donets Basin. Coal shipments represent up to 60 percent of the freight transported within the Kuznetsk Basin and from here to destinations in manufacturing centers of the MRW.[21] In 1975 the European part of the Soviet Union received 28 million tons of coal from the Kuznetsk Basin and 4 million tons from coalfields near Karaganda.[22] About 40 million tons of the coal mined in these areas went to the Ural Region.[23] Just how heavily the industrial regions depend on the raw material producing regions can be seen in the fact that, in 1975, the traffic volume of fuel transported on railroads and by pipeline between the Macro-Regions East and West reached the equivalent of 360 million tons of mineral coal after an increase of 4.5 times during a ten-year period. In the course of the tenth Five Year Plan traffic volume is expected to double again.[24] In addition, the cultivation of agricultural land, about 42 million hectares in Kazakhstan and Siberia, helped grain transports to the western industrial regions increase considerably; in 1972 these transports amounted to 5.5 million tons of grain.[25] Because of the long distances that have to be covered, the proportion of railway shipments which have to be transported over 3,000 km increased from 30 percent to 40 percent between 1960 and 1970.[25] Bulk goods such as mineral coal, timber, ores, and metals accounted for most of this increase. This caused marked changes on the communication lines between these two types of areas. Measures such as electrifying heavily travelled stretches of railroad and expanding junctions, as well as adding further lines or tracks to existing ones (f.i. double-tracking) and constructing independent new communications with higher standards of mechanization and automation were taken. Substantial effects of rationalization in long-distance traffic are being achieved by constructing oil and gas pipelines. They have become increasingly important since the early 1960's. New long-distance transport systems are emerging, and existing ones are being supplemented. The purpose of these projects is to make the connections with long-distance transport routes and the routes themselves function more efficiently, from both a technical and an economic point of view.

For railroad trunk lines connecting industrial and raw material producing centers, improvements during the Tenth Five Year Plan will concentrate on the following projects in particular: the last section of the South Siberian Railroad Main Line (Iushsib) from Beloretsk to Karlaman. This will greatly improve interregional transport for the coal shipments from Siberia and Karaganda via Magnitogorsk to industrial centers in the western part of the Soviet Union. The Uritskoe-Kustanai railway segment will create a third access route to the west for the Middle Siberian Railroad Main Line (Sredsib). The Pogromnoe-Pugachevsk railroad section goes from the southern portion of the Ural Region to the Volga Region. Freight transport from the Donets Basin to the western Ukraine and from there in the direction towards the Soviet border will be supplemented by the new Dolinskaia-Pomoshnaia stretch. It is a connecting link for a third key line between the Donets Basin and the western Ukraine. As is the case with new railroad construction, improvements like double- or multi-tracking and electrification of railroad lines are also concentrated on the above-mentioned long-distance route systems which regularly carry large quantities of bulk goods.

Besides these measures concerning long-distance railroad systems, efforts to rationalize transportation of bulk goods have been concentrated to a large extent on the development of long-distance oil and natural gas pipeline systems. In addition, installations of interconnected supply networks between power stations play an important role, as do significant efforts to catch up technologically in generating atomic energy in order to use it more efficiently and on a larger scale. However, this cannot be the subject of discussion in this paper, due to space limitations.

Since the mid-1950's structural changes in energy requirements[27] have led to an increase in petroleum and natural gas production, beginning at deposits in the MRW. Pipeline construction was initially limited to supplying consumers who were located near the resources (intra-regional), for example in the producing areas of Bashkiria, Tartary, Kuibyshev, Saratov, Volgograd, and Perm. Substantial expansion of pipeline systems based on purchases of Western pipe and equipment for oil and natural gas transport has actually begun since the Seventh Five Year Plan was launched. At that time a crude oil pipeline was build from Al'met'evsk (in the Volga Region), supplying refineries in Gor'ki, Riazan', Moscow, and Iaroslavl' with crude oil. At the same time construction was begun on the so-called Friendshop Pipeline from Kuibyshev to Brest and Ushgorod. This pipeline supplies crude oil to refineries in White Russia, in the Ukraine, in the Baltic Provinces, and in some of the socialist countries of East and Southeast Europe. A crude oil pipeline had already at that time been constructed eastward to Irkutsk in East Siberia via Petropavlovsk-Omsk-Novosibirsk-Krasnoyarsk. The Ukraine and the Black Sea ports were connected by pipelines with the Volga Region via the North Caucasus, as well as with oil wells in Transcaucasia. These pipeline systems have since had some sections improved by additional lines.

A decision by the Central Committee of the CPSU and the Soviet Union's Council of Ministers concerning the future development of the gas industry goes back to the Sixth Five Year Plan providing for construction of thirty-seven gas pipelines. At that time the pipeline Stavropol'-Moscow via Rostov/Don, Taganrog, Zhdanov, and Voronezh was, among others, one of the major construction projects. Since then gas pipelines connecting the Krasnoyarsk and the Krasnodarsk areas with the Moscow area and Ordzhonikidze with Tbilisi have also been constructed.

Pipeline construction gained a new and powerful momentum when the long-term development of petroleum and natural gas deposits in the West Siberian Lowlands was decided upon during the CPSU's XXIII Party Congress. In 1964 petroleum--and later natural gas--extraction began in this area. Already in 1975, 148 million tons of oil and 38 billion m³ of natural gas were produced. Planned output quotas for 1980 have been set at 310 million tons of petroleum and 125 to 150 billion m³ of natural gas.[28] In 1980 already, 50 percent of the Soviet Union's overall petroleum production is to be concentrated in West Siberia. The Tenth Five Year Plan provides for the construction of 15,000 km of crude oil pipeline or of 3,000 km per year on the average. This means that transport connections, especially between West Siberia and the industrial centers of the MRW, will be further supplemented and intensified as in previous years.[29]

The current Tenth Five Year Plan also emphasizes the construction of gas pipeline systems which originate in West Siberia and supply the industrial centers of the MRW with natural gas. There are three geographically oriented pipeline systems: the northern system leads from Ukhta to Torshok and supplies the Northwest, White Russia, and the Baltic Provinces with natural gas, some quantities of which will be exported. The construction of a gas pipeline from Punga to Vutkyl is planned for the purpose of connecting Torshok with the gas deposits near Medvesh'e. There are also plans to supplement the Ukhta-Torshok pipeline section by constructing a second line. The western system runs through Kirov-Gor'ki-Elets and supplies areas in the northern Ural Region, the Upper Volga, the Center, and the Ukraine with natural gas. This system is to be supplemented by the Urengoi-Nadym-Punga-Elets and N.Tura-Perm-Kazan'-Gor'ki gas pipelines. The southern system links Surgut, Tobol'sk, and Tiumen'. It will be connected with the gas pipeline running from Orenburg to the western border, which has just been completed and will supply the central and southern areas of the Ural and Volga regions with natural gas. Construction of a Urengoi-Cheliabinsk-Kuibyshev pipeline for consignees in the southern Ural and the Volga Region is planned.[30]

It is remarkable to see how many pipelines have been constructed for crude oil and natural gas transport since the mid-1960's. At present pipeline traffic amounts to 1,100 billion tkm, and the average length of haul to 1,994 km.[31] Ninety-two percent of all crude oil is already transported by pipelines. These performances also show to what extent they could relieve the burdens on the railroads.[32]

The development of the highway network by means of expansion and improvement has been very modest (2,300 km of mileage are assigned to the Tenth Five Year Plan). This will not lead to any fundamental variations of the transport system at the regional level. The same is true of river freight traffic, at least in the European portion of the Soviet Union where two-thirds of river freight traffic is concentrated on major navigable flood-controlled waterways. Their length represents only 13 percent of the total length of navigable waterways in the Soviet Union. The growing dependence of industrial centers on the eastern raw material producing regions, where 100% of the country's increase in oil and natural gas production as well as 90% of total production increases in mineral coal mining are projected to take place between 1976 and 1980[33] while, on the other hand, energy consumption in the western economic regions amounts to 80% of all energy produced, also caused the Soviet leadership to emphasize more strongly implementing changes in the relative proportions of energy used in the various economic regions, besides changes in the transport systems at regional level as discussed above. This is necessary, since it is said that otherwise after 1980 expenditures for transporting raw materials, fuel, and semimanufactured products from east to west, and also manufactured goods in the opposite direction, would increase enormously.[34]

The issues at stake are of fundamental significance for the Soviet Union's overall national and regional economic development in the future; that is, to what extent can further economic growth continue to take place in the industrial centers located in the European part of the Soviet Union, and to what extent must efforts to develop Soviet Asia's economic regions be intensified, so that production sites there can be expanded to take advantage of the cheap energy and raw material resources? Two fundamental alternatives for regional economic development can be distinguished in the Soviet Union, and each of these affects regional-level transport systems differently. In the Macro-Region West, land as a production factor is limited.[35] The fact that here agglomerated real capital (including transport infrastructure) and available labor force are to be combined to a large extent with raw material deposits situated in the Macro-Region East substantially burdens the national economy with extremely high costs for transport infrastructure and services necessary for hauling relatively low-value bulk goods in large quantities over long distances by land. This has been the usual course taken by regional economic development in the Soviet Union up to the present.

There is an alternative possiblity for regional combining of production factors: As factor labor is limited in the Macro-Region East,[36] combining it with raw material deposits (land factor) that are plentiful and workable, though it is to be done under sometimes extremely difficult climatic conditions (nature as a cost factor), would require substantial capital investments (capital factor) if eastward migration is to be stimulated successfully. A larger portion of the investments would have to be placed in the technical and social infrastructure. If differentiated production patterns could evolve in the eastern regions and interregional economic relations between them and western industrial regions could develop on the basis of higher-order manufacturing sectors, the burden of freight expenses would diminish. In this case relatively low-value bulk goods would no longer have to be transported in such large quantities over immense distances, but rather semifinished and finished industrial products could be shipped instead. Internal exchange of goods would rise.

Given the rising cost of carrying goods the Soviets seem to have set up the following guidelines for Soviet regional economic policy. In the western industrial regions, production targets are to be realized primarily by replacement and modernization of production facilities already in existence, and not by expanding them.[37] The expansion curb is aimed above all at types of production which require a great deal of energy and water. In the future, efforts will be intensified to locate such industry in the economic regions of Soviet Asia. At the same time the transport system is to be developed more efficiently. Therefore, to combat the western economic regions' energy supply problems and transport problems associated with them, regional policy is directed, on the one hand, at locating industries that require large amounts of energy and raw materials in the economic regions of Soviet Asia and, on the other hand, at making the transport system itself more efficient by rationalization. A main feature of this has been oil and gas transport by pipeline.

IV. Transport Development in the Economic Regions of Soviet Asia as Part of Their Overall Economic Development, Giving Special Consideration to the Territory Traversed by BAM

Industrial dispersion as a regional policy objective is to be achieved by establishing a larger number of industrial enterprises in Soviet Asia's underdeveloped regions. From 1976 to 1980, 30 percent of the national economy's gross investment is to be allocated in this area.[38] This, however, presents problems completely different from those involved in suburbanization of industrial centers in the European part of the Soviet Union.

The previous course of industrial development in Soviet Asia's economic regions has been marked by extensive exploitation of raw material deposits. Transport development was aimed at building trunk roads and connecting them to production sites. It is clear that deficiencies of the economic infrastructure in the underdeveloped regions of Siberia and Asia (material-oriented economy) are the cause of a relatively low level of capital productivity. In the Ninth Five Year Plan capital productivity for the Far East was 66.7 percent; for East Siberia, 84.6 percent and for West Siberia 97.4 percent of the RSFSR average.[39]

Regional development programs such as the railroad construction project Baikal-Amur Magistral (BAM) or the projects to exploit oil and natural gas reserves in the West Siberian Lowlands bring up the question about which developmental strategy should be pursued. In order to use capacity of new transport routes as fully as possible in backward areas, further economic measures are necessary. The transport factor must be combined with other factors promoting economic activities (capital, labor, etc.).

An economically motivated choice among alternative factor combinations must be based on research in comparative locational costs to determine the extent to which production should be substituted for transport. Even though raw material shortages are characteristic of the economic situation in the industrially mature regions of the Soviet Union, these shortages are not taken into account when costs for alternative industrial locations are being compared, allegedly for reasons of 'tradition'.[40] No attempt is made to evaluate natural resources, including land use, deposits and water. Expenditures for environmental protection also receive no consideration. If these regionally varying costs were included in economic calculations of alternate industrial locations, it has been pointed out that costs for certain production locations would be significantly higher in the western industrial regions. And, only when these comparative locational costs have been determined, would it be possible to decide to what extent and for which industries development of Soviet Asia's economic regions should be promoted and production substituted for transport.[41] On the other hand, it must be noted that the availability of raw materials is not the sole determinant, but that it is also essential to calculate comprehensively the costs of providing adequate working conditions in the eastern underdeveloped regions, because labor has an important indirect influence on location through various social investment requirements and skills. Therefore, these costs are also often much higher than in the Soviet Union's western industrial regions.

Experts feel that there are two principal alternatives for development of backward regions of Soviet Asia under discussion. On the one hand, they support the present locational practice which has been directing capital investment to the raw material deposits, taking into account their size, quality, and accessibility. Determinants for the locational pattern of an area in an economic region are then extractive industries and transfer (material) oriented branches. Whether a development project such as that in the West Siberian Lowlands attains national significance depends on the developmental objectives that have been set. In this case regional transport development measures are considerable. Inland navigation on the Ob' and the Irtysh has an important developmental function, since railroads are lacking. In 1975, 24 percent of total Soviet river transport (tkm and tons originated), took place on the river systems of Siberia and the Far East, compared to 17 percent (tkm) and 20 percent (t orig.) in 1960.[42]

Another strategic approach to develop backward regions in Soviet Asia has been suggested for more structural differentiation of production there. It does not start out with raw material deposits (transfer-oriented location), but rather the first step is to concentrate capital investment in the medium-sized and large cities in Siberia and the Far East. It has been pointed out that the continuing process of differentiating production is hampered primarily by a lack of skilled labor. For this reason, the industrial development of Siberia and the Far East has to start or continue with the formation of human capital. The conditions under which the economic factors relevant to production must be combined would make the development of completely different production techniques necessary, both in order to achieve minimization of labor input and to use productive assets effectively in a hostile environment. Therefore, some experts and planners feel it is imperative to mechanize and automate production extensively at every level. In order to achieve this, a comprehensive investigation into the natural and economic conditions in Soviet Asia's underdeveloped regions should first be carried out for generating appropriate techniques and technology for the extractive and processing industries. It is considered necessary to develop production methods which would minimize the demand for labor.[43]

Applying this concept, pioneer work in regional economic development would then no longer be done at raw material sources, but rather in the education, research and construction centers of the cities. Investments in the infrastructure would have precedence over investments in industry, i.e. for the creation of production units in which the scientific-technical, the social and the local transport infrastructure are involved. Therefore, if certain cities in the southern zone of Siberia and the Far East were to be chosen as developmental centers of the type described above, then production units at raw material deposits or in the cities themselves should be located after the technical basis for production, including transport facilities, has been developed.

It is expected that the creation of training centers and also of institutions for research and development of special production techniques in cities of Siberia and the Far East would arouse the interest of those who want to practice occupations of this kind. Once qualified workers were available, the preconditions for the establishment of higher order manufacturing branches would exist. In the long run, production centers could then arise on the basis of special production techniques applied to the spatial conditions in Siberia and the Far East.[44] If a more dispersed locational pattern were to be achieved, the composition of interregional traffic flows would change. Then the share of bulk goods transported would decline, in accordance with the above-mentioned alternative of regional economic development.

This locational concept is based on the consideration that, in the so-called age of the scientific-technical revolution, transportation as a locational factor has lost its former dominating importance in favor of other factors such as skilled labor, infrastructural facilities, research centers, etc.[45] As far as the regional development effects of BAM are concerned, it is not the purpose of this paper to discuss the technical details or any special aspects of the route taken by BAM. Rather, an attempt will be made to describe the regional economic effects BAM may be expected to have.

BAM's developmental effects on an area of approximately 150 to 200 km on each side of it are expected to be both extensive and varied. Therefore, BAM could carry large volumes of commodities originating in this zone, which would underscore its regional importance. However, there is no indication just now that a regional development program exists which could help to clarify when, where and which economic activities should be established within the BAM area, an area, it should be noted, in which present gross industrial output represents only 1.9 percent of overall gross industrial output in Siberia and the Far East.[46] Since the territory along the BAM route has not yet been prospected thoroughly enough, an essential prerequisite to formulate targets for regional economic development specifying localities, developmental objects, quantities and time periods does not exist.[47] Though the Tenth Five Year Plan provides for increasing coal production from fields in South Yakutia situated in the area served by BAM, and also for building a coal upgrading plant, a power station, and a branch line from Tynda northward to Berkakit, these measures are not part of a coordinated regional development program. The only hint we have is that provided by the Soviet economist Botvinnikov who gives some information about various economic development objects that might actually be realized by the year 2000.[48] His expectations refer to the Mid-Siberian Zone and the Far East and include the West Siberian Lowlands in addition to the BAM Zone.[49] In approximately twenty-five years, he feels it may be possible to attain the following annual output figures for individual commodities and products in this zone: petroleum 450-500 million tons; natural gas 200-250 billion cubic meters; iron ore 300 million tons; cellulose and paper 8-10 million tons; sawn timber 30-35 million tons; electricity from hydropower stations 45 million kwt; enough mineral coal and rock salt to meet the nation's increasing need for these products; 250,000-400,000 tons of beef; 160,000-180,000 tons of pork; 1.7 million tons of milk; and 15,000 tons of poultry--all very optimistic figures indeed! According to Botvinnikov, the realization of these objects will require various development measures. Thus, it would be necessary to add to the Zone's transport facilities 9,450 km of railway, 12,600 km of roads, 14 river ports and harbors and a number of airfields. The main axis of transport should consist of a North Siberian main railway line which could follow a route from Tiumen via Tobol'sk-Surgut-Maklakovo-Nishneangarsk-Tynda-Komsomol'sk/Amur to Sovetskaia Gavan'. In other words, it would include BAM and other stretches of railway already in existence. This transport axis would have to be connected to cities in the southern part of Siberia and in the Far East by means of branch terminal lines.

In addition to transport development, denser population is another essential precondition if the production targets assumed by Botvinnikov are to be realized. In Siberia the tendency of out-migration has become much stronger since the 1950's. Most of the migration is from rural areas in Siberia. Within eight years, from 1959 to 1967, the able-bodied population of West Siberia's rural areas, with the exception of the Tiumen' area, decreased by 550,000 persons.[50] Therefore, there is a considerable labor shortage, not only in industry but also in agriculture. This undesirable population loss is explained by the fact that the branches of industry which dominate here require heavy work and unskilled labor.[51] At present approximately 1.6 million persons live in the Mid-Siberian Zone. If this Zone were to develop as Botvinnikov indicates, his opinion is that the population must grow to 6 or 7 million people.

The factor capital can be considered from two points of view. The first aspect concerns capital input in connection with the choice of production techniques, as referred to earlier. The second aspect concerns the financing of capital investment. In this respect, participation of foreign capital by both 'capitalist' and CMEA countries in the development of Siberia and of the Far East is taken into account. Credits are to be compensated by raw material exports. As an example, the Soviet Union received a credit of 450 million dollars from Japan, which is to be partially compensated in the period from 1983 to 1998 by coal deliveries from South Yakutiia amounting to 5.5 million tons annually, and then with still larger deliveries thereafter.[52]

In raw material producing regions, too, the realization of development projects which are supposed to contribute to regional decentralization of economic activities depends on whether administrative behavior can be coordinated successfully. If industrial administrative organs (i.e., ministries) tend to realize production plans at locations where, from their point of view, the most favorable conditions prevail, such actions then threaten to intensify disparities in regional economic development to the detriment of the national economy. The shaping of a rational nation-wide framework for locating economic activities is strongly impeded by the diverging locational interests of individuals and groups acting on different administrative levels, interests which top decision-makers are confronted with. For better coordination of administrative behavior at the regional level, the production plans of industrial branches (sectoral plans) are to become integrated elements of regional development programs in order to be realized in 'program-regions' called territorial production complexes (TPK). Within economic regions, TPKs cover territories specified by size and availability of resources, with which sectoral plans should be coordinated. Yet, whenever attempts have been made to coordinate sectoral regional production plans, they have turned out not to be very successful. Up to this point no suitable organizational form has been found for managing a territorial production complex.[53]

So far, there are no indications that economic development along the BAM trunk line will be based on the creation of human capital prior to raw material production at deposit locations. Rather it can be assumed that raw materials will be exploited before new production techniques are generated. Since a development program for the BAM Zone can only be realized over the long run due to high capital expense, Sobolev recommends establishing production units simultaneously, with BAM sections starting in operation before the entire trunk line is completed. The operational basis for economic development of the northern zone of Siberia and the Far East must be, in any case, cities of their southern zone.

BAM's effects on economic development along both sides of its route will probably be quite limited at first. From the economic point of view, it is not a matter of any urgency to speed up economic development in this area. The energy and raw material needs that could be satisfied by products of this kind in which TPKs along BAM's route might specialize[54] can be met in other areas under more favorable conditions and/or at lower development costs.[55] for example, there are the raw materials and energy development projects Saian-Shushenskoe (Abakan), Kansk-Achinsk (Krasnoyarsk), and Bratsk-Ust'-Ilimsk, all in East Siberia. In addition, there are extractive and basic industries in West Siberia. There is also no compelling reason to urge on economic development of the BAM Zone specifically for the sake of raw material and energy exports. Because of the unfavorable conditions under which this development has to be done, substantial capital investment will be necessary. If a policy of development were pursued vigorously, then much of this capital would have to come from foreign sources. However, the greater the amount of foreign capital necessary, the more difficult it will be to compensate granted credits from foreign countries by deliveries of raw materials, since the Soviet Union's export capability is limited.

After completion in 1982, BAM's real significance will lie first of all in its transit function, improving transport capacity between East Siberia and the Far East by 40 to 50 million tons in both directions. Freight traffic will consist primarily of petroleum, timber, building materials, metals, and coal. Estimates are that it will amount to 35 million tons annually, with petroleum alone accounting for 25 million tons of this freight volume. The petroleum originates in West Siberia, is carried from here to Taishet, where it will be transshipped on the BAM and, after another transshipment at Urgal, is destined for refineries about 1,000 kilometers distant, as well as for export from eastern seaports.[56] The new seaport Sovetskaia Gavan' will be the central terminal for petroleum. Even at the present time petroleum and petroleum products account for about 40 percent of all commodities shipped to destinations in the Far East.[57]

Because the Siberian land bridge will be improved by BAM, it will also be possible to increase the transit traffic between Japan and West Europe which currently is carried by the Main Siberian Railroad (Transsib). The harbors of Nakhodka and Vostochnyi are now equipped for container shipments, and together they have an overall capacity of 200,000 containers annually. There can be no doubt that shipments of this type further burden the already heavily-travelled freight lines which lead westward from Siberia. However, apparently this disadvantage is outweighed by the opportunity to earn foreign currency.

V. Summary

The Soviet Union's regional economic development is characterized by the important ilndustrial agglomeration centers with highly differentiated manufacturing structures which have evolved in the European part of the country. In the industrial cities which form these aglomeration centers, population and production are concentrated within a fairly limilted space, while their surrounding areas are less developed in terms of industry, transport, and housing. The industrial regions form a contrast to economic regions in Soviet Asia with poorly differentiated production structures, where extractive and basic industries dominate. A high degree of economic dependence exists between the industrial and raw material producing regions.

These disparities in the Soviet Union's regional economic development are increasing as agglomeration in the nodal regions becomes still more pronounced and as their dependence on raw material regions continues to grow as well. Therefore, the overall process of economic growth in the Soviet Union will be impaired considerably. All this is reflected in the situation of intraregional and interregional transport systems.

Thus, at the intraregional level, transport services in the industrial centers, for example, deteriorate where the access and/or exit roads to or from large cities become crowded and the railroad junctions in them exhausted. On the other hand, the extension of such transport facilities proves to be difficult whenever space is limited in the centers themselves. Decentralization of industries by locating them in peripheral zones outside the nucleus is then unavoidable. However, dispersion in this way will only be possible if the areas surrounding large industrial cities are made accessible by more efficient transport development, which has been badly neglected in the past. This now is fostered through road construction programs which have been decided upon and may be realized during the Tenth Five Year Plan in, among others, rural areas and in the Non-Black-Earth-Zone in order to promote various economic activities there. It is said to be especially important to succeed by such measures in keeping labor from migrating to the cities.

The high costs connected with making transport infrastructure and services available for improvement and expansion of interregional communication also have detrimental effects on the overall process of economic development. Continuous expansion of transport infrastructure and services is required, because ever-increasing amounts of bulk goods must be shipped from raw material producing to industrial regions in order to meet the constantly growing demand of the latter for raw materials and fuel. It is for this reason that variations of transport systems between economic regions are concentrated primarily on rationalization together with expanding the capacity of long-distance transport to make it more efficient. One especially impressive example of how facilities for transporting raw products and fuel have been rationalized and expanded is the construction of long-distance crude oil and gas pipeline systems which connect West Siberia and Central Asia with industrial regions in the western part of the country. The cost of transporting crude oil by rail is in most cases considerably higher. However, increases in capacity and efficiency have not yet been great enough to ease operational transport dislocations because there are virtually no transport reserves and capacity remains heavily over-utilized. Since economic dependencies between industrial and raw material producing regions continued to grow, and transport problems associated with this became still more aggravated, it is considered necessary to emphasize industrial dispersion by accelerating economic development in Soviet Asia as well as measures for expanding capacity and increasing efficiency of interregional transport systems.

The course transport development takes in the process of making resources in certain areas of Siberia and the Far East accessible will depend on the principles followed in locating industries and other economic activities there. In the past, transport development has been directly associated with establishing plants at raw material deposits (material-oriented locations) to supply them with transport services. For example, the current economic development of the West Siberian Lowlands is proceeding in this manner. Together with localization of extractive industry, considerable transport capacity is being created in this area by means of pipelines, railroads, and inland navigation. At first it was necessary to connect pipelines and railway lines with long-distance transport systems outside of these producing areas which lead westward and eastward. But recently, for example, lon-distance pipelines have been completed which run directly from the oil and gas fields to industrial regions in the European part of the Soviet Union, supplying consumers there with petroleum and natural gas.

However, experience shows that, beyond extraction and processing of raw material, higher-order manufacturing activities prove difficult to locate, above all because skilled labor is not available. Therefore, another principle for regional development of economic activities has been suggested to overcome those obstacles. According to this proposal, capital input should not be immediately concentrated at the raw material basis, but in cities in Siberia and the Far East to create human capital first of all. The purpose is to generate production techniques which are applicable to different industries, including engineering, under the specific environmental conditions of the eastern regions. The infrastructural basis (research centers, trainging centers, etc.) would have to be built up or expanded in cities of the southern zone of Siberia and the Far East as a matter of prime importance. In following this principle for regilonal development of economic activities, it is considered useful, as with generation ofproduction techniques on the basis of human capital, to carry on transport development prior to establishing production units at natural deposits or in the cities themselves. Whether a regional policy which aims at decentralizing economic activities in suburban areas of industrial centers or in the eastern backwark regions in successful depends to a large extent on whether it is possible to coordinate administrative behavior effectively on different levels of decision-making.

With regard to the construction of the Baikal Amur-Main Railroad Line in Siberia and the Far East as part of their overall economic development, this railroad will remain an isolated development project for the time being. Though it is said that various economic activities should be promoted within the BAM Zone, apparently no development program exists which specifies development projects. It can be concluded that previous developmental actions which have been clearly oriented toward raw material deposits, rather than towards adapting techniques to the spatial conditions of Siberia and the Far East on the basis of human capital, will continue to receive priority, with cities in the southern zone of Siberia and the Far East as operational bases. Consequently, there is no reason to accelerate industrial development in the BAM Zone, either on general economic grounds or for the sake of exports. Siberia has workable deposits at other locations which can be exploited under more favorable conditions. After BAM is completed, its primary regional economic significance will lie in its transit function. This trunk line will strengthen the Siberian land bridge, ease operational transport dispositions between East Siberia and the

Far East, and improve the connection between the Far Eastern coastal zone and its hinterland.

Footnotes

1. MRW: Balticum, White Russia, Southwest, Northwest, Center, Central-Black-Earth, Donets-Dnepr, Moldavia, South, North Caucasia, Transcaucasia, Volga, Volga'-Viatsk, Ural;
   MRE: Central Asia, Kazakhstan, West Siberia, East Siberia, Far East.
   In Soviet literature, the economic regions of Soviet Asia are often referred to simply as the "East". In this case reference is made to the following geographic zones:
   1. Central Asia and Kazakhstan with their special, highly distinctive demographic and socio-economic characteristics;
   2. the northern areas of Siberia and the Far East, which are characterized by extreme climatic and economic conditions;
   3. the southern areas of Siberia and the Far East, where there are more favorable living conditions, and economic and cultural centers have already reached a somewhat higher level of development.
2. E. Lauschmann, *Grundlagen einer Theorie der Regionalpolitik,* 2nd ed. (Hannover, 1973), p. 95. (1st ed. Mannheim 1970).
3. V.L. Stanislaviuka, *Razvitie ednoi transportnoi seti SSSR v desiatoi piatiletke,* (Moscow, 1977), pp. 92-93.
4. *Transport i sviaz' SSSR,* (Moscow, 1972), p. 213, 262; *Narodnoe khoziaistvo SSSR v 1974 godu,* p. 471, p. 491.
5. Estimated (trucks, automobiles and buses).
6. "Vagon v oborote", *Pravda,* Feb 18, 1979.
7. Out of 5540 railroad stations, centralized rail/motor road trans-shipment operations took place at only 740 stations in 1970. A.N. Markova, *Transport SSSR i osnovnye etapy ego razvitia,* (Moscow, 1977), p. 164.
8. *Materialy XXV S'ezda CPSU,* (Moscow), p. 256.
9. Stanislaviuka, *op. cit.,* p. 93.
10. O.S. Pchelintsev, "Urbanizatsiia, regional'noe razvitie i nauchno-tekhnicheskaia revoliutsiia", *Ekonomika i matematicheskie metody,* 1 (1978), 6.
11. Markova, *op. cit.,* p. 210. The first percentage figure refers to the Ukrainian Republic. The second figure reflects a broader regional average.
12. Pchelintsev, *op. cit.,* p. 11.
13. *Ibid.,* p. 9; this refers to local passenger transport as well as to local freight traffic systems.
14. Markova, *op. cit.,* p. 213.
15. *Ibid.,* p. 206. Reference is made to hard surface roads that will be needed in agricultural areas. Approximately 5 million hectares of agricultural acreage are concerned, or about 50% of the land cultivated by kolkhozy and sovkhozy.
16. *Pravda,* Oct. 22, 1978. Motor roads to be constructed in rural areas during the tenth Five-Year Plan will be administered on republican, oblast, local, and farm (kolkhoz and sovkhoz) levels.
17. General plans for urban development are referred to. See Pchelintsev, *op. cit.,* p. 9.
18. The length of industrial railroads nearly corresponds with that of 'common carrier' lines administered by the Ministerstvo Putei Soobshcheniia and amounting to 138,500 km (1976).
19. This includes the Ural Region. A. Gladyshev, V. Loginov, "Razvitie ekonomiki Sibiri i Dal'nego Vostoka", *Voprosy ekonomiki,* 9, (1978), 24.
    See also V.P. Orlov, "O tseliakh dolgosrochnogo razvitiia khoziaistva Sibiri", *Izvestiia sibirskogo otdeleniia Akademii Nauk SSSR,* [Seriia obshchestvennykh nauk, 2nd ed.], 6 (1973), 14 ff.
20. As a rule long distance transport systems comprise several connections and in some cases more than one carrier (at junctions).
21. Stanislaviuka, *op. cit.,* p. 10.

22. *Trudy IKTP pri Gosplane SSSR*, 50th ed., p. 19, p. 82; cited by Markova, *op.cit.*, p. 117.
23. A.D. Danilova, V.V. Kistanova, S.I. Ledovskikh, (eds.) *Ekonomicheskaia geografiia SSSR*, (Moscow, 1976), p. 338.
24. V. Pavlenko, "Sovremennyi etap territorial'nogo razvitiia ekonomiki", *Kommunist*, 4 (1978), 19.
25. Markova, *op. cit.*, p. 114.
26. *Ibid.*, p. 113.
27. These changes have been caused substantially by transportation itself. Air and maritime traffic developed rapidly, broad introduction of diesel locomotives took place, and the use of motor vehicles increased significantly.
28. V. Udovenko, "Sdvigi v rasmeshchenii proizvoditel'nykh sil SSSR", *Voprosy ekonomiki*, 8 (1977), 25.
29. During the period of the ninth Five-Year Plan, 1600 km of oil pipelines were built on an annual average.
30. Stanislaviuka, *op. cit.*, p. 117.
    p. 402.
31. Markova, *op. cit.*, p. 114; *Narodnoe khoziaistvo SSSR za 60 let*, (Moscow, 1977), p. 402.
32. According to plan targets, the crude oil pipeline system will be extended to about 60,000 km and the natural gas pipeline system to about 135,000 km by 1980. Then 35% of all oil pipes are to have a diameter of 1220 mm. Of the gas pipelines laid in 1975, 40% (39,000 km) had a diameter of at least 1020 mm. See Stanislaviuka, *op. cit.*, pp. 39, 114, 119. Official Soviet statistics already indicate 61,900 km of crude oil main lines in place by 1977 with plan forecasts of approximately 70,000 km by the end of 1980. See *Narodnoe khoziaistvo SSSR v 1977 g*, (Moscow, 1978), p. 318.
33. L. Gramoteeva, "Effektivnost' razmeshcheniia proisvoditel'nykh sil", *Planovoe khoziaistvo*, 11 (1978), 31.
34. Gladyshev and Loginov, *op. cit.*, p. 24.
35. Known and exploited natural resources concentrated in the Macro-Region East include 75% of the nation's coal; and 80% of the total petroleum, natural gas, timber, and waterpower. On the other hand, 76% of all exploited iron ore deposits and 70% of arable land are to be found in the Macro-Region West; Siberia's share of arable land is only 12.5%.
36. Eighty percent of all residents of the country live in the European part (including the Ural Region); 8% are settled in Siberia.
37. During the present plan period, the following regional industrial development projects are mentioned as exceptions. Kurskaia Magnitnaia Anomaly, the so-called territorial production complexes at Orenburg (gas) and Timan-Pechora (oil and gas).
38. "Razmeshchenie proizvoditel'nykh sil v strane i povyshenie effektivnosti obshchest-vennogo proizvodstva", *Planovoe khoziaistvo*, 11 (1978), 4.
39. Gladyshev and Loginov, *op. cit.*, p. 25. We learn from this that average capital productivity in the eastern regions is relatively low; however, the basis for calculating these percentages is not clear.
40. G. Tarasov, "Kompleksnoe razvitie dal'nego vostoka", *Planovoe khoziaistvo*, 11 (1978), 50.
41. *Ibid.*, p. 50.
42. Stanislaviuka, *op. cit.*, p. 18.
43. Pchelintsev, *op. cit.*, p. 13.
44. *Ibid.*, p. 15 ff.
45. *Ibid.*, p. 13.
46. V.S. Katargin, L.I. Iurkevich, "Territorial'no-proizvodstvennye kompleksy tsentral' noi chasti zony BAM", *Izvestiia Akademii Nauk SSSR*, [Seriia ekonomicheskaia], 5 (1977).
47. For economic development of the BAM Zone, Sobolev suggests forming the following plan-regions (territorial'nye proizvodstvennye komplektsy/TPK and promyshelnnye uzly/PU):
    1. TPK Upper Lena—lumbering, cellulose production
    2. TPK North Baikal—ore mining, nonferrous metallurgy

3. PU Udokan—nonferrous metallurgy
4. TPK South Yakutiia—coal and ore mining
5. TPK West Amur—lumbering
6. TPK Zeisk-Svobodensk—lumbering, cellulose production
7. PU Urgal—coal mining, lumbering
8. TPK Komsomolsk/Amur—ferrous and nonferrous metallurgy, lumbering, cellulose and paper production, petrochemicals, engineering.
See Sobolev, *op. cit.*, p. 41.

48.   V. Botvinnikov, "K voprosu o kontsepsii ekonomicheskogo razvitiia srednei polosy Sibiri i Dal'nego Vostoka", *Izvestiia sibirskogo otdeleniia Akademii Nauk SSSR*, [Seriia obshchestvennykh nauk, 2nd ed.], 6 (1973), 28-32.

49.   The mid-Siberian Zone largely corresponds with the northern areas of Siberia and the Far East, as was mentioned above. See footnote 1.

50.   B.P. Orlov, "Tendentsii ekonomicheskogo razvitiia Sibiri i povyshenie ego roli v obshchesoiusnom proizvodstve", *Izvestiia sibirskogo otdeleniia Akademii Nauk SSSR*, [Seriia Obshchestvennykh nauk], 1 (1969), 10.

51.   Pchelintsev, *op. cit.*, p. 15.

52.   The USSR and Japan have agreed to promote six cooperative projects to develop natural resources in Siberia and the Far East. Three agreements concern lumbering, the others coal mining and geological prospecting in South Yakutiia, and offshore gas and/or oil exploitation on the Sakhalin peninsula.

53.   Kolosovskii defines a spacious intraregional TPK as a well-organized totality of stable interconnected, interdependent, and coordinated productions of different economic sectors (industry, agriculture, construction, transport, and services) which realize one or several economic tasks. N. N. Kolosovskii, *Modelirovanie, formirovanie territorial'noproizvodstvennykh kompleksov*, (Novosibirsk, 1971), p. 16.

54.   See footnote 47.

55.   Cost for creation of additional employment includes, besides establishing production units, housing construction and the provision of other infrastructural facilities.

56.   "Die Magistrale des Jahrhunderts", interview with W. E. Biriukov, member of the State Planning Committee of the USSR, in *DDR Verkehr*, 8 (1975), 519 ff. See also: C. Chr. Liebmann, "Die Baikal-Amur-Eisenbahnmagistrale (BAM), Trassenverlauf und wirtschaftliche Erschliessung entlang einer sowjetischen Bahnlinie", *Die Erde*, 109 (1978), 222.

57.   Iu. D. Kuznetsov, G.P. Kobylkovski, *Planirovanie razvitiia transportnoi seti v ekonomicheskom raione*, (Moscow, 1975), p. 103.

233

Dr. John Hardt

Current position:
Congressional Research Service,
Library of Congress,
Washington.

Main field of work:
East-West Trade and Political
Implications for the West; Soviet
Energy.

**Publications during
the last two years:**
"Techonolgy Transfer and Change in
the Soviet Economic System"
(Written with George Holliday), in
Joint Economic Committee (ed.),
Issues in East-West Commercial
Relations, (Washington, 1979), 59-91.

Transportation and the Military
Significance of Regionalization

The Military-Economic
Implications
of Soviet Regional Policy
Dr. John Hardt

I. Policy Alternative Overview

Economic performance may well become a major issue in the inevitable
succession process in Soviet leadership. Falling economic performance is a
concern to all groups in the leadership, as well as the population as a whole.
An 'industrialization debate,' such as influenced the succession to Lenin
may not be precisely revisited, but every period of change seems likely to
concentrate attention on vexing economic problems. A profound change in
political as well as economic policy is possible in the wake of Brezhnev's exit
from the scene. Moreover, the time of succession is likely to coincide with a
period of potentially sharp deterioration in economic performance. According to pessimistic U.S. intelligence estimates of energy and agricultural
production and changes in the efficiency of labor and capital, the aggregate
growth rate may be halved in the next decade to an average of little more
than 2 percent, or less per annum in specific years with some years potentially evidencing negative growth. On the other hand, others in the West
with similar data conclude that a continuation of a 4 percent growth rate is a
reasonable expectation. [2]

An assumption that underlies the more negative Soviet prospects is that
although better performance may be possible with change, the necessary
changes are not likely to be forthcoming. A recent CIA publication
forecasts a very narrow range of potential economic growth options for the
next Five Year Plan period to 1985. I associate with the general observation
on the uncertainty of forecasts:

> Any analysis of the prospects for Soviet economic growth is
> very speculative. This uncertainty is simply a reflection of the
> many unknown events and reactions--some under the control
> of Soviet policymakers and some not--that are likely to have a
> profound influence on growth over the next decade. [3]

I do not identify with the CIA implicit assumptions that policy changes are
not likely to affect performance. Let us then explore some of the changes in
policy and performance necessary to check the retardation and possibly to
rise Soviet performance closer to its full potential:

1. *Regional policy.* The resource potential of Siberia in energy, metals, timber--indeed all materials--is as yet only partially explored and largely untapped. The The labor potential for such economic expansion is largely in the seven Republics of the Caucasus, Central Asia and Kazakhstan. European Russia is deficient in both natural resources and labor, but has the established capital plant and infrastructure of the Soviet economy. Efficient adaption to these regional disparities in resource location will be a fundamental factor in growth determination.

2. *Military Support Policy.* With some variation during the post Stalin period, the trend has been to allocate in successive years a growing share of high-quality capital and labor resources to military pursuits. The military 'burden' deterring economic growth is substantial, as may be the opportunity costs. A shift of resource allocation priority for high-quality investment and labor resources from military to economic modernization activities would be important for the improvement in economic performance.

3. *Economic Reform in Planning and Management.* With better economic data, improved analysis, modern econometric tools, and appropriate computer application, planning might be more efficient. With more authority for the enterprise managers and improved incentives, managerial efficiency might be improved. How much improvement is possible with more efficient planning and management is hard to estimate, but I assume it would be substantial and is an important variable in economic performance.

4. *Western Technology Transfer.* Judicious imports of western technology, application of western management systems for utilizing the processes, coupled with investment from domestic capital of high-quality plant and equipment might accelerate technological change and improve economic performance. The measured gains from inter-dependence involving western inter-relations might not equal the 'economic miracles' of western economic developments, but technology transfer will surely have a growth-accelerating effect.

5. *CMEA Policy.* In the short run, Eastern European requirements for energy and other goods the USSR can export for hard or convertible currency are a drain on the Soviet economy. They divert resources such as

energy from domestic consumption or western markets supplying foreign exchange for high-technology product imports. In the longer term, however, to the extent East European economies modernize and supply their modern economic products and systems to the Soviet Union in a more absorbable or adaptable technological form, intra CMEA relations may have a growth-stimulating result. A positive Soviet balance of growth stimulating benefit from East Europe may provide a major boost to Soviet economic performance. In order to obtain the long-term benefit of intra CMEA modernization and integration, however, a substantial short-term burden of diverting hard goods to Eastern Europe may be necessary for the Soviet Union.

Each factor influencing economic performance may be considered in the context of Soviet regional policy. Traditional adherence to established priorities and institutions in the old European Russian emphasis may assure a deepening rather than an amelioration of the crises impending in Soviet economic performance. Change in regional emphasis may be intertwined with modification of the economic policy choices discussed above.

In factor endowment for national economic development, the Soviet Union may be said to be divided into three distinct economic areas with sharply disparate endowments of capital, labor, natural resources, and technology. The classic economic factors required for increased output are a developed capital base (C); an available, adequately skilled supply of labor (L); adequate, economically exploitable natural resources (R); and advanced technology. If the Soviet Union were divided into three regions they would be blessed with one of the factors and more or less deficient in the others: European Russia (including the Baltic Republics, Ukraine, Belorussia) (C+,L-,R-); Southern Republics (the Caucasus, Kazakhstan and the Central Asian Republics) (L+, C−, R+); Siberian RSFSR (East of Urals, North of Central Asia) (R+, C-, L-).[4] All regions would be deficient in technology by western industrial nations' standards, except in the military sector. The regional consideration also interacts with other elements of policy, e.g. to develop industry where the natural and labor resources are abundant involves sharply increased costs, preference for development of areas not dominated by central Russian power, and may involve a measure of foreign economic dependence.

In broad terms, what would be required in these various aspects of effective Soviet economic development is an application of at least some of the other economic policy changes, including: some priority change in resource allocation policy, in particular away from the traditional priority of military or heavy-industrial claimants for high-quality resources; erosion or restructuring away from the traditional dominant role of the Party and the all-pervasive Stalinist governmental bureaucracy at all levels of the

Soviet economy; further modification of the traditional Stalinist policy of economic independence from the West; and effective integration of the modernizing sectors of the smaller CMEA economies with that of the Soviet Union.

The changes in resource allocation policy, the institutions of planning and management, and the policy of foreign economic independence--the first three performance variables--tend to encourage a regional economic emphasis away from the predominantly Slavic, European heartland of the USSR to the outlying Siberian and southern regions. CMEA integration might, in contrast, tend to fortify continued regional emphasis on the European Russian areas of the Soviet Union.

Although the leadership in their policy statements seem committed to proceed toward modernization during the Fifteen-Year Plan period, projected changes have not consistently received high priority resources in practice.[5] Modernization through emphasis on higher technology projects related to western imports is official policy and the programs are authorized and underway, but there have been persistent deferrals or stretching out of aspects of these major modernization projects, including giant Siberian projects. The specific delays have probably had negative effects on entire complexes for which western technology is critical. Examples of these project stretch-outs include, but are not limited to, the following major deferrals within the Siberian regional and specifically energy-related priority areas: delay in development of the power-consuming industries and resource development industries in East Siberia and the region around the Baikal-Amur railroad; delay in the development of long-distance AC and DC transmission facilities for bringing cheap hydro and coal generated power from Siberia and European Russian markets; delay in importing transmission, exploration and extraction equipment and other facilities for petroleum and natural gas complexes to meet the projected plan of energy output increases, both onshore and offshore; and delay in the construction of the Baikàl-Amur railroad.

What are the costs of further Soviet delays and equivocation in opting for priority for western-related projects to achieve economic modernization and development? The costs are high, indeed, if the expensive multi-billion projects, in some cases well underway, are not soon brought to a level of effective production. The gestation periods for these major projects, so central to improved future Soviet performance, are long in any event, but the possibility for converting facilities or utilizing partially completed facilities and transportation facilities are sunk costs. The full returns come only after completing the economic complexes which provide them. Meanwhile, the projects are referred to by the Soviets as 'frozen assets.'

In each of these major complexes western technology plays an important, even critical, role in the likely cost and effectiveness of the projects. To be sure, less advanced metallurgical, energy, automotive, agricultural, computer and construction technology could be obtained from domestic

Soviet sources, either now or at a later date. However, the preference that Soviet planners have already shown for western technology imports for these projects suggests that the costs of relying on domestic technology must be substantial. To use imports of western technology more effectively, Soviet planners must revise traditional resource allocation policies and reform the institutional context in which the new complexes operate. The large western-assisted complexes place a heavy new demand on high-quality domestic inputs, such as technicians, materials, and machinery. If such inputs are currently under the control of traditional high-priority sectors of the economy, Soviet planners will have to make difficult choices on resource allocation. Moreover, traditional Soviet enterprise management practices do little to provide effective utilization of foreign technology. More effective absorption of western technology could be facilitated by significant enterprise-management reform, including the borrowing of western management techniques. One approach to reform might be the creation of foreign-technology-related 'enclaves' which operate on a new style of management outside of the present bureaucratic chain of command. For example, the degree of independence and enhanced authority granted to the managers of the Volga Automobile Plant and the Kama River Truck Plant appear to be a limited step in this direction. The longer-term, more active technology transfer mechanisms with which Soviet officials are experimenting could also help to facilitate more effective technology transfers. Although such changes will undoubtedly be seen by some Soviet officials as threatening the traditional bureaucracy and Party role in the economy, they may represent a necessary condition for effective modernization.[6]

Thus, western technology has a potentially greater role to play in the Soviet economy, if Soviet leaders are able and willing to make significant policy changes in resource allocation and enterprise management. While the rationale for change is compelling, and some Soviet leaders have expressed their commitment to economic reform, there is still only limited evidence of fundamental progress in this direction.[7]

Regional development of modernization projects in Siberia may draw resources from the scarce pool of quality products and manpower usually reserved for the military and reliance on western technology and systems may reduce the traditional role of the Party and the bureaucracy in planning and management. These kinds of changes may also be at stake in the investment in new facilities in Central Asia and the other Southern Republics designed to use their ample but presumably immobile labor supplies.

However, is there any credibility to the hypothesis that resource priorities as between defense and modernization projects may be reordered? There are indeed some technical limitations on defense allocations. Decisions to allocate investment resources to long-term defense projects have become increasingly difficult to reverse. With respect to strategic weapons systems, modern naval developments--and even the equipping of modern conventional forces for the China border--the options for conversion of economic resources from military to non-military have become increasingly limited once the project is initiated. The gestation period from decision on strategic weapons buildup after the Cuban missle crisis to deployment and utilization in some political sense may have been a decade or more. Writing at the time, I noted that, "Premier Khrushchev is using up today in weapons systems decisions many of the options of his successor and pre-conditioning the resource allocation pattern that will be his successor's inheritance."[8]

However, the fact that potentially competitive programs have been approved in long-term modernization projects and long-term defense programs does not mean that important choices may not be made on the margin. Specifically, a decision may be made to slow down or defer the expansion of agricultural equipment output, as it was in 1966, presumably to speed up the production of armored tracked vehicles, e.g., tanks, often made in the same plant complexes. Conversely, the priority for moving ahead on the Siberian Baikal-Amur railroad (BAM) appeared to be spurred in 1974 with a step-up in imports and use of military construction crews to facilitate progress on that so-called 'project of the century'. On several occasions the West Siberian petroleum development has been accorded top priority, e.g. in January 1970 and December 1977. In each case resources, contruction facilities and infrastructure development were all accorded leadership priority. The crash effort--referred to characteristically as 'storming' by the Soviets--probably drew from deferred civilian and/or military projects. In a 1970 Party and Government decree, according priority to the West Siberian development, the support of the Ministry of Defense Industries was specifically referenced as well as the cooperation required of the relevant civilian ministries.[9]

Resource overcommitment to meet the economic expansion targets of the Soviet economy is not a new phenomenon. Tautness in planning or systematic overcommitment is traditional. More projects have always been authorized than could be funded. The operational priority was established by the choice among projects to be preferred or deferred. The new characteristic, in the Brezhnev period, appears to extend the choice to competition between civilian and military projects. This may be described as the emergence of a marginal 'Guns' or 'modernization' choice in the current Soviet resource allocation.

II. A New Soviet 'Guns' or Modernization' Choice

The rate of progress in major large-scale modernization areas may be given alternating priority status. Indeed, it is my observation that a variety of large-scale projects fluctuate from low priority (deferral) to high-priority ('storming'). In the latter case, priority is given to supply of hard-currency imports and world market level quality, domestic intermediate products and skilled construction crews. The size of these latter claims on high-quality Soviet domestic resources is roughly three to five times the value of hard-currency imports for such projects as the Kama Truck Plant, comparing reported imports and domestic investment figures.[10] When priority or 'storming' status has been given to the commencement of projects, such as the Tolyatti Auto Plant (1968), Kama Truck Plant (1971), Baikal-Amur Railroad (1974), and Kursk Metallurgical Plant (1978), considerable increments of hard-currency outlays are required for imports and a substantially larger demand on world level or domestic 'hard goods and services' are required for effective implementation of the 'storming' decision. As all Soviet planning has been characterized by a conscious policy of overcommitment or 'taut' planning, no major levies on the domestic plan may be made without shortfalls or deferrals elsewhere. I assume that some shift in resources from other civilian projects may fill part of the needs of the 'storming' projects, but then the magnitude and quality of the resources required suggests that the Ministry of Defense Industries and the military builders would likewise have to play a contributing prominent role.

There may indeed be frequent deferrals in major defense programs. If the priority to the major modernization projects is to be upgraded, it is assumed that there is likely to be an increase in western imports and a diversion of resources from other domestic projects. Where the resource shift of sophisticated materials and labor is large-scale, then it is assumed that some deferral in defense-related projects is involved. The political decisions to approve a speed-up or 'storming,' either of civilian-modernization or defense programs, imply a slowdown, deferral or stretch-out in other programs.

To prepare for deferral or 'storming,' we note that a special, Soviet-style 'debate' occurs. This one-sided public discussion on behalf of the incremental commitment or 'storming,' and implying deferral of other projects, is the form we assume the Soviet modernization or defense resource debates have taken.

The assumptions made on the nature of the defense/modernization debate are the following:

1. More high-priority defense and modernization projects are approved than there are high-quality resources to fund at a planned or optimal rate. This tautness in planning, so characteristic of long-term Soviet practice, is especially intense for long-term, large scale, defense and modernization projects requiring access to high-quality resources and manpower approaching western levels.

2. Resources are distributed very unevenly among major projects and sharply change from time to time from deferral (low priority) to 'storming' (high priority) within Five-Year and longer plans.

3. Defense or 'guns or modernization' debates largely take the form of institutional contests to raise projects to the 'storming' level or remove projects from deferral status.

Illustrations of this kind of phenomenon may be of the following:

Agricultural Debate in 1966, unsuccessful in avoiding

agricultural equipment program deferral;
Western Siberian energy debate, 1968-69, successful in 'storming' energy;
Naval Debate, 1973-74, successful in 'storming' naval buildup;
West Siberian energy debate, 1977, successful in 'storming' energy.

In the agricultural debate of 1966, Politburo member Dimitri Polyansky, responsible for agricultural performance, argued against the apparent down-grading of priority for production of agricultural equipment to facilitate the efficiency of future harvests. The 'other people' he referred to as carrying the day may have argued for acceleration in the buildup in production of tanks and other conventional weaponry.

In the late 1960's, as the Ural-Volga oil fields began 'peaking out' well before expected by Soviet planners, the argument was pressed by many Soviet planners that the major new fields of West Siberia should be brought into production at forced draft. By January 1970, by joint Party and Government decree, the industrial and construction ministries, including defense industries, were directed to facilitate this 'storming' effort.

Admiral Gorshkov, the Soviet Naval Chief, argued in his house organ, *Naval Digest (Morskii Sbornik),* for a new, expanded navy and thus an accelerated program of shipbuilding. Although he may not have received all he asked for, it appears that priorities were changed to facilitate his program. Continued building of the Soviet Merchant marine suggests a sharing of joint construction facilties that may have a part in the accelerated naval shipbuilding that was apparently approved.[11]

Since 1973-74, when it became clear to the Soviet leaders that an energy problem was forthcoming unless high priority was given either to a broad comprehensive energy buildup or to a selected program of energy development, there have been many proposed and approved new energy programs, together with some deferrals. However, in 1977 the apparent focus on the short-run petroleum output problem led in December to an accelerated program stepping up exploration and bringing in new output in West Siberia.[12] This 'storming' effort may draw from other energy projects more than from defense-related efforts, at least in the short run. But keeping the broader, comprehensive energy program active, and raising it to the 'storming' level, would more than likely raise the competitive demands on defense-related activities as well.

Our hypothesis herein is that factors triggering increases in defense priorities that might lead to 'storming' are largely international, whereas the factors elevating the modernization priorities are largely domestic. These may be illustrated by the following examples:

International-Defense Heightening Factors
1. New concern or opportunity from the Chinese border, or other Asian areas.
2. New concern or opportunity from new, technologi-

cally advanced American strategic programs.
3. New concern or opportunity from Europe, especially
    Germany.

Modernization Heightening Factors
   1. Economic growth crises, e.g., sharp industrial slow-
       downs.
   2. Factor deficiencies, e.g., critical energy, metal, or
       labor shortages.
   3. Natural disasters, e.g., crop failures, including feed
       grain deficiencies.
   4. Dramatic shift in export prices for domestic output
       e.g., balance of payment crises, including non-
       payment of debts by East European nations.

The dynamics of the above is assumed to be related to a security priority. If neither a clear threat or vital international opportunity exists, then the domestic priorities may dominate resource allocation policy.

Therefore, if Soviet leaders are assured that military parity is stable, poltical stability on their borders is assured, and opportunities for security are limited, they will be less likely to approve 'storming' on defense projects. If the perceived threat of opportunity is persuasive, they will then give defense buildup a high priority. The lesson of Soviet action after the Cuban missle crisis is presumably that the strategic buildup was given priority because of the unfavorable Soviet military position in 1962. In the future, if the West Germans gained access to nuclear weapons and the command position in NATO (an unlikely prospect) or formal military supply or alliance relations developed between the PRC and the United States (an even more unlikely prospect), the high Soviet priority to military projects would be clear. Any tempting power vacuums in strategic areas, such as the Middle East or Africa, would likewise generate a pattern of attractive foreign opportuntities, thus enhanced military priorities might follow.

If, however, the reverse were true--no new concerns or opportunities-- then the urgent needs of economic modernization might lead to a high priority or 'storming' for one or more of the major civilian projects or complexes. This might not add up to an economic transformation or miracle, but the downward spiral of economic performance could be arrested. What is suggested is that defense priority heightening is influenced mainly by international affairs, modernization priority heightening by domestic affairs, but not the reverse. Thus, NATO and China may directly influence the Soviets to increase their defense allocations, but only indirectly influence them to decrease them. Pressures to stretch out military projects and increase the priority to modernization are likely to come from domestic forces.

We also assume a change in the traditional short-term aspect of 'storming,' e.g., an annual shift in tractor factories from tanks to tractors and back. This short-term 'storming'/deferral cycle often had a 'rob Peter to pay Paul' character within a given ministry or set of enterprises. The temporary shift of oil drilling crews from the Ural-Volga to West Siberian fields is such an example. What is implied in our use of 'storming' is a shift for sufficient time to bring a large project into production (the Soviet term *pusk* applies) and shift from outside the civilian ministries, especially the Ministry of Defense Industries.[13] By bringing large projects on line earlier in time a surge effect may be felt in the Soviet economy.

If resource allocation policy is shifted in some fashion from the trend of the past, permitting some significant economic growth stimulating development even in non-European regions, can the traditional system of Party and bureaucracy dominated planning and management be revised to facilitate more productivity and adoption of more efficient production modes? The foreign enclave approach coupling foreign technology and management has been noted, but are there domestic mechanisms for more efficient use of resources? There is, paradoxically, some potential in a *greater* rather than a diminished central Party role and *expanded* military involvement in economic management. The military may adopt a policy favoring civilian modernization as it promises a broadening of the narrow technological base from which future Soviet military needs must also be served. In this role of advocacy for modernization and civilian technological change the military may accede to a broader role in the administration of civilian projects such as BAM. The military may indeed seek an expanding managerial role, especially if resource claims of competitive military projects are being deferred. This expanded military role in economic administration may not be opposed by the Party. John Erickson argues that Party leaders, long wary of Bonapartism involving military intervention in major political decisions, may accede to 'managerial Bonapartism'--the traditional meaning in the West when we establish economic 'Tsars.'[14]

The role of the military in the BAM and related Siberian projects is supported or complicated by the enhanced role of the central Party. The responsibility for construction, manpower supply, and the provision of infrastructure has been partly assured by the Ministry of Defense and its related agencies. The Central Committee of the Party has become involved in the BAM development and appears to play a coordinating role. The Komsomols are an important part of the skilled manpower. Local Siberian Party and regional ministerial involvement is no doubt for accelerated development, but without the military and Party support from Moscow, a 'storming' policy for BAM would probably not be effective. Also paradoxically more central Party involvement may favor the modernization process and change in traditional resource allocation and management. The increasing involvement of sections of the Secretariat of the central Party in economic planning and administration may be an important factor in fostering change and increasing efficiency.[15] The appointment of Yakov P. Ryabov to be first deputy chairman of Gosplan, while retaining his functions in the Secretariat of the CPSU, may be a step in the centralization process of economic modernization.[16] The earlier appointment of N.N. Inozemtsev as deputy chairman of Gosplan to facilitate the integration of foreign trade and domestic planning was probably an early step in the same direction.

III.   The Economic Dilemmas of CMEA and the Warsaw Pact

Soviet policies for economic modernization under Khrushchev and Brezhnev defined the limits within which the smaller countries of the Council of Mutual Economic Assistance (CMEA) could adopt their own new economic strategies. The new East European strategy emphasis is selective modernization, using western technology and managerial techniques. East European efforts in the 1960's, designed to achieve modernization, were forcibly stopped by the intrusion of Soviet tanks into Prague. The Prague approach to economic modernization on a broad front was part of a larger policy of change which proved to be too provocative to the Soviets. Moreover, broad economic reform and structural change likewise appeared to be too much for East European leaders to accomodate simultaneously. In its place, the East European countries adopted a strategy of selective emphasis on growth areas and economic reforms in specific planning and management sectors for the current decade.   The New Economic Mechanism in Hungary, for example, emphasizes selective reform.

The East European countries also embarked, albeit somewhat unevenly, upon large long-term projects for development of selective sectors with special emphasis on western technology transfer. They likewise adopted consumer-oriented programs designed to provide increasing incentives, which generated substantially increased expectations as well as increased productivity. A modern industrial structure, an accelerated rate of economic growth, and, especially an increase in visible consumption--including availability of meat and other quality products--become characteristic goals of East European economic policies.

In 1975 the East European leaders and planners were no doubt chagrined when the Soviet Union, in the wake of the significant increase in world energy prices, radically changed the terms of trade against its East European partners. In 1973-74, when OPEC prices increased, CMEA prices were stable and payment to the USSR by East European nations was permitted through export of goods not necessarily marketable outside of CMEA.   In 1975, this situation was revised by a planning arrangement whereby the prices paid to the Soviet Union by the end of the decade would significantly close the gap with the current OPEC prices and presumably increase the requirement on East Europe to make hard good deliveries to the Soviet Union. The Soviet bargainers in the annual trade agreements also sought, and apparently obtained, enhanced industrial cooperation and investment in joint CMEA projects, such as the Orenburg natural gas pipeline and other Soviet resource projects. Soviet planners had been pushing each of these projects for some time, as they had the advantage to the Soviets of being a part of their domestic economy. One meght wonder if those Soviets pressing integration also tended to favor the regional dominance of European Russia of for various reasons did noo support accelerated development of Siberian projects.

One might expect the East Europeans to reduce their imports from the West in the face of pressing new requirements from the Soviet Union and irreducible, indeed, increasing requirements in their domestic economies. Some East European economic planners are doubtless drawn to the more secure, predictable CMEA markets.[17] But modernization and improved consumer performance are tied to the elimination of bottlenecks in East European plans which only western imports can effect. By the end of this five-year plan period, hard currency debt of the East European countries from the West may well increase from $18 billion in 1975 to over $60 billion in 1980.[18] The indebtedness of the East European countries has risen sharply, although unevenly. The Polish debt has increased from less than a billion when Gierek replaced Gomulka in 1970 to the highest East European level today. Credit worthiness of all CMEA countries is considered important by the Soviets so that the USSR can retain its option for increased indebtedness to the West. Likewise, in the last several years most East European countries have had balance of payments deficits with the USSR and some have a certain amount of hard currency debt.

Several questions may be asked in the above context. One is: Why do the Soviet negotiatores not extract the maximum short-term economic returns from Eastern Europe? The answer may lie in a Soviet sensitivity to the political vulnerability of the East European Parties and in a Soviet desire to benefit from increasing long-term productivity of the East European economies. The Soviets provided about 1.3 billion rubles in credit to the Poles in the fall of 1976 after the food price riots, presumably to keep Polish Party leader Gierek in power. The Soviets have also permitted East European economies to build up substantial deficits in their current accounts, especially GDR and Poland. Another factor may be the increasing divergence between Soviet and East European leaders on the utility of Warsaw Pact allocations--especially relative to non-European concerns--and the joint CMEA projects located in the USSR. In the longer terms, the Soviet Union will benefit or suffer from the ability of the East European economies to produce more 'hard' goods or products that can be sold under world market conditions. If they are politically committed to East European economic plans, then they might wish to maximize their long-term economic returns from this continued alliance or at least minimize the East European burden on the Soviet economy.

East European political stability has been shaken by the response of their people to 'Basket Three' of the 1975 Helsinki CSCE agreement. The reactions and public demonstrations, at considerable personal risk, of leading citizens in the German Democratic Republic and Czechoslovakia suggest the extent of the impact throughout Eastern Europe of the human rights aspect of these agreements. Economic improvement of the citizen's lot has become important to relative political stability. Indeed, economic performance is linked to stability in other ways. The agreement, long sought by the Catholic Church, to have churches built in new Polish towns, was a concession that seems to have a political-economic rationale. The potential of Vatican-East European relations is especially important in Poland, Czechoslovakia, Hungary and parts of the USSR, particularly in light of the successful trip of the Pope to Poland in June.

The fear of political instability in Eastern Europe appears to make the Soviets cautious in pressing their advantage over East European economic life. It may also partially account for the buildup of Warsaw Pact forces in recent years as a mechanism through which Soviet control can be reasserted by force if necessary. This area of interaction between CMEA and the Warsaw Pact as instruments of Soviet policy is a constraining and influential factor in the short run.

Some of the East European contributions to the Warsaw Pact forces are probably based on some common perceptions of the threat--especially the West German capabilities. However, military modernization and strengthening of Warsaw Pact forces, strategic missile and naval buildup, and preparation for manning the China border probably exceed shared East European/Soviet concerns. Contributions and burden sharing may thus be a part of the broader negotiation at the leadership levels; e.g., oil delivery and pricing may be tied into political instability and Warsaw Pact needs. The potential benefits from a reduction if Warsaw Pact forces under an MBFR agreement would probably be welcomed at least as much by East Europeans as Soviet planners. In contrast, increased Warsaw Pact defense outlays, especially if forces were shifted from Europe to Asia by Soviet decisions, would be unpopular in most smaller East European nations. Likewise, use of surrogate forces, such as the GDR personnel in the Middle East and Africa, is not likely to be universally popular.

IV. Choices for Brezhnev's Successors: A New 'Industrialization Debate'?

One factor in assessing current Soviet choices between short-term military and long-term economic improvements is the age of its leadership and the imminence of succession. The Brezhnev era has been characterized by consensus and status quo policies. Soviet acceptance of global economic interdepedence must be assessed against this resistance to change. In projecting future Soviet policy, Marshall Shulman, a special advisor to Secretary of State Cyrus Vance on Soviet affairs, appears to view economics in the transitional policy of Brezhnev's successors as crucial:

> The impulse toward modernizing the country along Western lines also cuts across other divisions in the political spectrum.

These divisions have their effects on two of the most interesting questions affecting the present and future development of the Soviet Union.

The first of these stems from the fact that the Soviet Union is on the threshold of a wholesale generational turnover at the upper levels of its power structure... Whether they will tend to move toward nationalism and orthodoxy, or toward Western-style modernization, we cannot now predict. All that we can say, perhaps, is that to the extent they see their interest in a responsible involvement of their country in the world economy and the world community, they should not feel from wahat we do or say that this option is closed to them.

This is related to the second question: how the Soviet leadership will deal with some fundamental structural problems in the Societ economy... While we should not underestimate the capability of the Soviet system to manage its problems on a day-to-day basis without any clear-cut solutions to these choices, it may have some relevance for our policy choices that the development of economic relations with the advanced industrial societies of the West is bound to have some influence on the directions that will emerge.[19]

The succession to Brezhnev may not develop immediately into a firm, stable leadership. A rocky transition may follow his political or physical demise. Whoever eventually succeeds him will inherit Brezhnev's long-term commitments to competing military and economic programs. A poorest (the worst) policy for Soviet leadership would then be one of continued equivocation. The Soviet leaders seem to have limited choice, and the policy of over-commitment and deferrals now followed is a very costly one. Watershed policy changes toward modernization seem unlikely for Brezhnev's successors, but important incremental changes influencing allocation and the conduct of the economic political system are quite possible, perhaps likely.

If the Soviets choose to stay on their current course of military superpower augmentation, they must defer of forego the option of joining the western industrial nations--as an economic superpower. If economic interdependence and economic modernization were to become not only a priority aim but an operational program of the Soviet leadership, their country might in time join the western industrial nations as an economic superpower. This would probably require a budgetary emphasis upon, and raised priority to, economic modernization rather than military augmentation. It would also require an expanding program of western technology imports which could affect both the economic and the political system in the Soviet Union. This, in turn, would require a pattern of accelerating or 'storming' modernization projects and delaying or deferring competitive military programs. This presumably might occur, especially in a succession period, if neither a threat nor an opportunity for effective use of additional military power were evident. The earlier words of Secretary Kissinger after the Moscow Summit in 1972 might be relevant,

But now both we and the Soviet Union have begun to find that each increment of power does not necessarily represent an increment of usable political strength.[20]

Dr. Kissinger also saw enhanced security in the collective benefits or linkage among various agreements, such as those on arms limitations, trade and the environment:

> We hoped that the Soviet Union would acquire a stake in a wide spectrum of negotiations and that it would become convinced that its interests would be best served if the entire process unfolded. We have sought, in short, to create a vested interest in mutual restraint.
>
> ...The SALT agreement does not stand alone, isolated and incongruous in the relationship of hostility, vulnerable at any moment to the shock of some sudden crisis. It stands, rather, linked organically to a chain of agreements and to a broad understanding about international conduct appropriate to the dangers of the nuclear age.[21]

The process of creating a 'vested interest in mutual restraint' is likely to be a very gradual and protracted one. Moreover, future changes in Soviet foreign policy and the motivations of Soviet leaders in their conduct of diplomacy will not be easily discerned. But this is the positive aspect of the international security environment that might turn Brezhnev's successors' policy toward emphasis on economic modernization. The more immediate impact from changes in policy may come from the regional emphasis, especially focusing on the rate of completion and effective use of the Siberian projects opening new resources to exploitation, bringing more energy, metals and other materials into Soviet domestic economic use and providing export potential.

A new 'industrialization debate,' if it occurs, may find its forum in the Central Committee of the Party. All the important regional, institutional, governmental interests are represented in this elite institution. Just as names of successors to Lenin, Stalin, and Khrushchev were difficult to foretell, identifying the personalities of the eventual successors to the Brezhnev generation will have to await the unfolding of events. It does seem likely, though, as in previous succession crises, that economic issues will be intertwined within the political succession debate.

In this new 'industrialization debate,' if it does occur, what the new generation of leaders may see and wish to act on is a widening gap between perceived economic needs and potential and actual performance. The emerging new post-Brezhnev generation may be able to overcome the institutional stagnation and traditionalism of the Brezhnev generation which is still rooted in the Stalinist system. This kind of fundamental change in the objectives, priorities, institutions, and cadre of the Soviet leadership may not prove possible. However, recent economic developments in Hungary, Poland, and the People's Republic of China illustrate the possibility of major change without abandoning the system. Closing the economic performance gap through basic changes in traditional economic priorities and institutions may be a central issue in a post-Brezhnev policy debate.

Footnotes

1. General sources for this essay include the various triannual compendia of the Joint Economic Committee, including the forthcoming *Soviet Economy in a Time of Change*; H. Hunter (ed.), *Future of the Soviet Economy*, (Boulder, Colorado, 1979). Earlier papers of the author given at NATO-SHAPE and the U.S. Military Academy were drawn on liberally. See J. Hardt, "Soviet Economic Capability and Defense Resources" in Grayson Kirk and Nils H. Wessell (ed.), *The Soviet Threat, Myths and Realities*, Academy of Political Science, (New York, 1978); "Military or Economic Superpower: A Soviet Choice", in Senior Conference of U.S. Military Academy, *Integrating National Security and Trade Policy*, Final report, June, 1978, (West Point, New York).

2   .Donald W. Green, "The Soviet Union and the World Economy in the 1980's: A Review of Alternatives", in Hunter, *Ibid.*, p. 42.

3. National Foreign Assessment Center, *Simulations of Soviet Growth Options to 1985*, (Washington, D.C., March 1979), Report No. ER 79-10131, p. 22.

4. Different regional groupings may be considered for various purposes. The Soviet planers now speak of seven regions; Theodore Shabad considers in this volume three macro regions: European USSR, Central Asia, and Siberia.

5. Although the Fifteen-Year Plan (1976-1990) has not been published, I believe that planning has been made in that time context and a formal plan may be released. Officials in Gosplan assured me that it did exist and will be released coincident with the next Party Congress and the Eleventh Five-Year Plan.

6. J. Hardt and G. Holliday, "Technology Transfer and Change in the Soviet System", in Frederic Fleron (ed.), *Technology and Communist Culture, the Socio-Communist Impact of Technology under Socialism*, (New York, 1977); reprinted in Hardt, Bresnick, Holliday, and Joint Economic Committee, (eds.), *Issues in East-West Commercial Relations*, (Washington, 1979), pp. 59-90.

7. George D. Holliday, "The Role of Western Technology in the Soviet Economy" in *Issues*, pp. 46-58.

8. John P. Hardt, "Strategic Alternatives in Soviet Resources Allocation Policy" in Joint Economic Committee, *Domensions of Soviet Economic Power, (Washington, 1962), p. 19.*

9. *Pravda*, January 15, 1970.

10. Holliday, *Issues*, p. 58.

11. See M. McGwire, "Naval Power and Soviet Oceans Policy" in *Soviet Oceans Development*, prepared for Committee on Commerce and National Ocean Policy, (Washington, October 1976), pp. 80-182.

12. See *Pravda*, December 18, 1977, p. 2.

13. I am indebted to Gertrude Schroeder-Greenslade for clarifying the point.

14. John Erickson was the primary discussant of this paper in Brussels.

15. Hardt, Holliday, *op. cit.*, pp. 89, 90.

16. See *Pravda*. March 7, 1979, p. 4; *Sobranie postanovlenii pravitel'stva SSSR,* Nos. 6 and 7, 1979.

17. A point made by Zbigniew Fallenbuchl in the Colloquium discussions.

18. End of 1980 debt of $60,695 billion ($13,289 USSR; $20,414 Poland; $26,992 other East European). See Allen J. Lenz, "Potential 1980 and 1985 Hard Currency Debt of the USSR and Eastern Europe under Selected Hypotheses" in *Issues*, pp. 188-191.

19. Statement to House International Relations Committee, October 26, 1978. See also *Congressional Review*, H-11883 ff., October 31, 1978.

20. Kissinger briefing to Congressional leaders, *Congressional Record*, June 19, 1972, p. S-9600.

21. *Ibid.*

Comment

Dr. Holland Hunter

The papers by Dr. Westwood and Professor Tismer contribute very solidly to this symposium. They provide detailed information on many basic aspects of the way the transportation sector fits into the Soviet economy in its regional dimension. Professor Tismer, among other things, identifies the geographic imbalances that have created huge freight transportation demands in the USSR for the last half century, and pinpoints the policy alternatives Soviet authorities now confront in planning future Soviet output and transport expansion. Dr. Westwood's deeply informed analysis places the currently hard-pressed Soviet transport system in historical perspective, noting the high costs associated with the long-standing Soviet policy of stringency in expanding transport capacity. In addition, both provide useful insights into the glamorous but dubious 'project of the century'--the BAM. Their judgments and their references will be very useful to many students of the USSR.

Soviet regional development reflects the basic policies that have governed Soviet economic growth for over half a century. Heavy industry and national defense have had first claim on resources; agriculture, housing and transportation have had secondary status. These priorities have shaped the geographic pattern of Soviet economic expansion, focusing development in specific regions and slighting many others. Moreover, these 50 years of distorted development have produced a transportation system unlike any other in the world.[1]

The Soviet railroad system has been forced to carry huge volumes of freight traffic, primarily concentrated on a skeletal network of major trunk lines connecting fuel and raw material sources with heavy industrial centers. In freight traffic density (ton-kilometers of annual movement per kilometer of first main track), Soviet railways far outdistance any other rail system in the world. Unit costs have been brought very low, and for many years the railways have returned substantial net income to the central budget. Capital for additional motive power, rolling stock, and line facilities has been only grudgingly allocated to the railways, however, forcing them to achieve remarkable levels of capital and labor productivity. The other carriers perform less impressively.

Railroad efficiency has unfortunately been obtained at the cost of substantial inconvenience for shippers and receivers. Freight cars must be loaded and unloaded very quickly on pain of large fines or even jail sentences. Railways are reluctant to pick up and deliver individual cars, though large, intermittent consignments disturb plant scheduling and raise storage costs. Dr. Westwood cites recent instances of railway refusal to deliver to small stations, where consignees face major problems in obtaining their needs.

The unremitting growth of heavy industrial freight traffic, pressing on a transportation system with no slack in it, is now producing bottlenecks here and there at peak periods. Lack of slack is a chronic deficiency observable in other sectors of the economy as well. It is laying steep costs on the economy, in the form of delays, idleness when inputs fail to arrive, impaired output quality as corners are cut, and sluggish technological progress.[2] It now seems evident that added transportation capacity at many specific points would pay for itself very quickly through reducing congestion, lowering production costs, and improving product quality.

Soviet regional development also reflects a traditional Bolshevik urban bias. Geographically, Bolshevik expansion, based on the urban proletariat, has moved out from cities to get the fuels and natural resources that are scattered over vast 'empty' spaces. A policy that concentrates on heavy industry and slights agriculture has obvious transportation consequences. Soviet heavy industry only requires inter-regional arteries (to use an anatomical analog); the capillaries in a circulatory system designed to serve agricultural districts have been deliberately neglected. The roadlessness inherited by the Bolsheviks has been a problem for centuries, but the USSR has done very little toward solving it.[3] In addition, as Professor Tismer points out, the lack of paved roads now hampers the spread of industrial development around existing cities. Again it is evident that transport stringency is raising costs and clogging expansion.

As many of the colloquium papers attest, mal-location of Soviet population with respect to natural resources, together with the maldistribution of many fuel and resource deposits with respect to each other, places very long run regional dilemmas before Soviet decision-makers. The old populated centers of the USSR, west of the Urals, require fuels and raw materials that increasingly must come from deposits hundreds or thousands of kilometers to the east and north. The eastern regions need a labor force, food and consumer goods to support the population, and capital plant and equipment for facilities to extract and process the fuel and raw materials. The transportation implications of these widely scattered requirements are quite serious. While it is true that 'complex development' around rich resource deposits in the east can convert weight-losing inputs into semi-fabricates or commodities easier to transport, there must still be a very heavy flow of westbound freight traffic to old developed centers of the European part of the USSR. The people and capital stocks in the Western USSR are not going to move east to be close to natural resources. The practical question, rather, is how to minimize the cost of developing Siberian resources and moving them to the Western USSR.

From a transportation point of view, it might be noted that Soviet Central Asia and the Trans-Caucasus are not likely to play a major role in meeting the resource needs of the USSR west of the Urals. Modernization and development of the Caucasus and the Moslem republics east of the Caspian Sea will no doubt continue, with particular resource deposits making a national contribution, but the massive flows of resources for the western regions seem sure to come from the east and north. As for labor, the expanding pool of non-Russian labor, as others have argued, seems unlikely on present evidence to be willing to migrate to the old centers in the European part of the USSR. My guess is that underemployed men and women in non-agricultural sectors of the existing labor force are a more likely reservoir to be drawn on as the labor shortage grows more severe.

One final observation on the transportation aspects of recent Soviet regional development relates to the freight traffic requirements that are coming increasingly from the periphery of the USSR. On the western edge of the USSR the pulls come from her neighbors and from the world market. Similar pulls are beginning to be felt in the east, from the Pacific. While it may be said that the Baikal-Amur Magistral' 'starts at' Taishet, where it leaves the old trans-Siberian railway, the first substantial traffic will move south along the 'little BAM' carrying coal to the Pacific coast for Japan.[4]

The 'little BAM' starts from BAM station on the old trans-Siberian about 25 kilometers west of Skovorodino and runs north 178 kilometers to Tynda and beyond to new coal deposits at Neryungri.[5] When the difficult central portion of the BAM comes into operation, the main traffic between Taishet and Tynda will consist of tank cars carrying crude oil from west Siberia to the Pacific coast.

The freight traffic pull from the west involves substantial flows of coal and iron ore from the Donbas in the Eastern Ukraine to several Comecon countries. Similar flows of raw materials, coming from as far east as west Siberia, the Urals, and Soviet Central Asia, move across the European USSR to Eastern Europe through Brest, Chop, and Baltic and Black Sea ports. Major petroleum and gas pipe lines play significant roles as well. An appreciable amount of internal waterway traffic now moves between the Volga and the Danube, making use of the Volga-Don Canal, the lower Don River, the Sea of Azov, and the Black Sea.

In summary form, then, Soviet regional economic history records the massive expansion of economic activity in selected regions, primarily industrial, drawing on fuels and raw materials scattered over a sprawling land mass of continental dimensions. The distances between material inputs and major concentrations of labor and capital have been gradually increasing. It looks as though the ratio of freight transportation to GNP will continue to increase, especially if Soviet authorities continue to stress material production rather than 'unproductive' services.[6] Technological progress could fend off real transportation cost increases, but as others have shown, technological progress comes slowly under the present Soviet system.[7] The spatial aspects of future Soviet developments are thus likely to involve problems that will not be easy to solve.

Footnotes

1. For background, see Ernest W. Williams, Jr., *Freight Transportation in the Soviet Union,* (Princeton, 1962), and Holland Hunter, *Soviet Transport Experience,* (Washington, 1968).
2. See my review essay in *Problems of Communism,* XXVII, 2 (March-April 1979).
3. The contrast with China is noted in my paper: "Chinese and Soviet Transport for Agriculture", University of Pittsburgh, Center for International Studies, 1974.
4. See Theodore Shabad and Victor L. Mote, *Gateway to Siberian Resources (The BAM),* (New York, 1977), pp. 3, 78, 81.
5. See Min. Putei Soob., *Ukazatel' Zhel. Pass. Soobshchenii,* (Moscow, 1977), pp. 517 and 689.
6. For discussion of the evidence through 1965, see H. Hunter, *Soviet Transport Experience, op. cit.,* pp. 35-43.
7. See, for example, Joseph S. Berliner, *The Innovation Decision in Soviet Industry,* (Cambridge, Mass., 1976).

Comment

Professor John Erickson

Whatever the discrepancy in opinions about the actual scope and purpose of present Soviet military policies, few if any will deny that these same policies continue to have a considerable impact on Soviet society at large. Certainly, the figures of what is loosely called 'the Soviet military build-up' are huge: 4.8 million men under arms, a massive reserve program, an ICBM force passing now into its fifth generation of missles with a numerical strength of some 1,400 intercontinental missiles, over 900 SLBMs (submarine launched ballistic missiles) in a growing fleet of nuclear submarines, a mighty array of air defenses (including an anti-ballistic missile system), air defense fighters with a strength of about 2,700 and a tactical air force furnished with about 5,000 combat aircraft (many of them modern types with even more advanced models under development) and then the Ground Forces, with 167 divisions backed with a tank-park of over 40,000 armoured fighting vehicles. Should this not induce a *frisson de terreur*, then there is the Soviet Navy with some major surfact combat warships and almost 250 submarines, quite apart from the ballistic missile submarine fleet. There is also the matter of the level of Soviet defense expenditure, which is again a matter of furious debate but none doubts its relatively high level.

These are the trappings and appurtenances of a superpower, the Soviet superpower in this instance, but in several respects this arrangement and accumulation of military power and capability is a 'regional' phenomenon, with profound implications for regional development in the USSR. Certainly, there is substantial justification for considering the regional aspects and impact of Soviet military organization (though 'territoriality' might be an equally acceptable description). Indeed, in the wake of the Civil War and in the flush of victory, the Soviet command set about debating the relationship between military and economic organization: at the beginning of 1920, Vatsetis (an ex-Imperial officer and then a Bolshevik commander-in-chief) argued the case for reducing Soviet vulnerability by setting up a 'military-administrative centre' in the region of the Urals, the Kama and the Volga as well as creating a unified 'state military-technical base' in the area of Vyatka-Perm-Ekaterinburg-Chelyabinsk-Ufa-Simbirsk--a remarkably prescient opinion but one which was not realized at the time. In fact, the Soviet government settled for the 'regionalism' inherent in the old Tsarist system of military districts (*voennyi okrug*) and a form of 'territoriality' implicit in raising militia units on a territorial basis.

The military delineation of Russia has always presented problems to Imperial and Soviet authorities alike. 'Regionalization' proved to be the answer, again under both regimes, the basic unit being the 'district', *okrug*, devised from the Imperial Russian reorganization set in motion in 1861 under the aegis of Count Dimitri Miliutin and designed to rationalize *deployment, mobilization* and *training*--the Military District. The first three MDs were set up on July 6, 1862, when First Army formed the Warsaw MD, the 1st Corps (First Army) and Vilno MD (originally designated the Baltic MD) and 3rd Corps the Kiev MD: the Odessa MD was established in December 1862 and exists even now with full 117 years of history behind it. In a matter of months after the Bolshevik seizure of power the MDs reappeared and have remained part of the Soviet military structure ever since—expanding to the grand total of thirty-two during the 'Great Patriotic War' but cut back thereafter to the present total of sixteen.

Merely to catalogue the existing MDs in the Soviet Union does not, of course, explain either Soviet military anatomy or its regional impact and implications. The military map, if it can be called that, proves to be quite complex. Soviet forces are divided basically into two components, the strategic offensive and defensive elements (ICBMs, SLBMs and *PVO Strany*, the latter the air defense command) which are not regionally or territorially deployed (at least not on first sight and the general purpose forces, army, navy and tactical air force grouped into either Military Districts or the four Fleet commands (Northern, Baltic, Black Sea and Pacific)--sixteen Military Districts and four Fleets. Yet geography itself imposes a form of regionalism even on the strategic forces: for reasons of basing and targeting, ICBM missile 'fields'[1] extend into a sidelong 'T' as it were, running from the north down to the center, south and southeast: the air defense system is organized into two major Air Defense Districts, Moscow and Baku, whose early warning radars reach out far to the northwest and the southwest respectively, while for air defense requirements the Soviet Union is severally divided into 'air defense districts' for the emplacement of radars, surface-to-air missiles and interceptor aircraft. Forward air defense runs most thickly through European Russia and along the southern/southeastern borders, so on to the Far East. The three 'air armies' of long-range (strategic) aviation are located in European Russia, in the north and in the Far East.

In some respects, this configuration of strategic forces could be regarded as belonging to the main 'regions' of the USSR--the north, European Russia, the south/southeast and the Far East. This, however, is somewhat simplistic and we shall return to the subject with yet another type of definition involving yet another geographic quartering of Soviet territory and its adjoining spaces, namely, 'theaters of military operations' (TVD). The sixteen military districts present less difficulty, being aligned more or less with the organization of the Soviet Republics: from west to east there are (with their headquarters) Leningrad MD (Leningrad), Baltic MD (Riga), Carpathian MD (Lvov), Belorussia MD (Minsk), Kiev MD (Kiev), Moscow MD (Moscow), Odessa MD (Odessa), North Caucasus MD (Rostov-on-Don), Trans Caucasus MD (Tbilisi), Volga MD (Kuibyshev), Turkestan MD (Tashkent), Central Asia MD (Alma-Ata), Ural MD (Sverdlovsk), Siberian MD (Novosibirsk), Trans Baikal MD (Chita), and the Far Eastern

MD (Khabarovsk). Before looking at the composition of these districts in detail, it is worth remarking on the nature of the MD organization as such, for it is a particular gloss on 'regionalism'. Though headed by a senior military officer, the MD is essentially an interlocking military-Party-administrative directorate, disposing of military and civilian resources alike: the Military Council (*Voennyi Sovet*) presided over by the District commander, includes the chief of staff, arms and services commanders together with the First Secretary of local Republc or *oblast* Party organizations--all collectively charged with ensuring that Party, government and Defense Ministry instructions are strictly carried out. The Military Council is, therefore, an important body responsible for coordinating the work of the military command and regional Party leadership, a function which is greatly expanding due in no small part to the expansion of the Soviet *civil defense program* which demands military-civilian integration.

Before going on to discuss the problem of the allocation of effort and resources within this whole system, it is worth noting that two other military entities should be added to the array of Soviet strength--the four 'Groups of Forces' abroad (Group of Soviet Forces/East Germany, Norther Group in Poland, Central Group in Czechoslovakia and Southern Group in Hungary, with twenty, three, five and four divisions, respectively) and the Warsaw Pact organization. Both of these present a very special form of military 'regionalism', but having included them in the total configuration of the Soviet effort, we can now see how this effort is distributed (itself a commentary on regional groupings and agglomerations):

Strengths of Forces (abroad)

GSFG (Group of Soviet Forces / Germany)

HQ Zossen-Wunsdorf

Five armies:

2nd Guards Tank Army (Furstenberg),
20th Guards Army (Eberswald),
1st Guards Tank Army (Dresden),
8th Guards Army (Weimar)

Strength:

10 Tank Divisions,
1 Artillery Division (34th Guards)

Air order ob Battle:

16th Air Army (approximately 900 combat aircraft)

Total strength GSFG:

370,000 men
7,500-8,000 main battle tanks
2,350 BMPs (infantry combat vehicles)
200 plus helicopters

Central Group (Czechoslovakia)
>HQ: Milovce (near Prague)
>3 Tank divisions,
>2 Motor-Rifle divisions

Total strength:
>55,000-60,000 men,
>2 Air Divisions (to replace 10th Air Army)

Northern Group (Poland)

>*HQ: Legnica*
>*2-3 Tank Divisions*

Total strength:
>32,000-35,000 men, supported by
>37th Air Army (350 aircraft)

Southern Group (Hungary)

>HQ: Budapest-Matyasfold
>4-5 Divisions (2-3 Motor-Rifle Divisions,
>2 Tank Divisions)

Total strength:
>40,000-50,000 men,
>
>2 Air Divisions (270 aircraft)

Soviet Military Districts (MD)

Leningrad MD

>6th Army HQ: Petrozavodsk
>8 Motor-Rifle Divisions,
>1 Tank Division
>1 Airborne Division
>1 Naval Infantry Regiment
>13th Air Army (300 aircraft)

Baltic MD

>HQ: Riga
>8th Guards Army: Kaliningrad
>6 Motor-Rifle Divisions,
>3 Tank Divisions,

2 Airborne Divisions (one a training division),
2 Artillery Divisions
30th Air Army (300 aircraft)

Carpathian MD

HQ: Lvov
8th Guards Tank Army (Zhitomir)
13th Army (Rovno),
38th Army (Ivano-Frankovsk)
7-8 Motor-Rifle Divisions,
3 Tank Divisions,
1 Artillery Division
57th Air Army (350 aircraft)

Belorussian MD

HQ: Minsk
5th Guards Tank Army (Bobruisk)
7th Guards Tank Army (Borisov),
28th Army (Grodno)
2-3 Motor-Rifle Divisions,
7-8 Tank Divisions,
1 Airborne Division (103rd Guards)
1st Air Army (300 aircraft)

Moscow MD

HQ: Moscow
4 Motor-Rifle Divisions,
2 Tank Divisions,
1 Airborne Division (106th Guards)
Attached Air Army (200 aircraft)

KievMD

HQ: Kiev
1st Guards Army (Chernigov),
2nd Guards Tank Army (Krivoi Rog) plus
1 Tank Army
4 Motor-Rifle Divisions
6 Tank Divisions
1 Artillery Division
17th Air Army (about 100 aircraft)

Odessa MD

HQ: Odessa

7 Motor-Rifle Divisions,
1 Tank Division
1 Airborne Division (102nd Guards),
1 Artillery Regiment,
1 Naval Infantry Regiment
15th Air Army (250 aircraft)

North Caucasus MD

HQ: Rostov
5 Motor-Rifle Divisions,
1 Tank Division

Trans Caucasus MD

HQ: Tbilisi
9-10 Motor-Rifle Divisions
1 Tank Division
1 Airborne Division (104th Guards)
34th Air Army (300 aircraft)

Turkestan MD

HQ: Tashkent
7 Motor-Rifle Divisions,
1 Tank Division
1 Airborne Division (at Fergana)
6th Air Army

Central Asian MD

HQ: Alma-Ata
6 Motor-Rifle Divisions,
1 Tank Division

Volga MD

HQ: Kuibyshev
3 Motor-Rifle Divisions

Ural MD

HQ: Sverdlovsk
2 Motor-Rifle Divisions,
1 Tank Division

Siberian MD

> HQ: Novosibirsk
> 4 Motor-Rifle Divisions,
> 1 Tank Division

Trans-Baikal MD

> HQ: Chita
> 8 Motor-Rifle Divisions
> 2 Tank Divisions
> (*Note:* In Outer Mongolia, the Soviet command stations three divisions--with one tank division and one motor-rifle division at full combat readiness.)

Far Eastern MD

> HQ: Khabarovsk
> 19 Motor-Rifle Divisions,
> 2 Tank Divisions
> 1 Airborne Division
> 2 Artillery Divisions
> 2 Naval Infantry Regiments

At first sight this is a colossal panoply of force in the field, but there are some important reservations to be made. Not all the divisions are at full combat readiness--indeed, this would be a physical impossibility--so that the Soviet command pursues a policy of deliberate *under-manning* and these forces, formidable though they may seem, have a wide variety of tasks to perform. Indeed, one can look at them as a series of 'regional packages', assembled for both offensive and defensive tasks. Notice, for example, that in the 'frontier regions', the Leningrad and Far Eastern MDs, the tank divisions have been thinned out in favor of the more versatile motor-rifle division:there is also an intriguing pehnomenon in that the Belorussian MD has a higher ratio of armor to motor-rifle troops than in GSFG, the basic Societ 'shock force'. What is puzzling in this consideration of 'military regionalism' is the degree to which these manning levels—combat-ready divisions, less fully manned divisions and 'cadre divisions'—are dictated either by manpower flows or by operational requirements, or a combination of both.

This necessitates a closer look at the Soviet MDs and their 'regional' impact. Certainly the MD system and these 'regional packages' is a method of maintaining a combat-ready order of battle with the minimum stress on military manpower, namely, the 'mix' of fully manned with under-manned divisions (the latter being fleshed out with reservists called to the colors in the shortest possible time). The mechanism to carry this through is the *voenkomat*, the military commissariat, which is inlaid at every level of the Soviet administration and is supervised by the 'military commissar'--what an anachronism!--at Republic level. The MD is thus a system for the optimization of manpower management in gross regional terms, with the *voenkomat*(s) taking account of local variations to fit the military manpower flow with special requirements: by the same token, the military manpower management system and the MDs can provide labor to deficit areas, either in the form of construction troops or additional labor reserves--in other words, the Soviet military can effect the *short-term* transfer of labor and offset dysfunctional territorial dispersal of labor.

The second function of the MD-*voenkomat* combination is to facilitate mobilization, for the *voenkomat* not only keeps the mobilization 'rolls' of men but also the lists of vehicles needed for mobilization and also a check on dumps, stores and war-stocks. Thus, at the regional level (and lower) there is a 'shadow' organization for mobilization (military and economic), with military representation at many levels and an interface between the military and civilian agencies: the *voenkomat* system, spread throughout every region of the USSR, has some 3,700 branches, staffed by 22,000 military officers and about 75,000 support personnel. There is presently much talk of the demographic crisis awaiting the Soviet Union, with serious regional implications: certainly the 'pool' of conscripts will fall in the early 1980's, impinging heavily on the nationality problem--some have pointed to the preponderance of Kazakh tank drivers and so on--but it should be said at once that the Soviet armed forces have a great deal of slack to take in or utilize before the manpower situation becomes really serious. Rather the military will be under pressure from three directions, the increased competition with the civilian sector for recruits, the problem of quality in military manpower (with a larger contingent of recruits from Central Asia and the Caucasus), and the growing need to plug gaps in the civilian labor force by the use of military-directed labor.

This, of course, must be a prime concern for the Soviet command, not least the Mobilization Directorate (3rd Directorate) of the Soviet General Staff which is generally charged with manning/mobilization planning in the Soviet forces and is in control of the whole mechanism of the *voenkomats*. Additionally, however, the MD system seems to be taking on a further responsibility, dealing with *post-attack recovery*, or, at the very least, a deliberate effort at damage limitation through an extended civil defense program--in several Military Districts, the post of Deputy Commander/Civil Defense has been established and military Civil Defense units trained and deployed (probably in battalion strength). This presupposes fairly close collaboration between the military and civilian authorities at Republic (and lower) level, with the 'statewide civil defense system' involving the strengthening of territorial organizations and their staffs, command structures built into Military Districts and machinery established to ensure close coordination between civil defense elements and military units in both peace and in war. The territorial plan is concerned with the protection of individual enterprises and territorial civil defense organizations are responsible for ensuring that these plans are carried out: in war the Military District assumes command and control of these functions which are otherwise in peacetime limited to *planning* and *training*.

We have thus seen, in simplistic style, how a military overlay can be placed upon the 'regions' of the USSR to provide a more complex map, one which should take account of the military input and influence. But this is not the end of the story. These military 'regions' can now be concentrated or collected into what might be called 'super-regions', to be exact, 'theatres of military operations' (TVDs)--one more overlay upon the map of the USSR. More important, this is the principle of Soviet organization for war.

Obviously, a Military District could not sustain wartime operations in isolation, whatever its peacetime role in maintaining particular forces-in-being and a mobilization apparatus. Perhaps a clue is provided by the organization of the Operations Directorate of the Soviet General Staff, which is divided into six 'operational branches'--the Northern, the Western, the Balkans, the Near East, Central Asia and the Far East: for the conduct of strategic operations we might reasonably assume tht the NATO area consists of at least three and probably four TVDs--one on each flank (north and south) and two in the center, thus involving the 'military region' of the Groups of Forces abroad, the Baltic, Leningrad and Carpathian MDs, as well as part of the Kiev and Odessa MDs: China will form one if not two TVDs, with additional TVDs prescribed for Japan, Korea and Okinawa. Again, the MD forces will be 'grouped' to deal with set missions within these areas, utilizing their missile, air and ground components. Nor is it possible to ignore--though this is frequently done--the existence of 'maritime theatres of operations' (MTVDs), extending now to 'oceanic theatres of operations' (OTVDs) where the ballistic submarines and long distance anti-submarine warfare (ASW) come into play.

Massive though the Soviet Military establishment may seem, this array of strength must be set against the several demands of the multifarious TV-Ds for *both offensive and defensive operations*. This set of 'regional overlays' is probably the best solution to Soviet military problems and provides a regional factor in its own right, a regional development which has already impinged substantially on Soviet life and which will continue to

Soviet Military Districts and Divisional Strengths

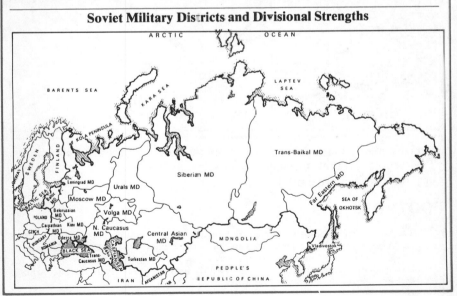

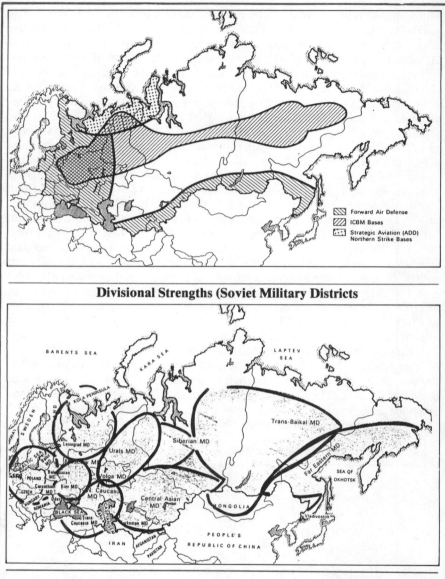

Divisional Strengths (Soviet Military Districts

exercize a marked influence on Soviet political and economic developments. The degree of that influence--or its possible curtailment--is the next questions to which we must attend.

FOOTNOTE

1. The Soviet Strategic Missile Forces are presently organized into six *operational armies* (complete with their own regiments) and three test armies: the ICBM armies consist of 'missile fields' or complexes and regiments down to launch control posts, while the Intermediate Range Ballistic Missile (IRBM) elements are organized into armies, divisions, regiments and launch control posts.

Peter G. Beazley

Current position:
Research Fellow, Royal Institute of
International Affairs
Chatham House
10 St. James's Square
London SW1
Conservative European Parliamentary
member
Previously Director ICI Europa at
Brussels, and General Manager ICI
Europa Fibres GMBH; Deputy Chair-
man and Managing Director ICI's
South African Fibres and Textiles
interests.

Main field of work:
Western European industry and commerce Transfer of technology to Soviet
bloc

Publications during the last two years:
"The Role of Western Technology in
the Development of the Soviet
Union's Chemical Industry", Chatham
House

Trade Aspect of Regionalization
Impact and Importance of Regional Development for Soviet Trade: A Commercial Assesment

Peter Beazley

It is characteristic of Soviet industry that as compared with that of other major Western Countries and of USA in particular, its branches are less concentrated in particular specialist regional areas. This arises for a number of reasons. The USSR is a vast continent whose natural resources are widely spread. Concentration of a branch of industry—steel or heavy engineering for example—within a particular area would put undue strain on the Soviet transport system. So whilst 90% of the US steel industry is concentrated within a radius of 250 miles of Pittsburgh and at Chicago, there is no single dominant steel region in USSR. Forty-two percent of Soviet steel is made in the Donbass-Dnieper region of the Ukraine, 32% in the Urals region a thousand miles further north-east and 6% on the Kuzbass coalfield in Siberia 1,200 miles east of the Urals. Other industries are similarly widespread throughout the USSR. This means that despite the great importance of the further development of Siberia and the Far East, the older established areas such as the Central or Moscow district, the Ukraine, the Volga and the Urals are still predominantly important.

However, in order to try to assess the importance and impact of regional development on Soviet trade I should like to concentrate on the industry which I know best and which perhaps best illustrates the widespread regional nature of Soviet investment in a particular industry, i.e., the chemical industry. Since the time of Khrushchev's chemicalization program in 1958 it has received priority in investment. Not only does it illustrate the widespread regional pattern I have mentioned for other industries but it is particularly important in regard to Soviet trade.

The regional development of the Soviet chemical industry has naturally owed a great deal to the way in which oil exploration and production have developed. From 1950 to 1970 oil production increased more than nine times—from 38 million tons (760,000 barrels per day) to 350 million tons (7 million barrels per day). The increase came firstly from the old oil fields around the Caspian Sea and from large fields in the Tatar and Bashkir republics but the rapid growth was only really made possible by the discovery of the extremely rich and accessible oil deposits in the

Urals/Volga region. Here the output grew between 1950 and 1970 from 5 million tons (100,000 b/d) to 210 million tons (4.2 million b/d). However, as the size of discoveries fell off seriously in this region from the mid 1950's, so the growth of output slowed dramatically here in the early 1970's.

During 1972-75 the USSR failed to meet its original targets for output. Production in the Urals/Volga region levelled off whilst production in the older regions like the Ukraine, North Caucasus and Azerbaidzhan actually declined. The Western Siberian oilfields—in particular the giant Samotlar field producing 110 million tons (2.2 million b/d) in 1976—enabled the USSR to come close to meeting its national plans in the period 1972-75.

The maintenance and possible increase of oil production for the future—that is the late 1980's and 1990's—are thought to depend on the development of the Arctic offshore regions, on the East Siberian lowlands, on deep structures in the Caspian Sea and perhaps off Kamchatka and Sakhalin in the Seal of Okhotsk. although oil technology may be developed for the pack ice, the permafrost and the rough sea conditions which these areas imply, they will obviously cause many problems for other types of industrial production located there than solely their distance from consuming markets.

Whilst an increasing percentage of Soviet industry has moved Eastwards and the most dramatic developments of the petrochemical industry are being planned in Western Siberia, it must be recognized that other factors also have strong influence on the location of industry. Some industries benefit from their being located close to the sources of raw materials, particularly if transport to the consuming market does not present serious problems. It was natural for the inorganic chemical industry to be sited from its early days close to mineral deposits and sources of energy. From this sprang up many of the early industrial sites well spread across the Continent from the Western borders down to the Caspian Sea and Baku skilled work forces and industrial organization were built up. and baku skilled work forces and industrial organization were built up. Large scale modern plants are being erected in such places today.

Similarly it was to be expected that fertilizer plants would be distributed in locations with reasonable proximity to the agricultural areas where their products would be used. Hence the majority of the 40 new 450,000 ton/year ammonia plants based on Western technology which are scheduled to be built over the next four or five years will be in the Western regions of Byelorussia, the Ukraine, North Caucasus, the Central region and the Black Earth Zone. Nine are destined for the Volga economic region. Three for the Urals and only four in Western Siberia.

The chemical industry only consumes between 5 and 10 percent of oil production. Whilst there are obvious advantages in locating low labor intensive petrochemical production close to the well head as is happening on the largest possible scale in Western Siberia, there is also a very good case for capitalizing on those production centers with specialist capabilities, on locations with integrated processes from basic raw materials or which are in relatively close proximity to the downstream user plants or the centers of population, which may provide the main market for the product.

Such is the case with the synthetic fiber industry. The main production of polyester fiber is at Mogilev in Byelorussia. The original work undertaken by Soviet scientists on polyester fiber was carried out at Kursk in the Moscow economic region and although it was used for the first small scale commercial production (which was unsatisfactory), it was then abandoned as far as further polyester production was concerned. The first major polyester fiber plant was installed here by the British in the late 1960's and the site has since been further developed by big extensions made by the West Germans. There are now plans to use Kursk for new West German polyester fiber extensions but no other sites are envisaged. The polyester fiber raw material DMT (dimethylterephthalate) is made at both Mogilev and Kursk with additional production at Novomoskovsk also in the Moscow Central economic region.

Otherwise the manmade fiber sites are well distributed geographically. Their locations, however, often seem to have been dependent on historical decisions related to earlier chemical and fiber plants or to textile areas rather than to a specific coordinated plan. Viscose rayon is made at Ryazan in the Moscow Central economic area and cellulose diacetate and its offspring triacetate are made in a variety of locations from Kaunas in Lithuania, Korovakan in Armenia, Fergana in Uzbekistan, Novopolotsk in North East Byelorussia, Svetogorsk, North of Leningrad and Severodonetsk in the Ukraine. Centers like Saratov in the Volga economic region make both cellulose acetate and acrylic fibers as the British and Italian firms which installed the processes also make both products. The chemical raw material for acrylic fibers—acrylonitrile—is also made in Novopolotsk as is cellulose acetate, whilst Barnaul in Western Siberia produces cellophane, cellulose acetate and nylon 6. Tashkent in Uzbekistan also makes caprolactam, the raw material for nylon 6 and will install a big nylon 6 fiber plant in 1980. At Balakovo and Naberezhnye synthetic nylon tire cords are made in close proximity to the tire production for the respective passenger and commercial vehicle production. At Chernigov in the Ukraine nylon 66 yarn and tire cords are also made, whilst the intermediate for nylon 66—A.H. Salt—is made at Novopolotsk.

The location of petrochemical plants with their downstream products like plastics and synthetic rubber has naturally been greatly influenced by the availability of oil. Similarly the production of a wide range of chemical products such as methanol and ammonia has depended on gas supplies. In the 1960's and early 1970's plastic products like polythene, polystyrene, PVC and polypropylene were manufactured throughout most economic regions where ethylene and styrene were readily available from oil. The early polythene plants for example were installed at Kazan and Ufa in the

Volga region, at Polotsk in Byelorussia and at Sumgait on the Caspian Sea. These sites have become polythene centers. Kazan has become very important with a second and a third plant of increased size as Western technology has developed and with a further very large plant to be completed in 1981. New ethylene streams have of course been built and additional products such as ethylene oxide added. An ethylene pipeline linking Kazan to Nizhnekamsk and later to Ufa, Sterlitamak and Salavat is being constructed. Nizhnekamsk has its own ethylene stream and is planning to manufacture ethylene derivative products on large scale plants. Ufa likewise is a very important chemical center with two polythene plants and other products based on petrochemicals. Sterlitamak has acetylene as well as ethylene and produces appropriate derivatives. A further polythene plant is situated at Kuibyshev with PVC at Volgograd in the same region. Western involvement in this very important area is considerable. It is a traditional chemical center which will continue to expand but its product range is repeated at other centers. Sumgait on the Caspian Sea for example added a PVC plant to its original polythene plant at the beginning of the 1970's and is at present constructing a large new ethylene plant using Soviet technology and due to be completed in 1980. The downstream products are intended to be specialized resins.

In the Volgo-Vyatsk region at Dzerzhinsk PVC is manufactured and at Gorkii in the same region there is also large production of ethylene derivatives. At Budyonnovsk near Prikumsk in the North Caucasus a large scale polythene plant is also due to come on stream this year whilst Severodonetsk in the Ukraine is developing into an exceptionally big petrochemical center.

What is true of the plastic products is largely true of synthetic rubber where butadiene and styrene are similarly derived from oil. For example at Guryev, Pavlodar and Shevchenko in Kazakstan, one of the Soviet Asian Republics, a particularly large styrene and polystyrene complex is due to be completed in 1980. At Yerevan in Armenia, chloroprene synthetic rubber capacity is being extended.

It is unnecessary to provide further examples to illustrate the fact that these chemical sites West of the Urals are all becoming very important centers in their own right and are being expanded regularly as new investments can be made.

Meanwhile it must be pointed out that the development of Siberia and the Far East is seen by the Soviet planners as a precondition of further growth of the Soviet economy. The region has vast deposits of raw materials and minerals of all kinds. It is extremely rich in oil, natural gas, coal and has cheap energy with the five biggest hydroelectric power stations in the USSR and plentiful water supplies. Extraction and transport of raw materials however present very considerable problems due to the unfavorable climatic conditions and the long distances involved. Chemical and petrochemical production make however ideal projects with their heavy dependance on oil and gas supplies and their very low labor intensity. They also do not present serious transport problems as their end products are easily packaged and transported. Ethylene can be cheaply transported by pipeline from one production center to user centers as is projected between Kemerovo and Tomsk on the one hand and between Irkutsk, Angarsk and Zima on the other. Irkutsk and Barnaul were already being developed in the early 1960's. Omsk is already an important polystyrene producer and a range of products based on benzene and xylenes is due to be produced there in 1980.

Tobolsk and Tomsk are planned as the two major developments for the future. Tobolsk will be a most important synthetic rubber center. Construction was started in 1972 and it is significant that relatively greater use is to be made of Soviet technology and some of the processes used will be Soviet designed but western companies will also play a significant part in the development of this center. Tobolsk will manufacture the usual wide range of petrochemicals on plants of the maximum size available.

Tomsk has been the favorite project of the Chemical Minister Leonid Kostandov. It was originally a US $4 billion investment in a wide range of petrochemical products based on a 10 million ton per annum oil refinery. It was Kostandov's intention that the whole cost of the project should be covered by compensation trading. The Western contractors who would build the plants would be paid back in product from the same plants over a period of approximately ten years. A consortium of leading West German contractors had set out to win the contract but strong objections were made to the West German Government by both the leading West German chemical manufacturers and the West German trade union involved. The manufacturers were concerned at the likely damage which would be done to Western markets from such a large volume of products being sold through merchants associated with the contractors, whilst the trade unions feared that such form of payment put the jobs of German chemical workers at risk. When the identical agreement was finally made in mid-1978 the scope of the project had been scaled down to DM 2-3 billion or US $1-1.5 billion but the 100% compensation trading method of payment remained.

Enough has been said about the location of chemical plants to establish the fact that major chemical centers have been built up in all industrial areas of the USSR. New large scale developments like those planned for Siberia will still be additional. The very low per capita consumption of consumer goods in the USSR makes this both possible and necessary. For example, only half the area sown with grain at present receives any fertilizer at all and where fertilizers are applied the dosage is small by Western standards. The internal market available for the Soviet Chemical manufacture is enormous.

On the other hand chemicals present a very convenient way of earning hard currency. The USSR has recognized since the early days of Khrushchev's Chemicalization Plan that it cannot maintain its chosen growth rate without Western technology. A slackening of the growth rate would have dire consequences both in the USSR's capability to maintain parity with the USA in defense matters, as well as limiting the availability of consumer goods below an acceptable minimum level. The import of the large volume of machinery that is required to install plants based on Western technology in the USSR—despite the fact that an ever increasing percentage of the equipment and machinery specified is produced in the USSR—has caused a heavy drain on the Soviet foreign currency resources. In the case of the large contracts which the French, Italians, and Germans obtained for the shipment of large diameter steel pipes for the Orenburg gas pipeline repayment was largely made in gas and oil products. However, as Soviet indebtedness to the West increased to levels which made it unlikely that they could be repaid from anticipated foreign currency earnings, the Chemical Ministry decided to ask for the same type of compensation trading terms for the transfer of technology from the West which were becoming normal with Comecon projects. In scarcity economies such as those of Comecon countries, payment in the form of the product may well be valuable, particularly if the project concerned has been based on the real requirements of the countries supplying management, labor and machinery. This is not however the case with Western suppliers. The USSR is now supplying Western markets products which have been in surplus supply since the recession hit the West at the time of the oil crisis in 1973/74. In many cases they are only being produced in volume in the USSR some 15 to 20 years after they had been introduced into Western markets. They are therefore 'mature' products without novelty or speciality. On the other hand they are products which have been manufactured by Western technology to Western specifications and so are eminently saleable in world markets if offered at suitably low prices.

It may well be asked why the Western contractors accept this form of payment. Obviously they would not do so if cash payment was available and if their resources were sufficiently well occupied in other markets. It is, of course, a consequence of the oil crisis and the recession which has hit Western countries that there is not a genuine mutual benefit available on such trade with the USSR. Because of the recession, resources of all types are only partially occupied in the West. This applies equally to men, money and machinery. Governments make guaranteed credits available on favorable terms to avoid unemployment in the machinery sector, banks are pleased to find projects at minimum risk against which they can lend their surplus funds, the contractor keeps together his skilled designers and project engineers, the chemical manufacturer earns a license fee or sells know-how.

The Soviet Ministry is in the happy position of being a monopolistic buyer with each of its potential suppliers selected from the leading manufacturers or contractors in the West competing with each other. The USSR can therefore optimize its position in the different financial markets of the world as well as obtaining the best technology at a very keen price. In practice whilst the USSR is a very hard bargainer on these matters, it is essential for it to be assured of completion of the project and start-up of the plant on time. So the Foreign Trade Organization (FTO) which handles these negotiations will normally maintain a short list of highly experienced and reliable contractors and manufacturers from different countries from which to make their choice. An important aspect of the FTO's decision is the capability of the supplier in handling the 'buy back' contract. Some contractors are extremely experienced in this field and have very considerable facilities for placing products across the world with the minimum of market disturbance. Others are less skilled. Manufacturers themselves sometimes are keen to undertake the 'buy back' contract either to fill a gap in their own investment plans or to act defensively by handling the sale of the product themselves to ensure orderly marketing.

It will be noted that the USSR not only benefits from the supplying countries finance but also in such compensation business automatically obtains a share of world export markets. In most contracts the 'buy back' of product under compensation agreements covers the complete cost of the project plus design and license fees, the charge for handling the 'buy back', interest charges, etc. This normally means that 10% to 12% of the plant's announced production is exported over a period of about 10 years. The USSR can therefore purchase the largest available plant and run it at full capacity even if there are delays in the downstream processing plants coming into operation on time. It should be noted, however, that the western plant loses a good deal of its 'modernity' if the Soviets contact to build it. Construction delays are notorious and the technology transfer can often take up to seven years before it is implemented.

In the case of the 40 Western ammonia plants which are planned eventually to supply nitrogen for USSR's own fertilizer industry a high proportion of their initial capacity—up to 40% in the days when only a quarter of the plants are on stream—will be used for export.

Part of the lack of mutual benefit lies in the fact that the USSR permits no 'BUY FORWARD' of product from Western suppliers' plants to prepare the Soviet market prior to the start up of the local production. Whilst this would be normal in a Western market economy system, in a scarcity market which is centrally planned, demand can be built up from scratch immediately production is available.

When the earlier 'buy back' contracts were signed for the Kazan and the Severodonetz polythene plants, the quantities of product involved appeared to be very small in relation to world demand. The increased weakness of Western markets changed the situation which resulted in a much harder line being taken by all chemical manufacturers. Many preferred not to be involved in technology transfer where 'buy back' of the plant's product was a condition of payment. The Tomsk project where the scale was so great may well have proved to be a watershed in this type of business.

Should this be so the options open to both sides are limiting. In principle the USSR would be faced by the necessity of restricting here imports from the West, whilst increasing her exports. During 1977 it did in fact reduce its short term hard currency balance of payments trade debt to $3.3

billion although its net hard currency indebtedness increased to $16 billion from $15 billion.

It must be concluded that the regional development of Soviet industry, in particular of the chemical and petrochemical industry, is both a necessary and desirable feature. In such a large continent, concentration of industry—irrespective of defense considerations—would not bring real benefits. It would add further burdens to an already difficult transport problem. It would make unduly heavy demands on labor in particular regions without helping to enlarge the skilled work force, which is so badly needed over the widest possible area of the USSR. The opening up of new areas such as Siberia together with the further development of all existing areas is necessary to maintain USSR's growth. This does give great opportunities for the West to provide the know-how and machinery necessary to exploit Soviet resources. There can be little doubt that this expansion will increase trade in both directions. This will be essential as it produces the only way in which the USSR can hope to pay for the benefits it receives from the West.

Nevertheless the major problem rests in the difficulty of providing mutual benefit in trade between a centrally planned and a free enterprise economy. The USSR will have to expand its hard currency earnings from world trade in order to purchase the Western technology and machinery needed to exploit its natural resources. The West will not wish to provide this technology at an unacceptable cost to its own manufacturing capacity and its share of world markets. A compromise solution must therefore be found to satisfy these conflicting interests.

Trade Aspects of Regionalization
Impact and Importance of Regional Development for Soviet Trade: An Economic Assessment

Dr. Alastair Mc Auley

There are two ways in which this topic can be approached. Either one can ask how the existing level, pattern and structure of Soviet foreign trade (and, particularly, the institutional mechanisms through which it is organized) impinge upon regional development in the USSR. Or, one can examine how the existing pattern of regional development and likely future changes will affect the level and structure of Soviet foreign trade. This paper will concentrate upon the first interpretation although the last section contains a few comments upon the second.[1]

The paper is organized as follows: in Section 1, I raise certain questions associated with the organization of Soviet foreign trade, particularly the so-called foreign trade monopoly and its impact on regional development. Section 2 is concerned with changing Soviet attitudes to foreign trade, again in relationship to regional development. Finally, Section 3 deals with the other side of the coin, I suggest certain ways in which the salient features of Soviet regional development may influence the course of Soviet foreign trade over the next decade or so. At the outset, however, I should say that I do not consider the linkage between the two halves of the topic to be strong. That is, I do not see regional factors as providing any very strong stimulus to trade; nor do I believe that trade constitutes an important motive for or constraint on the pattern and rate of regional development.

I. The Foreign Trade Monoply and Regional Development

The participation of the Soviet Union and other socialist countries in foreign trade can be explained in terms of the same factors that determine the participation of market economies (that is, size in some suitable measure, level of deveopment and so forth). But, it is generally accepted that foreign trade plays a smaller role in the USSR than would have been predicted for a market economy with similar characteristics. This is ascribed to the institutional structure by means of which economic activity is organized in the USSR and, in particular, to what is known as the foreign trade monopoly. It is also due to the attitudes that successive Soviet leaderships have had towards foreign trade. In this section I set out briefly the relationship between Soviet-style central planning and the control of trade and raise certain queries about its likely impact upon the pattern of regional development. The question of attitudes, of what used to be known as the search for autarky, is discussed later in the paper.

In the Soviet system it is the supply plan, the system of *nariady,* that ensures Gosplan control over the allocation of resources. If this latter is to be retained, it is important that the central authorities should have the power to specify which enterprises or ministries are entitled to obtain allocations of key intermediate products and investment goods. Such power cannot be reconciled with free access to Soviet domestic markets by foreign organizations. Nor is it consistent with free access to foreign markets by Soviet production organizations. Access of either kind might frustrate planners' intentions. That is, central planning implies commodity inconvertibility.

Two further consequences flow from commodity inconvertibility. First, if foreign enterprises are not allowed access to Soviet domestic markets, they will have little incentive to hold Soviet currency balances; *ceteris paribus,* this will tend to make the ruble weak. Further, it is always possible that holders or ruble balances might be able to obviate central controls and thus frustrate the intentions of planners. This is more likely if ruble balances are freely transferable. Thus, commodity inconvertiblity needs to be reinforced by currency inconvertibility. The need for this is reinforced by Soviet domestic price-setting practice and its introduction permits the divorce of domestic and world market price structures. Second, if Soviet enterprises are not to be permitted to engage in direct relations with foreign firms while trade is to take place, specialized foreign trade organizations must be set up. It is the channelling of international transactions through such bodies that is referred to as the foreign trade monopoly.

In the Soviet Union, these foreign trade enterprises (FTEs) exist primarily at the All-Union level and with certain exceptions (notably *INTOURIST* and *SOVFRAKHT,* the Soviet shipping agency) are subordinate to the Ministry of Foreign Trade in Moscow. But it is not clear that the logic of the system necessitates this. It seems to me that all that is required is that the FTEs be established at the same level as the supply plan. All that is required, surely, is that import-export decisions be integrated into the formal resource allocation procedure? Since there exists a hierarchy of supply-planning organizations (corresponding roughly to the hierarchy of priorities: funded, planned, decentrally planned, etc.) one might expect to observe a similar hierarchy of FTEs.

The only regional-local foreign trade organizations of whose existence I am certain are located in Leningrad and the Far East. As far as one can gather both *Dalintorg* and *Lenfintorg* are restricted in their export operations to the products of local industry and imports consist primarily of consumer goods for the local market. That is, they operate in accordance with the principles set out in the last paragraph.

Actually, the network of local trade organizations may be more extensive than suggested here. I vaguely recollect reading about a Ukrainian organization (located in Lvov) during the *Sovnarkhoz* period but have been unable to track down the reference. Also, travellers returning recently from Tashkent report that it is possible to buy various Chinese consumer goods there. Is this an example of locally organized trade? Perhaps there is scope here for further enquiry.

Whether or not there exists a network of local-level foreign trade organizations, the vast bulk of Soviet foreign trade passes through the hands of the various All-Union FTEs located for the most part in Moscow. What effects does this institutional framework have on the level and structure of foreign trade originating in individual regions of the USSR?

This is clearly an impossible question to answer with any degree of conviction partly for lack of the relevant information and partly because it is imprecisely formulated. But certain speculations can be advanced. Consider the following hypothetical situation: suppose that each of the Soviet republics (and each of the economic regions of the RSFSR and the Ukraine) was an independent country with its own customs, currency, commercial law and so on. In such a situation, the relative advantages for Georgians, say, of trade with Turkey and Armenia would differ from those that would exist if one postulated the existence of the USSR with its economy organized on market lines. In this case, the USSR might be thought of as a customs union. Given the existence of a common currency, a unified commercial law and so forth, my guess is that there would be substantial trade diversion. (The analogy might be drawn with the impact of the existence of the federal government on the trade of individual American states with third countries.) Although I know of no empirical work on the topic, I feel sure that the trade participation of individual states with countries outside the USA is substantially less than would be predicted if they were independent countries of the same size and level of development. Similarly, I would suggest that, given membership of the USSR, the bulk of Georgian (or Estonian or Ukranian and so forth) trade would be with other Soviet republics, however foreign trade was organized. It is for this reason that I do not believe that trade and regional development are strongly linked.

This general point having been made, it remains true that Soviet trade is lower than might be predicted on the basis of the standard trade participation model, and hence, the external commerce of one or more Soviet republics musts be less than it otherwise would be. In part, this is presumably due to the tendency towards bilateralism which results from currency and commodity inconvertibility engendered by central planning. In addition, the fact that import-export decisions are made overwhelmingly in Moscow must surely result in decision-makers being less well informed about regional trade potential than if they were resident in specific regions.

Both a tendency towards bilateralism in trade and a lack of commercial acumen on the part of those responsible for the initiation of trade will result in Soviet (and hence republican) trade flows being lower than might be expected. But I do not regard either of these factors to be sufficient to explain observed disparities. For this one much also consider Soviet attitudes to trade; and this topic is taken up in the next section.

Before turning to this issue, however, there is one further point that should be mentioned. It is certainly possible for centralized control to be used to impose trade imbalances upon particular regions (or, to offset the consequences of trade imbalances that occur for other reasons). That is, in the interests of a particular policy, say development beyond the Urals, the foreign exchange earnings derived from the export of the products of Ukrainian industry might be used to purchase investment goods subsequently installed in Siberia. While the Soviet system facilitates such practices, they are not unique to the USSR. Nor do I regard them as fundamentally an element of the regionalism-trade nexus.

II. Foreign Trade Policy and Regional Development

The institutional framework within which Soviet foreign trade is organized is not sufficient, in itself, to account for the low level of participation observed in the past (and, to a lesser extent, at the present time). Certainly bilateralism and over-centralization will result in a reduction of trade flows and this will be accentuated by the irrationality of Soviet domestic prices (making it more difficult to determine which products should be exported and which imported). But, had the Soviet leadership or its planners been convinced of the desirability of the international division of labor, had they accepted the doctrine of comparative advantage, foreign trade flows would have occupied a more central position in the construction of material balances, international linkages would have played a more prominent part in Soviet development strategy. That is, Soviet attitudes and policies as well as Soviet institutions are needed to explain Soviet trade participation.

The set of Soviet attitudes to which I am referring used to be described as a striving for autarky. But, it has been pointed out that this apparently simple term conceals a great deal of conceptual ambiguity. (For more details, see Brown, 1968, pp. 58-59 and the further sources cited there.) More recently, observers have preferred the term "trade aversion." This is usually ascribed to two factors. First, observers have commented on the apparent Soviet desire for strategic independence, their unwillingness to rely upon product flows from potentially hostile countries. This was most marked in the pre-1940 period when the doctrine of capitalist encirclement was most forcibly stated. Second, observers have noted the importance of economic nationalism. While I would not, perhaps, go so far as Harry Johnson and suggest that domestic manufacturing capacity was seen as a public good, it seems undeniable that Soviet leaders (and, I suspect, many Soviet citizens) derived satisfaction from the knowledge that the USSR itself produced an array of industrial commodities. The fact that Soviet production was inefficient and often irrational was probably irrelevant.

There is a third factor that contributes to an attitude of trade aversion, one that I have not seen mentioned in the literature--although I am sure that trade specialists are aware of it. The Soviet leadership is ostensibly Marxist and this heritage affects the way that they view foreign trade. Marxism emphasizes the exploitative nature of trade relationships. Within its analytical framework, the gains made by one party are seen as losses accruing to the other. It is difficult if not impossible to conceive of mutually beneficial trades. If trade is seen as a zero-sum game, then fair trade leaves a country no better off than it would have been in the absence of trade. If one has doubts about the skill of one's trade officials, the chances are that one will lose from such transactions. Better then, to reduce them to a minimum, to minimize the tribute that one pays to capitalists.

Marxism, economic nationalism and a concern for strategic independence imply a particular limited role for trade within a centrally planned economy. Imports are seen as a means of acquiring those essential goods that the economy is not yet in a position to produce. (Whether or not a particular product is considered essential is determined by reference to the overall development strategy, of course, and not in terms of individual preferences.) Imports also serve as a means of relieving bottlenecks caused by planning failures, unforseen events, natural disasters and so on. No special effort is made to develop export industries; imports are paid for with whatever commodities will find a ready market abroad, are in temporary excess supply or can best be spared from the domestic development program. For all its crudity, I believe that this is a reasonable characterization of the role and status of foreign trade in the USSR in the period 1930-1953 and it has retained some validity into the more recent period.

What may be called the Stalinist policy towards foreign trade has implications for the development of particular regions within the USSR. First, although it follows from standard analysis that a failure to take advantage of the principle of comparative advantage in determining production decisions and trade flows will result in welfare losses for the world as a whole, it is not clear that the USSR or individual republics within the Soviet Union must necessarily be worse off. After all, the optimal tariff literature shows that countries may gain from protection and the free trade theorem requires factor mobility for it to be valid. At a more concrete level, the principle of trade aversion has two consequences. It logically entails the preferential development of import-substitutes and it results in a neglect of potential export industries. Whether or not individual regions gain or lose from these two conflicting forces is an empirical question that can only be resolved on the basis of detailed study of the economic history of particular areas over the past half-century or so.

But one can offer the following reflections. A preoccupation with import substitution will result in the installation of industrial capacity (or the development of agricultural capital) that would not have occurred in other circumstances. Whether this is of benefit to the region in question or not will depend upon forgone alternatives, upon the way in which the resources would have been used under an alternative regime. For example, it might be argued that the very heavy concentration on cotton production in parts of Central Asia reflects Stalin's desire to be self-sufficient in this crop. Whether or not Uzbekistan has suffered, however, as a result of this policy depends upon what would have happened had the Soviet government been prepared to import a larger proportion of its requirement for cotton staple. If the resources at present devoted to the production of cotton had been used to develop productive capacity in which the marginal product of labor was higher than in cotton growing--and if that capacity was located in Uzbekistan--then it can be suggested that the Soviet desire for self-sufficiency has resulted in a welfare loss for Uzbekistan. If, on the other hand, a greater respect for the principle of comparative advantage had resulted in agricultural (and industrial) stagnation in Uzbekistan, in the persistence of agricultural under-employment and the non-development of indigenous manufacturing capacity, then it can be argued that the Soviet policy of trade aversion has resulted in welfare gains for Uzbekistan.

The failure to develop export industries is more clearcut. This derives from a fundamental lack of belief in the possibility of making gains from trade. It is compounded by the divorce of domestic and foreign markets that is both the result of and the justification for the foreign trade monopoly. It is also reinforced by another feature of Soviet economic policy--taut planning. If the principle of comparative advantage suggests that a particular industry could profitably be developed in the USSR, the failure to do so must result in a welfare loss. And this loss will also accrue to that region where the industry would have been located.

The stress on trade aversion as a characteristic of Soviet trade policy is perhaps more appropriate to the Stalin period than that of Brezhnev and Kosygin. Although there is a good deal of continuity in Soviet attitudes, there has been, I think, a shift in emphasis. The emergence of the Soviet Union as a world power and the recognition that trade, aid and influence are intimately connected has led to a greater involvement in international trade. In particular, the USSR has sought to expand its exports to third-world countries. This has necessitated changes in the composition of Soviet imports--and a change in emphasis upon domestic import substitutes. Second, both greater self-confidence among policy-makers and the growth in analytical sophistication among economists (the mathematical programming revolution) has led to an awareness of the possibility of making gains through trade. It is now accepted, I believe, that direct domestic production may not be the rational answer in all cases. In certain circumstances, it may be preferable to expand the output of commodity y, export it and then import commodity x rather than attempt to produce x directly. The existence of the Soviet bloc and continuing contact with East European economists has surely added to this awareness.

The primary result of these trends is, I think, an increased concern with the development of export industries; there has as yet been little suggestion that the Soviet authorities are prepared to let their import-substitute sectors run down. Perhaps I am ill-informed, but it also seems that the sectors that have been singled out as possessing the most immediate export potential involve the extraction and preliminary processing of raw materials. If this is the case, this would imply an increased emphasis upon the growth of North East Siberia, since it is there that major unexploited deposits are located. Perhaps the decision to construct the BAM can be interpreted as supporting evidence of this hypothesis.

On the other hand, it is possible to argue that the Soviet Union's apparently increased willingness to export raw materials is a response to other pressures; that it reflects an attempt to resolve conflicts arising out of domestic development policy. This possibility is examined in the next section.

III. Regional Development and the Pattern of Foreign Trade

So far in this paper, I have been concerned to outline some of the ways in which Soviet foreign trade may have influenced the development of individual regions in the USSR. In this section I consider the obverse: in what ways might the imperatives of regional development affect the level and structure of Soviet foreign trade in the next two decades? At the risk of pre-empting the purpose of the Colloquium, I first set out what I take to be the salient features of Soviet regional development at the present time and then go on to suggest their likely consequences for the development of foreign trade.

There are four features of the Soviet economy that merit recognition in this context. First, although all the Soviet regions have experienced rapid economic development in the past half-century, the operation of industrial location policy has resulted in a high proportion of manu-facturing capacity being concentrated in the RSFSR, the Ukraine and the Baltic States.[2] Second, as a consequence of geology and past economic activity, the major unexploited deposits of raw materials are to be found in Siberia, particularly North Eastern Siberia. Third, partly as a result of past development policy, and partly as a result of differences in cultural tradition, different demographic regimes operate in the European and Central Asian parts of the country. In particular, for the rest of the century, labor force growth will be almost exclusively confined to the latter area. Further, in the past, the Central Asian population has shown itself to be geographically immobile. There seems no reason to suppose that there will be a fundamental change in these proclivities in the next two decades. Fourth, past development and present demographic behavior have resulted in substantial disparities in regional living standards. While per-capita incomes in the Baltic States and Slav areas suggest a degree of affluence, those in Central Asia and parts of the Transcaucasus indicate persisting poverty, urban as well as rural. There are also differences in the degree of urbanization.

One might want to add a comment about the state of Soviet agriculture to this list of features. Again, partly as a result of geography but more as a consequence of organization and development policy, the growth of agricultural output in the USSR has been slow. Indeed, since the mid 1960's, the Soviet Union has been a net importer of grain.

This situation has certain implications for the development of Soviet foreign trade. First, it is clear that continued growth in manufacturing output will depend upon the growth of labor productivity in the Slav areas. This, in turn, entails the more efficient use of labor in existing plants and an increased emphasis upon labor-saving technology. Insofar as Soviet industry itself is unable to develop these processes, there will be continued (or possibly increased) reliance upon imports.

Second, it is usually assumed that marginal propensities to import are positive. Rising real incomes result in an increased demand for foreign consumption goods. (To put it crudely, in the 1950's, Russians wanted trousers, now, increasingly what they want is jeans.) To a certain extent, of course, the planners, and hence those responsible for import-export decisions in the USSR are autonomous; they can afford to neglect the pressure of consumer demand. But this autonomy should not be overstated. Since they have shown themselves unwilling to pursue a policy of flexible prices, planners must preserve market equilibrium through quantity adjustment. Failure to respond to the demand for increased availability of foreign consumer goods may also adversely affect morale and popular perceptions of the system's legitimacy.

Third, unless the planners can achieve a radical improvement in the performance of Soviet agriculture in the near future, there will be a continuing demand for food and animal feed imports. All three of these factors suggest that the Soviet demand for imports is likely to increase in the next two decades. Unless there is a corresponding increase in exports, the Soviet balance of payments is likely to come under increasing pressure.

Here, the Soviet system and its past history becomes relevant. For the reasons set out above, it is unlikely that the supply curve of manufactured exportables is particularly elastic. And if the depressed state of world trade continues, the USSR is unlikely to find new markets for her industrial goods. But, there are extensive deposits of oil, gas and other raw materials in Siberia and most of these will find a market in a world in which natural resources will become increasingly scarce.

However, the labor supply position is important. The development of the remote resources of Eastern Siberia will require considerable inputs-- both capital and labor. But the growth of the Slav labor force for the rest of the century will be negligible and Central Asians themselves have shown unwilling to move. Thus, as a result, jobs must be created in this region if structural unemployment is to be avoided. It is clear, though, that resources invested in Central Asia will not be available for the development of Siberia and there in not enough in capital to meet all the development demands coming from the various regions. In this respect, the Soviet balance of payments problem will constitute a continuing constraint on the pattern and rate of regional development for the rest of the century.

IV. Conclusion

A long conclusion would be out of place in a paper of this nature, but perhaps I can end by summarizing the argument. An analysis of the logic of central planning suggested that it was incompatible with decentralized decision-making in the area of foreign trade. The existence of the foreign trade monopoly has almost certainly resulted in a reduction in trade flows. But institutional factors alone do not account for the low levels of participation observed. As an aside, the actual organiztion of Soviet foreign trade appears to be more centralized than would be implied by the institutional logic of the system. This feature was noted, but no explanation was advanced.

The anti-trade bias implicit in Soviet economic institutions has been reinforced, in the past, by a policy of trade aversion. But an argument was advanced to suggest that the social factors responsible for this policy might have diminished in intensity in the recent past. Indeed, I would go so far as to suggest that the Soviet import demand function has shifted to the right in recent years and will continue to shift in the same direction in the next decade or so. In the near future, it is the availability of exports that will place the main constraint on import growth.

At the empirical level (and even conceptually) it is not clear that Soviet style control over foreign trade has adversely affected regional growth in the past. While all areas may be presumed to have suffered through the failure to develop export industries, some at least will have benefited from the development of import substitutes. In the near future, however, it is at least possible that attempts to develop Siberia for balance of payment reasons may adversely affect industrialization and the growth of urban employment in Central Asia. But, in the last analysis, it must be recognized that because the USSR is a "large" country, it is only weakly linked to the world economy and foreign trade factors will only marginally affect the course of regional development.

REFERENCES

Alan A. Brown: "Towards a Theory of Centrally Planned Foreign Trade" in Alan Brown and Egon Neuberger, (eds.), *International Trade and Central Planning*, (Berkeley, Calif. 1968), pp. 57-94.
D. Gale Johnson: *The Soviet Impact on World Grain Trade*, (British North American Committee Publication BN-20), London, 1977.

Comment

Professor Zbigniew Fallenbuchl

It is difficult not to agree with Professor Abouchar's opening statement that it is dangerous to accept "stated policies" and that it is more useful to infer policies from events. However, I feel that there is a certain danger inherent in this procedure. Sometimes it is possible to infer too much from observable facts and often different interpretations as to the objectives can be made on the basis of the same facts.

In Table I Professor Abouchar relates "observable Phenomenon," "policies that are consistent with this phenomenon" and "implications for investment allocation". Leaving the matter of policies aside for the moment, it may be useful to concentrate on column 3 (i.e., "implications for investment allocation"). These implications are presented in terms of the rates of capital stock in Group A and B (the production of industrial producers' and consumers' goods).

The whole concept of Groups A and B, as Professor Abouchar points out later on, is extremely shaky because various industries as a whole are classified as belonging to either A or B. The shares of the two types of goods in total output may, therefore, differ from the shares of the output produced by the two groups of industries if, for example, an industry classified as belonging to Group A produces also, as often happens in practice, some consumption goods.

The main criticism of the observations presented in column 3 is, however, that they may be misleading. For example, in the case of the "observable phenomenon" (b)--a shift in favour of "economically industrialized but already well established regions"--Professor Abouchar maintains that (1) capital stock in both A and B should grow faster in backward regions and (2) there would be no change in regional shares of capital stock of A.

This would not always be true. If a region develops textiles on the basis of the local cultivation of cotton, Group B can grow more rapidly in that region than in others. Group A does not have to grow at all if all producers' goods which are necessary for the cultivation of cotton and for the textile industry are imported from other regions.

Another region may develop on the basis of expanding the extraction of oil and natural gas. A large proportion of its labour force would be employed in this sector and perhaps in the petrochemical industry which produces some basic materials. All this is Group A. If all additional consumption goods which are needed are imported from other regions, Group

A can grow rapidly but Group B does not have to grow at all.

In the case of Phenomenon (c)--a shift in production to sparsely populated regions in the east--Professor Abouchar expects capital stock in Group A to grow faster than in other regions. This would, indeed, happen when the regions develop on the basis of the production of fuels and raw materials. However, when the development of sparsely populated regions is based on the cultivation of virgin land and the establishment of the food processing industry, Group B will develop more rapidly if, again, all producers' goods are imported from other regions.

In the Soviet Union there has been quite a strong disparity as to the proportion of Group A in different regions, sufficient to suggest the existence of some regional specialization. On the basis of statistics available for 1967, the proportion of "extractive industry" and "related to it heavy industry" (both belonging to Group A) varied from 41.9% in the Donetz-Dnieper region and 39.6% in the Urals to 4.9% in Belorussia and 1.5% in Moldavia. East of the Urals, in Professor Abouchar's less developed regions, the range extends from 29.3% in Khazakstan and 29.2% in Western Siberia to 18.5% in Eastern Siberia and 15.2% in the Far East.[1] In other words, there must have been considerable difference in the rates of growth of Group A and B as between those regions. These statistics do not seem to be consistent with the assumption that A must always grow more rapidly in an unpopulated new region.

The central part of the paper is the analysis based on Pearson rank correlation. Professor Abouchar accepts that when there is a faster growth of backward regions this suggests "a strong income distribution objective". Why should it be so?

Let us assume that there is an expansion in the production of fuels and raw materials in the less developed regions. The outcome of this policy will, indeed, be a more uniform distribution of production, and therefore income, throughout the Soviet Union but this result does not tell us anything about the motivation. The objective could have been the fastest overall growth which, because of the exhaustion of fuels and raw materials in the old regions, necessitated a very rapid expansion of new sources in the less developed regions.

Indeed, Professor Abouchar infers from his analysis various objectives, such as attempts to reduce inequality of income, or military and political objectives, which are supposed to be responsible for the development of the border republics that are exposed to potential adversaries or, in the case of Moldavia, are close to Romania, the "trouble maker".

Political and military considerations have always been important in all fields of economic activity in the Soviet Union. However, it is not necessary to use these arguments in order to explain regional disparities. There are some other factors which may be more important.

There is no reference in the paper to the distribution of natural resources, except that in the strange, from Professor Abouchar's point of view, case of Moldavia he has to explain the situation in terms of agricultural development rather than industrial, in other words with reference to the existence of good soil.

When Professor Abouchar finds that the 10th Five Year Plan envisages a faster growth of the backward regions, it is a sign for him that this "reflects greater concern with ameliorating inequalities of income." It is, however, more likely that the Plan envisages that the eastern regions must provide the whole increase in the output of oil, natural gas and aluminum, over 90% of the increase in the output of copper, 45% of the increase in the output of cellulose. In this situation there must be a rapid expansion in the development of new regions.

For example, Turkmenia whose growth Professor Abouchar explains in terms of its proximity to Iran and Afganistan, has large resources of natural gas. This region, together with Tiumen region, have 60% of total Soviet known deposits of this important resource.[2] Moreover, Turkmenia had the highest rate of growth of population in the whole USSR in 1970 (28.6%) and the projected average rates of growth of population in the Central Asian republics are 30.3% in 1980 and 31.3% in 1990.[3] At the time when there is a shortage of labour in the European regions it is not surprising that some labour-intensive industries are located in this region in addition to the energy-intensive and chemical industries based on natural gas. It is not, therefore, necessary to impute any military or political objectives to explain the high rate of industrial development in this case.

It is, therefore, possible to conclude that the factors that are discussed in the paper do not seem to be the most important ones, while those factors that are essential for the explanation of the Soviet regional investment policy have been omitted. It is impossible to discuss that policy without taking into consideration the three basic facts about the Soviet economy in the 1970's:

(1) A high level of capital intensity of growth and some determined attempts to reduce it which, among other things, imply giving priority to modernization and enlargement of existing plants; this factor tends to petrify the present regional structure;

(2) A fundamental regional maladjustment resulting in the situation in which 80% of energy resources are located east of the Urals, while about 80% of energy consumption takes place in the European Soviet Union and in the Urals; this factor implies the necessity of either moving industries eastward or transporting energy and other raw materials westward, both very capital intensive and conflicting, therefore, with the objective of reducing capital intensity;

(3) Recent and expected future demographic trends which suggest a very rapid expansion of population in Central Asia and a very slow growth and labour shortages in the European part, as well as inability to induce a sufficient movement of population to northern Siberia, where most of the development of natural resources will take place.

To discuss the impact of these three factors on the Soviet regional investment policy would require presenting, in effect, a separate paper and this has not been my present task.

Footnotes

1. S. Tokarev, "Zmiany w struckturze terytorialnej gospodarki narodowej ZSSR", (Changes in the Territorial Structures of the National Economy of the USSR), *Gospodarka planowa,* 10, (1967), 26.
2. A. Oborotov, "Kompleks paliwowo-energetyczny", (The Fuel and Energy Complex), *Zycie gospodarcze*, 44, (1976), 13.
3. M. Feshbach and S. Rapawy, "Soviet Population and Manpower Trends and Policies", in J.P. Hardt (ed.), *Soviet Economy in a New Perspective,* (Washington, 1976), p. 123.

Summary
Assessment of Soviet Regional Development

Professor Alec Nove

It is hard to compress into at most twenty minutes the intensive and interesting discussions of these few days. I shall mention just a few key points which seemed of especial importance.

The first concerns *labor*. Soviet planners well know that, because of the falling birth-rate, there is occurring a very marked slowdown in the growth of the labor force, that consequently economic growth will depend almost exclusively on labor productivity. They are also acutely aware of regional maldistribution of the labor force, and much is written about the tendency for enterprises to hoard labor, so that there is overmanning in many industries. Agriculture sheds labor only slowly, and at peak periods labor has to be drafted in from the cities, the army, etc., to help with harvesting. In some areas, for instance Siberia and North-West Russia, farms are acutely short of labor. There is an apparent surplus in Central Asia and Azerbaidzhan, areas of high birth-rate, but the native population are unwilling to move out of their republics, or even (in some cases) to industrial towns *within* their republics, and these attract Russian migrants, to the chagrin of the planners. It is widely assumed that the Uzbeks, Turkmens, etc., are immobile, and problems arise as to what kind of economic activity should be fostered in Central Asia. One wonders if the authorities might try to tempt some Central Asians to work in Siberia, for instance, by setting up compact settlements in which they could live their traditional lives among their own folk, analagous to the Polish miners' settlements in Northern France. But this may prove an impracticable notion.

Siberia rightly attracted much attention at the conference. To recruit and hold the necessary additional labor, to provide the essential infrastructure, new towns, roads, means of transport, building materials, under conditions of permafrost, remote from existing population centers, are formidable tasks. Though many problems exist, it is surely right to stress that there have been some major achievements, as a glance at the oil and gas production statistics amply proves. It is reasonable for them to try to develop Siberia with minimal additional permanent population owing to the high cost of attracting workers there, but some must, of course, be persuaded to stay, while others will come for the big money and then move back to European Russia to spend their savings. Siberia's enormous potential is clearly of the very greatest importance, and not for the USSR alone.

We had a good discussion on *regional inequalities*. Owing to the much larger number of children in Central Asia, incomes in these areas are low on a per capita basis, but look a great deal better if expressed per family or per earner. In fact, owing to the more or less 'standardized' wage scales, the USSR shows only modest regional income variations, especially if one bears in mind its size and heterogeneity. Other factors to take into account include availability and quality of goods and services, as well as their price. One of the relevant factors is 'hierarchical' distribution, with Moscow the best supplied by Soviet standards, though Muscovites complain of thousands of provincial crowding into its shops. Another is soil and climate:Central Asia and Transcaucasia have much more fruit and vegetables, with lower free market prices, which, together with the warmth and sunshine, attracts immigrants from the north. Then there is the *kulturnost'* and organization of services: in this respect, as well as in per capita income, the Baltic States are out in front. There were complaints about inadequate statistics, since data based on republics did not enable us to identify the diversity which certainly exists within the RSFSR.

Then what of *regional policy*? Some participants spoke of Stalinist policies of regional self-sufficiency, contrasting them with the present tendency to specialization, and also of the 'traditional versus Siberian option'. Some reference was made also to the Marxist ideology of the even spread of development by area and by national republic. My own view is that there had been a concentration on short-term results, which led (except in war) to concentration on already-developed areas and a relative neglect of Siberia. The 'Siberian option' was forced, by the location of reserves, especially of fuel, and the growing exhaustion of such reserves West of the Urals. There has been some increase in regional specialization, arising largely out of the location of fuel and other minerals, but because of the strain on the transport network certain remote areas are having to be made rather more self-sufficient: thus the Far East is developing food production, repair facilities, some machine-building, etc. So one cannot really generalize about 'Stalinist self-sufficiency' versus specialization. An interesting trend has been to devise better methods of economic calculation: thus for instance Siberian oil and gas investments have been 'revalued' by some economists in prices which take into account both the relative scarcity of fuel and the potential export earnings, and this makes Siberia more profitable, despite the high costs.

Regional planning problems have arisen, because of the dominance of the 'ministerial' system: on the separate ministries' provision of finance are based the production, supply and financial plans, yet the complex development of new production facilities (in Siberia especially) call for the closely coordinated activities of many branches. Neither republican nor provincial boundaries are suitable. There is much discussion about the creation of Territorial Production Administrations (*Territorial'no-Proizvodstvennye Upravleniya*), but how could they 'fit' into the ministerial system when inevitably they overlap the jurisdictional boundaries of several industrial ministries. Paradoxically, it seems easier for a Western corporation to achieve the desired administrative structure: thus the firm Exxon in Alaska can act as principal, using sub-contractors for specific tasks under its overall control.

The *external impact* of Soviet regional planning was discussed, especially in connection with the plan to supply Japan and the West coast of the United States with liquefied gas. East Siberia, because of its remoteness from European Russia, is likely to be export-oriented. There was discussion, too, of how far the Soviet system tends to 'trade aversion,' even though trade has increased greatly in recent years. The high level of centralization of foreign trade surely obstructs links between peripheral republics, such as the Baltic states, and their neighbors. We discussed also the impact of moves towards CMEA integration on Soviet regional plans, and vice versa. Siberia was seen as a potentially big source of hard-currency earnings in a world in which fuel and minerals might be increasingly short, but the issue is complicated by the rising demands of CMEA countries.

Finally, there were varying interpretations on *motives*, exemplified by the Baikal-Amur-Mainline (BAM). Was this great rail-building project essentially economic or military? My own view was that the economic aspect predominated given the mineral riches of South Yakutia and the export possibilities to the east, but it seems that the military press stresses the military aspect, such as the submarine base at Sovetskaya Gavan'. There was once a story that the chief imperial Russian delegate to the Congress of Vienna died, and Metternich (or was it Tallyrand) was heard to remark, "I wonder what his motive was?" It seems to me reasonable to try to find a normal or rational motive for Soviet actions, in regional development or elsewhere, and to examine more subtle explanations only if the more obvious ones did not fit the facts.